Pop

How Graphic Design Shapes Popular Culture

By Steven Heller

Published by Allworth Press
An imprint of Allworth Communications, Inc.
10 East 23rd Street, New York, NY 10010

14 13 12 11 10   5 4 3 2 1

Cover design by James Victore

Interior design/page composition/typography by James Victore

ISBN: 978-1-58115-715-4

Library of Congress Cataloging-in-Publication Data

Heller, Steven.
  Pop : how graphic design shapes popular culture / by Steven Heller.
    p. cm.
  "The essays in this book were written for various periodicals, Web site journals, and blogs, including *Print* magazine, *Eye* magazine, *Baseline* magazine, *Metropolis* magazine, *Grafik* magazine, DesignObserver.com, *Voice: AIGA Journal of Design*, and *The New York Times T Magazine*'s "The Moment" blog"--Acknowledgments.

ISBN 978-1-58115-715-4 (pbk. : alk. paper)
  1. Art and society. 2. Graphic arts. 3. Popular culture. I. Title. II. Title: How graphic design shapes popular culture.
  N72.S6H392 2010
  741.6--dc22
                         2010009935

Printed in the United States of America

Acknowledgments

This book would not be possible if not for the encouragement of Tad Crawford, publisher of Allworth Press. His support spans over thirty books I've done for and with Allworth. For this, and his generosity of spirit and humor, I am forever grateful.

The essays in this book were written for various periodicals, Web site journals, and blogs, including *Print* magazine, *Eye* magazine, *Baseline* magazine, *Metropolis* magazine, *Grafik* magazine, DesignObserver.com, *Voice: AIGA Journal of Design*, and the *New York Times T Magazine*'s "The Moment" blog.

I'd like to thank the following editors for their continued support (and great editing): Martin Fox and Joyce Rutter Kaye, Emily Gordon (formerly of *Print*), James Gaddy (*Print*), John Walters (*Eye*), Hans Dieter Riechert (*Baseline*), Martin Pedersen (*Metropolis*), Angharad Lewis (*Grafik*), William Drenttel, Jessica Helfand, Michael Bierut, Julie Lasky and Jade-Snow Carroll (DesignObserver), Sue Apfelbaum (*Voice*), and Pilar Viladas (*T Magazine*).

Also thanks to Sam Tanenhaus, Robert Harris, and David Kelly, my editors at the *New York Times Book Review*.

I could not accomplish any of my goals if not for the support of my "family" at The School of Visual Arts. First and foremost, Lita Talarico, co-chair of the MFA Designer as Author program. Our work together has been an exceptional experience. Much gratitude to David Rhodes, president, for his consistent presence in my career, and Anthony Rhodes, executive vice president of SVA, for his generosity. Also many tips of the hat to my other SVA collaborators, Alice Twemlow (chair of MFA D-Crit), Liz Danzico (chair of MFA Interaction), Debbie Millman (chair of MPS Branding), and Maro Chermayeff (chair of MFA Social Documentary Film).

Thanks also to Esther Ro-Schofield and Matt Shapoff in the MFA Designer as Author program.

Finally, but certainly never the least, love and respect to my wife, Louise Fili, for the requisite putting up with my obsessions and inspiring me in the bargain. And to my son Nick, the next great American filmmaker.

- Steven Heller

Table Of Contents

Snap, Crackle Pop!

Snap, crackle, pop is such a well-known "branded sound" of a certain familiar cereal that it is unnecessary to mention its name. How ingenious it is that these simple sounds have for so long reinforced such indelible recognition. With Pavlovian certainty, the snap, crackle, and pop in a bowl of freshly poured milk triggers a yearning (or at least an appetite) that would be difficult to replicate. How fortunate was the advertising copywriter tasked with conceiving the brand mnemonic. Ah, to be a fly on the wall when he heard the sounds for the very first time. Pop goes the slogan!

For generations snap, crackle, pop has been a kind of alarm, like the sizzling of bacon and eggs in a frying pan, announcing breakfast time! Of course it wouldn't be as effective without all three words, yet the third note in this melodic triplet is nonetheless the most resonant of all. Snap grabs attention. Crackle tickles the tongue. But pop is an uncontrollable burst of pent-up power. Think champagne. Or, if you prefer, think weasel.

POP is also the title of this volume of essays. And in this context it refers to a burst that stimulates our collective cultural senses. Pop is short for popular culture, which, although ostensibly ephemeral, also implies long-term acceptance of certain contemporary ideas and artifacts that have influenced social and artistic life. For purposes of this book, pop (which admittedly has other familiar meanings, like ice pop, soda pop, grandpop) implies two fundamental characteristics: Pop is the initial spark and the long-term consequence of contemporary public art and design on people like you and me. For me, this public (or popular) art and design tickles the fancy much like Rice Krispies (there I said it) tickles my ears, nose, and mouth.

My boilerplate biography states that I write about "graphic design, illustration, satiric and political art, and popular culture." That last category is somewhat redundant. While there is certainly more to popular culture than the categories in my bio (including film, games, literature, TV, and music), the "popular" or "applied art" that I specialize in exploring has been the key to mass cultural activity since the birth of so-called popular culture (which dates to around the middle of the nineteenth century, when printing technology made it possible to reach out to mass audiences rather than only a privileged few). I view graphic design, illustration, and satiric and political art as building blocks of popular culture. How these forms and genres have influenced or have been influenced by one another, and how the broad expanse of popular culture was impacted by graphic design, illustration, and satiric and political art is essential in defining the verbal and visual languages of our society.

The pop aspect of my writing is not only about what is ephemeral or happening now. Rather, I am concerned with what has occurred over the span of more than the 150 years during which popular culture has held sway over mass perceptions and behavior. To truly appreciate how significantly applied art and design have contributed to our quotidian history, it is important to view contemporary graphics with an eye to the past and future, as well as the present.

Therefore I look at the snap, crackle, pop of those cultural issues and artifacts with narratives that extend beyond the things themselves and influence a broader sensibility (and sensitivity). For example, in this volume I write about the late-nineteenth-century satiric art magazine *L'Assiette au Beurre*, because it helped alter the aesthetics of both fine art and cartooning as well as informed the public with ideas that went counter to officialdom. I juxtapose *L'Assiette au Beurre* with, among other stories on periodical publishing, an essay about the covers for *Weirdo* magazine, edited and illustrated by R. Crumb, who altered notions of comics and visual narrative. On another track, I discuss the recent reemergence of stencil type and lettering that has, in fact, been emergent for dozens of years as an alternative history of type. I also dredge up how a forgotten series of *Time Life* paperback covers from the late 1960s were illustrated and designed in such a way that they are classics today. They are also so "today" it is important to view them as models of this so-called dying art of book publishing. Speaking of classics, I also use a lost book about trademarks to show how "primitive" branding was just as effective as the more sophisticated variety practiced today. While on the surface the fifty or so essays in this book may appear disparate, in fact, they are only separated by six or seven degrees.

Pop culture is often maligned as fleeting. But history shows that sometimes what is pop in one culture has time-honored resonance in later ones. I will not claim that all my subjects and themes should be so remembered (indeed there are probably things discussed herein that are best laid to rest), but this book is an attempt to show that pop culture, especially as seen through the lens of design, illustration, and satiric and political art (and other things), is integral to a broader understanding of who we are and where we are going. Oh yeah, and it is key to being literate in the twenty-first century.

What's Cool and What's Not

In 2009 I wrote an essay for *AIGA VOICE* about when it was "cool" to say "cool" in a professional or academic situation, and when it was not professional or academic to do so. The term "cool" raises various issues. Often it is used as a means to indicate that something is merely interesting or extremely exciting (depending on inflection), other times it is verbal filler (because there is just nothing else to say given the context). But more frequently, it is an indication that something or someone is either in or out of cultural favor. Popular art is usually cool, insofar as it is "hot" in the eyes and minds of the critic and consumer. But when it is "cold" it is no longer cool. Double talk, you say? Maybe. But this is also a case of semantics. The word "cool" is a useful expression if only as an initial sign of widespread commercial or cult cultural acceptance. This section begins with the essay referred to above on the proper use of the word. Then it leads into a collection of reports on design and other cultural artifacts that are, were, or perhaps never will be cool. But that's the cool thing about cool—you never know.

When It's Cool to Say Cool

Being a successful popular culturist, no less graphic designer, is all about knowing whether something is cool or not. The word is as charged as the things it describes. So, when to use the word—indeed when to design in a "cool" manner—is key to being cool, and, by extension, being at one with pop.

It's never cool to begin an article with a dictionary definition of anything. It invariably sounds like the writer is unable to start the article with an original lede. Nonetheless, it is cool to provide the following definition of cool, so we are on the same page (which is a tired expression, and thus uncool).

The *Dictionary of Slang* says: From Black English usage meaning "excellent, superlative," first recorded in written English in the early 1930s. Jazz musicians who used the term are responsible for its popularization during the 1940s. As a slang word expressing generally positive sentiment, it has stayed current (and cool) far longer than most such words. In order for slang to stay slangy, it has to have a feeling of novelty.

Wikipedia says: There is no single concept of cool. One of the essential characteristics of cool is its mutability—what is considered cool changes over time and varies among cultures and generations.

The impetus for this article stems from a terse critical declaration—"that's cool"—I gave in response to a sketch for a book cover by James Victore that he sent to my publisher. This is what he wrote back to me: I had a workshop just recently and was showing some images. One was a GP race bike; very cool and sexy. A student asked why I showed it, and my only answer was that is was "cool." Of course a client wants a better answer, but how is it that sometimes an emotional response is sometimes the only and best answer?

Good question. And one that comes up often in both classroom and boardroom. When is it cool (meaning appropriate) to say cool (meaning capital, boss, hot, groovy, hep, crazy, sweet, nervous, far-out, rad)? And when is it, well, cavalier (meaning inappropriate, ignorant, flaky)?

Let's start with the classroom. When I was a kid, the use of slang was entirely forbidden in school, with penalties ranging from demerits to trips to the principal (i.e. the language police). Slang was not good English—at worst guttural, at best improper or mongrel. New York City schoolteachers were charged with turning out right-speaking-melting-pot-Americans void of any ethnic quirks whatsoever (there was even a class called "remedial speech"), and that meant none of those flagrant linguistic abuses so common among us first- and second-generation citizens. Of course, slang is vernacular language that distinguishes or defines groups and individuals—socially, culturally, economically, etc.—which today is usually a good thing. Every culture has slang in some form, and the most common indicate approval and disapproval and are comprehensible by all who subscribe to the language—dig it?

Slang is to language as handwriting is to type; it is unofficial. Yet it often becomes imbedded into everyday speech. Cool is certainly part of our shared Esperanto. It covers a multitude of concepts and emotions, the most common of which is high praise if indeed one is called "cool." Unlike groovy, fab, or gear, which sound positively antediluvian, cool never seems to go out of style. And still, cool does not convey the specificity necessary for making a viable criticism in the classroom.

When Victore abruptly responded with "cool" in response to a curious student's legitimate query, he broke the first rule of teaching. Rather than explain his rationale he relied on linguistic shorthand. Rather than examine motives that would prompt greater understanding, he used a code that while imbued with common meaning had no specific meaning. There had to be more to the image of that motorcycle than just its cool aesthetics—even though it was, for some, totally cool.

Or maybe not. Had Victore's class been in motorcycle maintenance, then a more detailed deconstruction of the vehicle and its infrastructure would have been necessary. But he was showing a class of graphic design students how common objects can be made to look uncommon through visual additives. Maybe calling it cool was sufficient for what he was attempting to do. Or, then again, maybe not. The fact is, the classroom is a place where even the most insignificant thing should be viewed as significant. While it is okay to use the word cool on the street ("hey that's cool, but I gotta go before the iPhone line gets too long"), it is wrong to rely on cool when deeper meaning is demanded. It's cool to show cool things in class, but its useful to explain their coolness. Too often throw-away responses are interpreted by students as a cold-shoulder, which is never cool.

Slang in business meetings is routinely problematic. Although a client—particularly a cool one—may understand and even use the code in private, when it comes to efficient client/designer communications, clarity, straightforwardness, and seriousness are imperative. Slang can easily ring the wrong chime. Too many "dude," "def," or "phat" suggests an informal, devil-may-care attitude that could easily trigger insecurity in the receiver. Or stated another way, if you don't want to sound immature stick to the King's English.

Nonetheless, cool can be an ice-breaker. In business situations, if the client initiates the talk then the designer should jump right in. However, that does not mean cool becomes a substitute for smart. Language—conversation—should be designed or fashioned with just as much care and forethought as type and image. Knowing when and where to use cool shows wisdom that only truly cool designers possess.

For many designers, being a decorator is the nadir of un-cool. The word decorator, like cool, has many—and not all good—connotations.

Curse of
the "D" Word

Do you make things look nice? Do you spend more time worrying about nuance and aesthetics than substance and meaning? Do you fiddle with style while ignoring the big picture? If your answers are yes, yes, or yes, then you are a decorator.

Being a decorator is not how graphic designers necessarily want to perceive themselves. But what's the big deal? Is anything fundamentally wrong with being a decorator? Although Architect Adolf Loos (1870 - 1933) proclaimed ornament is sin in his essay "Ornament and Crime," an attack on late-nineteenth-century art nouveau, in truth decoration and ornamentation are no more sinful than purity is supremely virtuous.

Take for example the psychedelic style of the late 1960s that was smothered in flamboyant ornamentation (indeed much of it borrowed from Loos' dread art nouveau), but was nonetheless a revolutionary graphic language used as a code for a revolutionary generation—which is the exact same role art nouveau played seventy years earlier with its vituperative rejection of antiquated nineteenth-century academic verities. Likewise, psychedelia's immediate predecessor, Push Pin Studios, was from the late 1950s through the 1970s known for reprising passé decorative conceits. In the context of the time it was a purposeful and strategic alternative to the purist Swiss Style that evolved into drab Corporate Modernism, which had rejected decoration (and eclectic quirkiness) in favor of bland Helvetica. Moreover, content and meaning were not sacrificed but rather illuminated and made more appealing.

Anti-decorative ideological fervor to the contrary, decoration is not inherently good or bad. While frequently applied to conceal faulty merchandise and flawed concepts, it nonetheless can enhance a product when used with integrity—and taste. A decorator does not simply mindlessly move elements around to achieve an intangible or intuitive goal but rather to optimize materials at hand and tap into an aesthetic allure in order to instill a certain kind of pleasure.

However, Loos and likeminded late-nineteenth and early-twentieth-century design progressives argued that excessive ornament existed solely to deceive the public into believing they were getting more value for their money, when in fact they were being duped through illusionary conceits. These critics argued that art nouveau (or later art deco or postmodern) decoration on buildings, furniture, and even graphic design rarely added to a product's functionality or durability, and also locked the respective objects in a vault of time that eventually rendered everything obsolete. Decoration was therefore the tool of obsolescence.

However, decoration also plays an integral role in the total design scheme. It is not merely wallpaper (and what's wrong with beautiful wallpaper, anyway?). Good decoration enhances or frames a product or message. The Euro paper currency, for example, with its colorful palette and pictorial vibrancy, is much more appealing than the staid U.S. dollar (even with the promised purple numerals). While the greenback is comprised of ornate rococo engravings, separately each bill lacks the same visual pizzazz as the Euro. Of course, if one is clutching a score of $100 bills in two hands visual pizzazz is irrelevant, but putting the respective face values of the currencies aside, the Euro is an indubitably more stimulating object of design. It is a decorative tour de force with a distinct function. One should never underestimate the power of decoration to stimulate the user of design.

Decoration is a marriage of forms (color, line, pattern, letter, picture) that does not overtly tell a story or convey a literal message, but serves to stimulate the senses. Paisley, herringbone, or tartan patterns are decorative yet nonetheless elicit certain visceral responses. Ziggurat or sunburst designs on the façade of a building or the cover of a brochure spark a responsive chord even when type is absent. Decorative and ornamental design elements are backdrops yet possess the power to draw attention, which ultimately prepares the audience to receive the message.

It takes as much sophistication to be a decorator as it does a wire-framer. A designer who decorates yet does not know how to effectively control, modulate, or create ornamental elements is doomed to produce turgid work. The worst decorative excesses are not the obsessively baroque boarders and patterns that are born of an eclectic vision (like the vines and tendrils that strangulated the typical art nouveau poster or page) but the ignorant application of dysfunctional doodads that are total anachronisms. A splendidly ornamented package, including the current crop of boutique teas, soaps, and food wrappers, may cost a little more to produce but have a quantifiable impact on consumers with discerning tastes who buy them (and sometimes keep the boxes after the product is used up).

There are many different kinds and degrees of decoration and ornamentation. While none of it is really sinful, much of it is trivial. And yet to be a practitioner of this kind of design does not a priori relegate one to inferior status branded with a scarlet (shadowed, inline, and bifurcated) letter "D." Some designers are great because they are exemplary decorators. And that can be very cool.

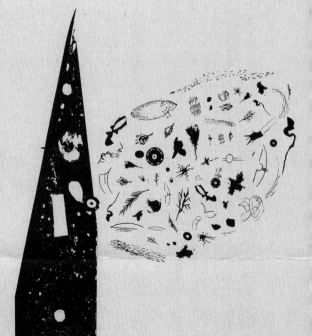

CERTAINLY TO A
A GREAT EXTENT
Fabul ous

The Decade of Dirty Design

Swimming with and against the current is endemic to a designer's role in society. Popular culture demands being in the moment, but often the moment is hard to pin down. Trends shift-shape at rapid clips these days and despite the popularity of one approach this year, next year will often be totally different.

Post-nostalgia stress syndrome for the '90s (a curious love/hate relationship with grunge type) is finally ending just as the first decade of 2000 is coming to a close. Nostalgia is so '90s. It is time for design pundits to start looking forward. Actually, I have dibs on being the first to offer some viable categorization. I know it is cheating to do so before 2010 is officially over, but I am looking forward. Furthermore, I hold that fairness is not an issue when staking out one's pundit-turf. So let's begin . . .

2000 began tumultuously with the contested election of George W. Bush. The nation was in fairly good economic health owing to the surpluses accrued by the Clinton administration, and graphic design was rolling merrily along with plenty of work for everyone. Stylistically, designers had just emerged from a period of hyper experimentation that pitted old Modernist verities, such as order and clarity, against computer-driven chaos, which some called postmodernism and others (myself included) sarcastically referred to as "ugly." Yet from a more sympathetic and reasoned perspective, "The early '90s was an extraordinarily fertile period," wrote Ellen Lupton recently at Printmag.com (*www.printmag.com/Article/Typography-in-the-1990s*). "In the U.S., a far-flung vanguard had spread out from Cranbrook and CalArts, where several generations of designers—from Ed Fella to Elliott Earls—had embraced formal experimentation as a mode of critical inquiry. *Emigre* magazine, edited and art directed by Rudy VanderLans, provided an over-scaled paper canvas for experimental layout, writing, and typeface design." And let's not forget David Carson's stinging jabs at typographic propriety. He significantly influenced a generation to embrace typography as an expressive medium.

No matter what side of the aesthetic or philosophical divide one was on, this was a critically exciting time to be a graphic designer. Although the computer was the dominant medium, during the early '90s designers were transitioning from the hand to the pixel, experiencing all the visual quirks and anomalies that came with technological unease. By the end of the decade and the beginning of the twenty-first century, despite the Y2K-end-of-civilization hoopla, the computer was firmly entrenched in the lives of designers. Not only was there an aesthetic calming down, but there was also a frenetic media migration. Designers were relying on the computer not only for clean, crisp, and flaw-free print work, but also to turn from the printed page to video, audio, and other motion and sound formats.

Mastery of the computer's options meant by the end of the twentieth century a new generation of designers were commanding much more than merely Illustrator, Quark, and Photoshop programs. They had figured out how to wed technique to concept, and produce design that often had an exterior life other than the client's message. The earlier grungy experimentation gave way to a new clarity and rationalism—even a new minimalism began to take hold with the return to Helvetica and other emblematic sans serif faces.

So arguably, neo-Modernism of the kind practiced in, say, *Wallpaper** magazine was the defining style of the decade. But actually that was not the case. Eclecticism was still in force and while some designers were out-of-the-closet Modernists, others followed an expressionist model. (You want names? Just look at the AIGA Graphic Design Archives for the evidence). But eclecticism is too broad a notion to be a decade-defining style. The '90s was clearly the digital decade with all that that represents—an evolution from embracing digital mistakes to practicing digital precision. Axiomatically, generations challenge one-another. If '90s is devoutly digital then, the 2000s should be the "anti-digital" decade.

Where's the proof, Mr. Pundit? Anecdotally, I draw the rationales from various students entering the MFA Designer as Author program I co-chair (with Lita Talarico). When asked why the first wave of students entered the program from late '90s through mid-2000s, the answer was, "To get back to the hand." Now, this does not mean a total rejection of the computer (for that would be professional suicide), but it does mean that the craft aspect of design was lacking in their formal educations and practices. With the increase of the D.I.Y. sensibility, with renewed emphasis on "making things from scratch," designers were feeling a need to make physical (not virtual) contact with their materials and outcomes. It is no surprise that sewing and scrap-booking emerged as popular hobbies, but it was somewhat novel that they were integrated into the graphic design practice.

Over the past five years I co-authored three books that support this "anti-digital" claim: *Handwritten* (with Mirko Ilić) and *New Vintage Type* and *New Ornamental Type* (with Gail Anderson). The first is totally focused on typography done by the original ten digits (although unavoidably it was scanned into a computer). The other two books revisit older styles and eras, and a good amount of the material is generated by hand with a D.I.Y. underpinning. Consistent with this assertion, hand typesetting, letterpress printing, and silkscreen techniques are on the rise in schools and workshops. And speaking of workshops, as a thesis, a former MFA Designer as Author student created a workshop titled "Dirty Weekend" (*www.dirty-weekend. org/*), a series of three weekend sessions that focus exclusively on painting, carving, cutting, and printing by hand. The recent turnout at the ADC in New York prove that the hand is at least as mighty as the pixel.

Why call this anti-digital? Isn't it just an alternative to the dominant medium, but certainly not a substitute for it? Perhaps. But since pundits like to sum up moments—especially decades—for purposes of further debate, I will refer to this as "The Decade of Dirty Design" until someone proves otherwise.

Give a Hand to Hand Lettering

The dirty decade is largely defined by a return to old digital lettering—that done by the ten digits on the hands. But type and typography is supposed to be a crystal goblet—transparent—seen and read but not heard. Type should not be boisterous or distracting, though it must be appealing. In recent years there has been movement away from the exclusive use of traditional typefaces (or fonts) to an increase in hand or custom lettering for advertisements, magazines, children's books, adult book jackets and covers, film title sequences, and package designs. Hand lettering is not just used, as it once was, for DIY youth cult concert posters and T-shirts, but the likes of Calvin Klein, IBM, Microsoft, even the Episcopal New Church Center have run entire ad campaigns using what might be viewed as sloppily scrawled, sketchily rendered, untutored lettering. Its applications are so widespread that a couple of years ago I coauthored a book about it (*Handwritten: Expressive Lettering in the Digital Age*, Thames & Hudson), and from what I can see there is no sign that the trend is waning.

Owing to its infinite capacity for perfection, the computer has made this kind of hand lettering possible and inevitable. Incidentally, this is not the beautiful hand-crafted calligraphy celebrated by scribes and hobbyists and used for wedding invitations and diplomas. On the surface this raw lettering looks like it was produced by those who are incapable of rendering letters with any semblance of accuracy or finesse. And while this may or may not be true, a decade or so ago, this lettering was a critical reaction to the computer's cold precision. It was also, in certain design circles, a means of rebelling against the purity and exactitude of modernism. Eventually it became a stylistic code for youthful demographics (the poster and title sequence for the film *Juno* stands out as a high-water mark in hand lettering, and before that the TV series *Freaks & Geeks* used the trope), but then was embraced by the mainstream (like the aforementioned IBM advertisements).

Some hand lettering derives from roughly sketching vintage and passé letterforms (including Victorian, art nouveau, or art deco styles), making them even more imperfect and by doing so injecting a contemporary aesthetic. Others are crazy and novel scripts and scrawls based on nothing other than an eccentric sensibility. Some look suspiciously like the kind of block letters with shadows one might draw on a doodle pad. With the popularity of comics and graphic novels, hand lettering of the comic strip variety has also emerged as en vogue.

Once designers replaced official typefaces with their own handwriting because it was too expensive to set type (see Paul Rand or Alvin Lustig). These days, it is not an economic decision at all. Hand lettering is seen as a means to distinguish expressive from non-expressive messages. Or conform to certain fashions. I recently rented *Nick and Nora's Infinite Playlist* because the poster reminded me of laissez faire lettering of *Juno*, which I liked so much. It said playful and youthful. Lettering can certainly trigger that Pavlovian response, and hand lettering can do it better than most formal typefaces.

I am a big fan of this anti-type-typography. This may be because I can do it without mastering complex techniques. But it is more complicated than that. Nonetheless, hand lettering is liberating. Sure, most official documents, in fact, most things we read, like books, magazines, and blogs, require "official" typefaces—the more elegant, readable, and legible the better. But not every type treatment needs to be standardized. Hand offers a more human dimension and individual personality. Of course, this will inevitably change. A popular design trope will be copied until it is overused and we're sick to death of it. But while it is still done well, my advice is to enjoy it. In another few years it may simply be that style of the early 2000s, quaint and old hat. For now it's cool.

You're Not Just a Designer Anymore ... or Are You?

Designers are free thinkers, and in this age of accessible technologies, controlling the media is a viable and enviable option. Whatever type or design style suits a particular fancy, designers are more than designers; they are increasingly major contributors to the popular culture as authors.

Part One

Graphic designers are faced with important choices these days. If you didn't already know it, we are in the digital loop. We can either move other people's words and pictures around on a computer screen or make words and pictures express our own ideas. With our design skills we routinely make other people's notions come to life, so why not our own?

It may not have been a viable option a decade ago. In fact, before the digital revolution changed the professional ground rules, we were content collaborating with (in the best situations) or serving so-called content creators. Today, graphic designers have the opportunity to be authors in the metaphoric and practical senses of the word. Our ability to package, organize, and aestheticize through the manipulation of type, image, and decoration is a foundation for more inclusive control of an entire creative process. Want to publish a book? Any designer can be a packager, producer, or editor in the desktop environment. And thanks to the Internet, publishing and distributing an e-book is potentially a breeze. Want to launch a retail shop? With less bureaucratic interference than it takes to open a storefront, a Web site can be launched to fulfill many desires.

Okay, a graphic designer cannot become an author or entrepreneur just by pressing a button—it does take considerable savvy and a great idea—but the digital world invites the ambitious to expand their expertise or passion into realms other than typographical or Photoshop servitude. And while every business venture has inherent risks, designers are in a better position now than ever to take steps that will lead towards independence—creative, monetary, or otherwise.

Nonetheless, the digital environment poses certain roadblocks for the auteur. As it is in film, design auteurship is bracketed by integral collaborations. It is certainly easier to be the sole creator when faced with paper and pen, or even with Quark, than in the multimedia realm. The creator relies on technical support to bring ideas to life and the expertise of others to transform notions into gems worthy of the medium. But ultimately this model is not that different from traditional authorship. In book publishing, for example, the writer is supported by editors who read copy for content, proof copy for sense, and check copy for facts. Often, the editor truly shapes and molds the finished product. Are these collaborators authors, too? Routinely they are simply considered part of the process. Regardless of writing ability, the main idea stems from the author of record. Likewise, an individual working in interactive media can retain sole authorship—only, given the range of opportunities, it's harder to do so.

There are many possibilities for authorship, yet no formulas. The first thing to understand, however, is that juggling is essential. Charles Spencer Andersen did not give up his design studio when he founded the CSA Archive. Tibor and Maira Kalman did not fold M&Co when M&Co Labs, the subsidiary that produced its popular watches, earned a modicum of success. Authorship can be something of a side project that grows (or doesn't) into a profit center, but it won't happen overnight. Which is to say that one's design business should, at the outset at least, support any entrepreneurial pursuits. The business of business may be business, but the business of design authorship is charting new territory. In the beginning it is simply good enough to create something that is one's own idea.

Funny Garbage, the New York multimedia design firm known for creating Web sites and CD-ROMs for high-visibility brands, recently launched a small subsidiary called Funny Garbage Books. Paradoxically, it used its success in the digital realm to create a print product. The first book on its initial list is a collection of comic drawings by Gary Panter, which has nothing whatsoever to do with the Web. Nonetheless, it was born of its creators' art and design passions. But it is one thing to get a very handsomely designed and produced volume into print, and another to sell it. FG used its organizational infrastructure to produce the volume, but must now learn about the publishing industry from the bottom to get the book into the market and sustain viability.

To be a designer entrepreneur ultimately means learning new skills that as mere designers we did not need to know. Most designers, after all, become designers because they like to play with form. Our fundamental concerns are more or less artistic, i.e. finding the perfect typeface to highlight a pristine layout. Most of us can spend the day noodling away repositioning a word by a quarter of a point left or right. Business issues are left to the bean counters. But in the new, holistic practice of authorship and entrepreneurship these concerns must not be ignored or set aside.

Three years ago, I co-founded the MFA/Design program at the School of Visual Arts, New York, devoted to "authorpreneurship." The overriding difference between this and other advanced degree study programs is that students are "trained" to be content creators. And trained is an apt word, because our students are former professionals who, for the most part, never imagined conceiving their own intellectual property. In a sense they must be reprogrammed to think of themselves as integral creators. But they also must be made aware that their products are not developed within the vacuum of an academy. Instead, under real life simulations, they must first (in year one) explore and find what they have to offer (and capitalize on it), and second (in year two) invent a product that will be promoted, developed, and marketed to a defined audience (whomever that may be). They are encouraged to use their design skills (and each student has very different abilities) to frame, package, and structure their ideas. But design is the vessel, not the end.

Given the prevailing fashions, most students focus on the Internet as their epicenter, but invariably, after reflection, it is only a component of larger ideas. With the rise and fall of dot-coms the designer authorpreneur must realize that the trendier the trend, the less the need over time. Web sites are good vehicles for transmitting and distributing ideas, but for the Web to be a viable end in itself requires much luck. Nonetheless, it can be a necessary hub of commerce. SVA students are, therefore, creating magazines, books, retail products, films, and videos that use the Web for promotion and sales but look to other media for the end product.

Whatever is produced and however it is accomplished designers in the digital age must be open to the redefinition of their roles. The graphic design paradigm from as early as a decade ago is no longer exclusive. Although not everyone can be an author or entrepreneur—not every designer wants to or can create unique products—pushing type or an image around on a PC or Palm Pilot display will yield fewer rewards. Then it will be time to give authorship a chance.

Part Two

One of my students who bought the author concept hook-line-and-flash and has devoted himself to doing an MFA thesis project that involves developing the concept, design, and content for an ambitious Web site. I cannot tell you the title or specifics of the project because the intellectual property lawyer on our faculty insists that students make us agree to non-disclosure pacts. Since the work is now in development and has not yet been awarded a copyright or patent, my lips are sealed. What I can say, however, is that if it works this will not be a huge dot-com profit center but could be an invaluable asset to graphic design pedagogy as both tool and resource. It has, therefore, become intellectually rigorous and incredibly elaborate—perhaps too elaborate for a single person to handle.

The project began modestly enough as a site that compiled various book essays and magazine articles. Originally it was going be a Web digest and reference outlet, something along the lines of artsandletters.com featuring a variety of scholarly and journalistic writings. The student is taking sole responsibility for accumulating, excerpting, indexing, and publishing this body of work and also the hands-on design of the site. For the final thesis he is required to create a homepage that links to various pages, each on a sub-topic, and then build supplementary visual content around these existing entities using various means. He must also provide an interactive component for users' commentary, such as "response" pop-up screens. The idea is viable if the outside writers agree to his terms, which includes non-exclusive rights to publish their work in full without a fee—he cannot afford at this time to pay them for subsidiary rights. He has received positive response from some of the "content providers" on his wish-list but a few rightfully want compensation for what amounts to unlimited distribution of their work.

The royalty issue was his first major obstacle. The so-called "Kinko's Law" stipulates that permission must be obtained from a copyright holder for any published material that is copied and distributed apart from the original venue (i.e. books or magazines). Some writers routinely suspend fees; nonetheless, others are sticklers for the small honorarium. Given the prospect of losing important content, however, the student decided to develop a venue, not unlike Contentville.com, that gives terse summaries of all texts, while the entire work is available for a nominal fee. This required that he investigate online methods of releasing information and "shopping cart" options. He subsequently learned that it would be quite difficult because these services require cash reserves. His alternative was to summarize some texts and link to authors' sites or other resource sites. He felt that this would compromise the idea to make a wide range of materials directly available, and yet linking is the only acceptable solution for now.

This glitch caused him to do further research on other Web sites where he found similar archival and distribution services. Although his material would be different, and while improving on an existing idea is perfectly fine, the student concluded that his first idea was not good enough. He, therefore, decided to expand the parameters to include original material that he will author—a virtuous goal with inherently profound challenges that proved to be his second obstacle.

It is one thing to be a warehouse (and the Web is perfect for that), another to be a retail store. Or, using another analogy, it is comparatively easy to write or edit a single book but taxing to shepherd a multi-volume encyclopedia. The pressures in terms of time, energy, intelligence, oh yes, and stress, decidedly increase. This is where the sole authorship paradigm is put to the test. In addition to assembling and writing the content— and writing in such a way that the audience will enjoy rather than feel obligated to read—the issue of maintenance is paramount. If the student found financial underwriting (which incidentally is encouraged but improbable), then he could hire an editor, designer, tech wonk, etc. But as a student project this must be a bare bones operation—though a highly sophisticated one. The students in this MFA program are encouraged to make their theses as unique and viable as possible, which often involves projecting their work five years into the future. But for the prototype the student was rightly convinced that this project would not stand a chance in the marketplace if he did not launch it with all the value-additives he now proposed. The faculty advisors agreed. So the question remains: How to make it work?

You might ask why this student did not team up with other students. Catch 22: The MFA/Design program promotes individual authorship. We do not restrict the use of outside assistance, including commissioning freelancers. But, at least for the time being, we prohibit joint authorship. The challenge is to do it alone, which in the digital medium increases the obstacles.

The upside and downside of digital authorship, as well as the computer's seduction, is the belief that one can do almost anything on the desktop. Our students are taught the benefits of collaboration, yet we believe that to truly master the authorial product they must have hands-on knowledge of all the components that lead to the success or failure of their thesis. In this case, the student made a decision to expand his fundamental idea to a theoretically solid place, but that severely challenged its overall functionally.

Obstacles arose in direct proportion to the student's increased ambition. The thesis advisory committee (which includes three or more "thesis faculty"—we employ five thesis teachers addressing different aspects of the work, business, concept, technology) sets the minimum standards. The students, however, must set their own high standards, so once this student announced his new direction, the additional goals became integral to his final requirements. Not only do the technological demands expand (more screens, more links, more visual effects), but also his knowledge base is duly challenged. So far, most of our students come from a print background with some training on the Web. This student had been in the corporate communications area but had taken a few HTML classes before applying to our program. During his first MFA year he took HTML and Flash, learning enough to know the capacity of the technology but not enough to be expert. He also took a course that taught him to graph and manage content. These skills had to be honed over time, which meant a lot of remedial work was necessary. Still, he would have benefited from more help from a dedicated tech person.

While he is on terra firma when acting as a compiler or editor of existing material, the development of original content requires more experience and greater understanding—perhaps more than he can acquire in two semesters, the allotted thesis preparation time. Good compilations require considerable research and reading, but being a confident writer takes experience. He entered this process without extensive knowledge of his theme, and over time he voraciously accumulated some of what he needed. While this is a valuable acquisition, his knowledge is tertiary in parts. Therefore, how to parlay his weakness into strength is his biggest challenge.

He is adamant that he will be the sole author because he came out of a background where every element of design was more or less predetermined. He has developed two overall design prototypes, which are navigationally sound and typographically handsome (without being overly stylized). The compilation of essays and articles is being accumulated, and he's uncovered more resources than he initially expected to find. He is also devising a way to add some original materials through interviews and reportage that introduce voices of others who possess some of the missing pieces, which takes some of the onus off his lack of knowledge. He is determining how many or few bells and whistles are needed to give the site extra impact—given his time constraints he will probably forego unnecessary Flash animations in favor of more conservative gifs. Some things are coming together nicely, while others could be greatly enhanced by more collaboration and better management.

This is indeed a learning process for the student and those of us who administer and teach in the program. It is one thing to espouse authorship (a few of our print-based authors have been fairly successful), another to put it into practice in the real world, and still another to develop a unique authorial voice in the digital environment. The goal for this student is to get the proper funding to launch his site. He says he'll do it himself in if he cannot raise the money. But the ambitious nature of this undertaking makes it imperative that he link up with a partnering institution. I wish I could tell you what this is (I could be sued and my Ferrari repossessed). If it never sees the light of day (other than its intranet test launch) it will be a loss to the design community. But if the student can make the pieces work together and find others with additional strengths, educators will definitely find it valuable.

Pop
Icons

What is a pop icon? It can be someone who has attained celebrity in the zeitgeist, or something that represents that timeframe. Personally, I prefer writing about the somethings rather than the someones. Objects are hardwired with so much history—from them I often link directly to the individuals who make them. Usually pop icons are ephemeral—hence the reference to pop—but sometimes they begin as ephemera and turn into something that transcends time. Graphic designers have been known to create images that are so considered. Signs, symbols, and marks can be described as graphic icons if they have resonance and relevance to the broader culture. This section is not a catalogue of the myriad icons I've collected and written about, but rather a few unique ones that have played or continue to play roles in the history of design—and popular culture.

Design for Obama

The term pop icon usually refers to celebrities who have transcended the usual fifteen minutes of fame to become natural (or manufactured) members of the cultural pantheon. Graphic designers help create icons of all kinds: the bigger than life personalities as well as objects that loom large in the world. Who can be more of an icon in the first decade of the 2000s than President Barack Obama? According to those who designed posters and images, he is "the man."

The astounding amount of art created in support of Barack Obama during the 2008 presidential campaign made me think of the nineteenth-century French poet Théophile Gautier's term *l'art pour l'art*, "art for art's sake," to describe the essence of pure art, rather than its functional or commercial counterpart. While the images and designs aimed at getting Obama elected were not pure in Gautier's sense, arguably they are pure given the designers' honest and fervent response to this unprecedented national candidacy. The work may have been "art for Obama's sake"—it may also contain a fair share of universal signs, symbols, and even clichés—but many of the Design for Obama posters (and others) are as impassioned as any personal or muse-driven expression.

This was not, however, the first time artists and designers supported a presidential candidate. Given the mediocre sameness of most graphics for contemporary political campaigns, which are usually laden with patriotic clichés—red, white, and blue, stars, stripes, eagles—their unceasing redundancy has a numbing rather than rousing effect. The reason for this design rut is simple: Conventional campaign imagery is usually produced by mainstream advertising agencies slavishly following old formulas lest they make a truly novel statement that might offend a single voter.

Almost from the very beginning, the Obama campaign sought to challenge the old-school cliché-mongers with a distinctively consistent typographic graphic identity (the typeface Gotham was a nice touch), and a startling Obama "O" logo, along with Obama Blue (not quite the flag's blue, but distinctive). Yet apart from the officially sanctioned designs, the campaign received a visual energy jolt from Shepard Fairey, the Los Angeles graphic designer and street artist, who on his own dime designed a social realist inspired portrait in blue and red with the title Hope. After allowing free downloads on his Web site, the poster seemed to post itself around the nation and in various forms throughout the world. Its viral popularity was unprecedented in American politics, but in spirit, it was not all that unique.

Artists and designers, for years, have been inspired by particular candidates and have designed posters that break the mold not only in terms of color and style but also in message and tone. Even during this campaign, a movement of grass roots poster artists came out in droves to support Ron Paul—and some of them were effective in raising consciousness for the rogue candidate.

Independent posters may not have the same ubiquity as the sanctioned ones (Fairey's is an anomaly, although the Internet has changed the distribution paradigm and may continue to do so in the future), but they are more memorable. While this is not always the case, the majority of posters reject bland tropes while making novel graphic statements that reflect the times in which the candidates are running. They also target audiences that may be oblivious to the standard options. Fairey's work appeals largely to young audiences, and his poster exudes a youthful cachet.

Eventually, the Obama campaign took some ownership of the Fairey poster, and even asked him to make Obama smile; but had Fairey been "art directed" at the outset, the poster may have been even more fettered by the usual committees—or not done at all. The Design for Obama artists' designs did not go through the routine vetting process; the images were uncensored and command attention because of their freshness. Arguably, not all of the images hold to the same conceptual or aesthetic standard. Some should have been art directed or never produced. But given the exceptional momentum of the Obama candidacy, and the hope that was promised, encouraging free expression was more important than design perfection.

Too many cooks, as they say, would have destroyed the immediacy of a 1968 poster for Eugene McCarthy by Ben Shahn. Rendered in his signature loose linear style, instead of a ham-fisted patriotic message, it exuded an image of hope—of change. Similarly, a poster that Andy Warhol produced in 1972—the hallmark of irony—was an impressionistic rendering of an official portrait of Richard Nixon under which Warhol roughly scrawled "Vote McGovern." The paradox was made more poignant years later when it was revealed that Nixon's CREEP was involved with dirty tricks.

Although not my favorite, in 1996, Peter Max, who gave signed copies of his Statue of Liberty prints to whichever president was in office, created a poster for Bill Clinton and Al Gore's re-election campaign. Mr. Max's post-psychedelic poster was a youth-directed alternative to the status quo methods that define campaign graphic inertia.

Granted, breaking from firmly held traditions of American official symbolism does not add votes to a candidate's column (maybe it even takes away in some quarters), but alternative graphic approaches are decidedly more eye-catching and can only have a positive public impact. Posters, banners, and buttons are not going to sway a voter, but they may touch responsive chords with those who have already made choices. They may also redirect attention, if only for an instant—yet, that instant could be all the time needed to wrest action from the jaws of indecision.

During the McCarthy campaign, I hung the Ben Shahn poster in my apartment window. I was not just showing support for the candidate, but allying myself with my generation, which the poster's artful graphics aptly telegraphed. The Obama poster, despite the subsequent controversy over whose image was used, served its constituency well. When it was street art, it was a kind of pure expression (not exactly *l'art pour l'art*, but close) that signaled a message directly to youth culture. Even for older voters it signaled change.

The Obama posters did that and more. They enabled the artists and designers a chance to take part in the electoral process, to make their feelings known, and perhaps even to impact others. At the very least, the myriad posters produced for this campaign proved that if candidates' messages are not so formulaic, the perception of business as usual might be moot.

IN LESSER GODS WE TRUST

THIS RANSOM NOTE IS WORTH EXACTLY WHAT
YOU ARE WILLING TO GIVE IN ORDER TO GET IT

OBEY FEDERAL RESERVE
CASH FOR CHAOS
PROP. MANUFACTURING
SUPPLY AND DEMAND

THIS IS YOUR GOD

OBEY

CAPITALISM WITHOUT DISCRETION IS AN UGLY RELIGION

Shepard Fairey Is Not a Crook

Even before Shepard Fairey's Barack Obama "Hope" poster became the focus of legal and ethical scrutiny—for Fairey's use of Mannie Garcia's AP news photo as the basis of the now ubiquitous image—some design critics and practitioners had already questioned the street artist's habit of "sampling" existing imagery. A scolding essay by Mark Vallen, entitled "Obey Plagiarist Fairey," which was published online in 2007 (*www. art-for-a-change.com/Obey/index.htm*), accused Fairey, who created the "OBEY GIANT" project in 1989, of "expropriating and re-contextualizing artworks of others." The booty in this alleged thievery is primarily propaganda imagery from the 1920s (Russian Constructivism and Bolshevist posters) to the 1960s (Chinese Socialist Realism and counter-culture rock posters). Vallen's harsh indictment, however, seems not to have hurt Fairey's reputation. If anything, the criticism enhances his subversive agenda as it fosters debate about the line between influence and theft in art and design.

Fairey's image-making follows the lead of earlier rogue art and design movements, like dada in the 1920s or psychedelia in the 1960s, as well as the situationalists in the 1970s, and even the retro/postmodernists (i.e., designers who borrowed passé commercial art styles) in the 1980s and 1990s. Some guerilla art is rooted in a romantic Robin Hood notion: steal from the powerful; tamper with sacred cows; and avoid getting caught. Fairey has been caught several times, and was arrested on his way to the February 6th opening of a retrospective exhibition of his work at the Institute of Contemporary Art / Boston. Comparisons have been made between Fairey and Andy Warhol's transfiguration of the Brillo Box into an evocation of pop culture; he is also linked to the skateboarder practice of ripping off and then satirically twisting mainstream corporate logos and brands by altering a name or symbol. His sensibility is perhaps even more reminiscent of the old *MAD* magazine advertising parodies and their derivative, *Wacky Packs*, which send up mainstream products by co-opting and changing their names.

Those who rebuff Fairey's work are angry that he misappropriates (read: steals) famous art and design works; they argue that Warhol changed paradigms while Fairey makes knock-offs. I did an interview with Fairey for his recent book, *Obey: Supply & Demand*, and I admit that on occasion he has come close to crossing the line from acceptable borrowing into murky infringement territory. But after seeing the satiric art barbs that he aimed at politics, cultural icons, and *bêtes noires* in his exhibition at the ICA (where I participated in a panel discussion on appropriation), I can say this: Shepard Fairey is not a crook.

He has indeed copied a number of established graphic works in art and design history, including Koloman Moser's emblematic art nouveau cover for the 1901 Vienna Secession magazine *Ver Sacrum* and the image (well-known in graphic design circles) of a pained woman holding her ears, which was taken from a poster cautioning against noise pollution by the Swiss designer Josef Muller-Brockmann. Yet these images are playfully twisted, not maliciously pilfered. The critics argue that literal replication of the originals—and this is true of Moser and Muller-Brockmann's imagery, among others—is ethically wrong, but that charge fails to take into account Fairey's fundamental ethos. His is a wink and a nod toward visual culture and media monopoly. No designer with Fairey's experience and historical knowledge could be so stupid as to pinch such visible historical artifacts and call them his own. On the contrary, Fairey sees popular visual culture in terms of what Tom Wolfe has called a "big closet" of shared objects. For him, the ubiquity of the graphic design and advertising art that he relies on for source material makes it a kind of commercial folk art. Although some of what he borrows is not as anonymously vernacular as one might like, Fairey believes that the fact that it is designed for public consumption makes it free for the taking.

In Fairey's parodies of Warhol's "Marilyn" paintings (where he replaces Marilyn Monroe with his famous Andre the Giant image over the headline "Obey,"), or of a popular poster of Jimi Hendrix by John Van Hamersveld, (in which he substitutes the familiar face of Che Guevara), it is difficult not to recognize Fairey's humorous intent, or his sly commentary on how media—as art and commerce—exploits everything that will turn a profit. Fairey is essentially arguing that icons can be conflated and repurposed to achieve manipulative results. His own appropriation refers to that which goes on in the mass media every day. At its most articulate, his work is a critique of image ownership.

But this does not mean the results are not sometimes simplistic. Indeed, some of his posters are ruefully naïve. Still, after seeing the last twenty years of Fairey's output at the ICA, the last thing I'd call him is a crook. What I would say, however, is that his "Obey" has evolved from a cultural critique into a successful commercial brand with anti-establishment overtones. To protect that brand, even he is now aggressively using legal means to stop other artists from appropriating his work. While there's nothing crooked about this, it is painfully ironic, if not disappointing, to see "Obey the Giant" co-opted by Obey the Brand.

Father of Shrek, Grandfather of Tweet

Instant messaging is the most popular communication tool today, and tweeting is its offshoot. The word itself, silly though it sounds, is now embedded in pop culture. But decades before cell phones cartoonist and illustrator William Steig (1907-2003) was way ahead of the curve. His book of drawings, *The Lonely Ones* (1942), prefigured the now common practice of satirizing personal neuroses; his children's book, *Shrek* (1990), anticipated Disney's success with slimy green Ogres; and his *CDB!* (1968) not only predicted vanity license plate abbreviations, it also suggested the rise of Instant Messenger, SMS, iChat, and Twitter shorthand. Although the last was his most prescient work, Steig never got the credit as grandfather of the tweet.

Those who missed his hilariously morose graphic commentaries in the *New Yorker* (starting 1930 he created over 100 covers and countless cartoons) may remember Steig as a children's book author and illustrator. He won the Caldecott Medal with *Sylvester and the Magic Pebble* in the early '70s and other honors quickly followed for his quirky takes on the venerable children's picture book. He often focused his pathos and bathos on innocent young folk and young folk-like animals as they routinely ran into problems and obstacles in their quests for happiness and fulfillment. Roland, of *Roland the Minstrel Pig*, narrowly misses being crushed; Sylvester, a donkey, is turned into a rock. Amos the mouse in Amos and Boris falls overboard mid-ocean while Boris the whale is beached on a beach after a hurricane. Abel, another mouse in *Abel's Island*, is marooned for a year, and Pearl, a very young pig in *The Amazing Bone*, is almost cooked by a pesky fox. Shrek was, of course, a poor, misunderstood ogre, who rises from the muck to become a wealthy, better-understood ogre. Eventually all find redemption, but you'll have to read them yourself to find out how (and why).

Steig had a keen ability to combine innocence and menace, and, like James Thurber, his sketchy line between the two captured the essence of emotion. His drawings were shorthand for expression; similarly, *CDB!* was shorthand for conception. For over forty years this book has both perplexed and excited its young and old readers, offering challenges and frustrations with a satisfying punch line. In the original Windmill paperback edition, a summary of the book reads as follows: "Letters and words are used to create the sounds of words and simple sentences 4 u 2 figure out with the aid of illustrations." This is a fairly accurate description of SMS-speak. Yet since the digital-age human capacity to perceive such word games without visual aids has evolved to such a high degree of mastery, pictures are no longer necessary. Nonetheless, in this earlier stage of development (since this was, after all, a picture book) Steig's pictures were necessary.

CDB! begins with a sketch of a boy and girl looking intently at a flower, as the boy says: C D B ! (see the bee) / D B S A B-Z B. (the bee's a buzz bee) / O, S N-D (author's note: this phrase has always confounded me). While the word games are not always easy (particularly if English is not your first language), solving them is habit forming. Here's another showing two boys in bed together (they're brothers!!): R U C-P? (are you sleeping?) / S, I M. (yes, I am) / I M 2 (I am too). Here's another with a picture of a proud chicken: D N S 5 X (the hen has five eggs). And here's my favorite—because it is so true—showing a little boy looking longingly up at a bigger girl who says: I M 2 O-L 4 U (author's note: you figure it out, I can't translate everything for you).

When SMS and Instant Messenger came to my household in the late '90s, I wondered how my son (who was then in his early double digits) picked up the abbrevi-language so quickly. Had he been reading the real estate classifieds (drmn bldg w/ rivr vw), or was it just in the air? I only realized recently, as I was re-reading *CDB!* (and was very proud of myself for deciphering I M N A T-P—okay, it's one of the easy ones), that this was the holy grail of this digital generation's mode of communication. It only goes to prove what the writer Wolcott Gibbs said about William Steig in his foreword to *The Lonely Ones*: "For a good many years, William Steig has been drawing rational, though occasionally disconcerting, pictures ... It is hard to define the special quality of these works since so many warring elements have gone into them—cruelty and compassion; burlesque and acute social perception." Or maybe it doesn't prove that. But it does prove that Steig was the grandfather of social networking. A N E 1 AV A P-LM W TH-T?

MONOCLE

politics, polemics & satire for the sub-influential volume 6 number 1 price: ($1.00)

"In the land of the blind the one-eyed is king." volume 6 number 1 price: ($1.00)

MONOCLE

When the One-Eyed Man Was King

America's most well-known type designer, Frederic Goudy, once said, "Those old guys stole our best ideas." Well, despite a whole lot of hoopla generated about *Monocle*, the art, culture, and issues magazine from *Wallpaper*'s creator Tyler Brule, the guy who brought neo-classic post-European modernism to lifestyle publishing, it was done before. Kind of. Although *Monocle* looks nothing like its predecessor, it promises to be the next new thing in integrated Web and in print publishing—a very laudable endeavor to be sure—deserving serious analysis and review. But this is not going to be that. In fact, this is not even an article about Brule's magazine at all, but rather a look back to another, virtually forgotten but decidedly important, magazine with the very same name— one that published under the motto, "In the land of the blind the one-eyed man is king."

This earlier *Monocle* was the smartly literate and hilariously funny American satirical magazine, published from the late 1950s (as a stapled pamphlet and assorted newsletters) through the mid-1960s (as a perfect bound magazine) edited by Victor Navasky, currently editor emeritus of the *Nation*. This *Monocle*, headquartered at 80 Fifth Avenue in New York City, had the distinction of predating many of the sixties' most important alternative publishing institutions, like the "new left" monthlies, *Evergreen Review* and *Ramparts*, and was precursor of The National Lampoon. Arguably, it also influenced *Esquire* (during its golden years under Harold Hayes, when George Lois conceived its covers), *New York Magazine* (under Clay Felker and Milton Glaser), and even *Spy* magazine (edited by Kurt Andersen and Graydon Carter). It impacted the look of some underground newspapers. Many of the artists, cartoonists, designers, and writers who contributed to this so-called "leisurely published" (at first lazily twice a year) *Monocle* seeded much of the alternative press and mainstream publishing industry, and many are still active today.

Monocle was started while Navasky was still a student at Yale during the tail end of the McCarthy period. "There was what I thought of as an 'irreverence boomlet' going on, and we thought we were part of it," he recalled in a career-spanning interview on the Web site of the Institute of International Studies at UC Berkeley. "Mort Sahl [the political monologist] was out in San Francisco at the 'hungry I' nightclub with the daily paper; Nichols and May were improvising in Chicago, and we started *Monocle* magazine. There was another little magazine called the *Realist*, a journal of free thought, criticism, and satire that Paul Krassner had coming out of New York, and we thought we could challenge the pieties of the day through satire, which didn't really exist in print in a serious way at that point."

Careers were made and styles launched at *Monocle*. The list of contributing satiric illustrators is a who's who of political acerbity and editorial acuity: Robert Grossman created the first African-American superhero, "Captain Melanin," and "Roger Ruthless of the C.I.A.," while Ed Sorel, David Levine, Paul Davis, Randy Enos, R.O. Blechman, Bob Gill, Milton Glaser, James McMullan, Tomi Ungerer, Lou Myers, Seymour Chwast, Marshall Arisman, and John Alcorn contributed covers, cartoons, and illustrations that poked gaping holes in the body politic and its sanctimonious leaders on both sides of the aisle, elected and otherwise. Together they triggered a golden age of conceptual editorial illustration eventually adopted by the *New York Times*' Op-Ed page (which today receives the lion's share of the historical accolades for this genre of art). Their trenchantly witty writers included some of today's literary and social comedic luminaries, Calvin Trillin, C.D.B Bryan, Dan Wakefield, Neil Postman, Richard Lingeman, Dan Greenberg, and humorist Marvin Kitman, who became a commentator and TV critic for *Newsday*. With wickedly comedic hubris, *Monocle* even ran Kitman for President of the United States in its Spring 1964 issue (the year LBJ ran against Goldwater), the first time in the twentieth century a comedian ran for a high office (pre-dating Al Franken by over forty years). In the same issue, Chas B. Slackman offered his timeworn vision of "The Composite Congressman," showing a faint heart, strong stomach, hip pocket in which he hopes to keep his district, and pocket bulging with franked junk mail for constituents, among other things. There were also parodies of certain verities, like Sorel and Chwast's "Cold War Cutouts," a patriot's pastime for people on both sides of the Iron Curtain, inspired by hyperbole in speeches by Kennedy and Khrushchev.

For *Monocle* looks were not everything, but the unique design gave the magazine great allure. As art director, Phil Gips, later of Frankfurt, Gips, and Balkind, introduced Victorian wood types to the layout, which was a revelation. The eclectic typefaces supplied by Morgan Press, the leading distributor in the United States of vintage type, were a fresh alternative to the Swiss style with its preponderance of Akzidenz-Grotesk and Helvetica. Five years before the hippie flea market aesthetic and twenty years before postmodern "retro," Gips introduced nineteenth-century pastiche—and did it beautifully. Sorel (who spent considerable time sleeping in the *Monocle* office) also helped compose the ornamental display typography. When I was first starting out as an art director for underground newspapers in the '60s I'd buy second-hand issues of *Monocle* simply to cut out the type and paste them onto my own layouts.

Vintage type was endemic to the magazine's personality, but when *Monocle* became a quarterly in 1963 it adopted an unconventionally tall narrow format developed because, Navasky said, being "as tall as *Time* and as wide as *Reader's Digest* we thought we could sell ads prepared for both [of these publications]." But it didn't work. In fact, it "caused problems with the printer because we wasted paper." Few paid ads were ever realized and the magazine was chronically in the red.

Finances aside, *Monocle* was neither ideologically red or pink but rather contrarian. In the Summer/Fall 1963 issue, only months before John F. Kennedy's assassination, the "Lord of the Hawks" article sharply critiqued Kennedy and his brain trust for saber rattling in the Vietnam War. *Monocle* also took no-holds-barred swipes at both Johnson liberals and Goldwater conservatives, CIA interventions and civil rights disruptions—one issue included Tomi Ungerer's famous commentary, Black Power/White Power, was a pox on both houses. In Kitman's ongoing campaign, it was never clear exactly what side he was on—the right? Left? Libertarian? Or was he just plain-old independent? "At *Monocle*, we [thought] that the ideal magazine should be like the UN police force and come out whenever there's an emergency, or come out when we had something to say," said Navasky, explaining its irregular schedule and regularly skeptical stance.

So today a new *Monocle* is on the stands and the Internet, which its publisher and investors hope will be as popular and influential as *Wallpaper*. But I wish they had selected another name. Like great sports figures' jersey numbers, *Monocle*, which ceased publication in 1965, should have its name exempt from appearing on any other magazine (unless, of course, it's as great as the original).

INTER/VIEW

ANDY WARHOL'S FILM MAGAZINE

JULY 1971 VOLUME II. NUMBER 4 50¢

A Snippet of
Interview History

Speaking of the past influencing the present, the long-running magazine, *Interview*, was once on the edge, then on the ledge, and now, well, marginal. But its legacy says a lot about pop culture history. I played a fairly minor role in the history of *Interview* magazine, and this is as good a time and place as any to toot my own horn. In three or four issues published in 1971 my name appears on the *Interview* masthead under "layout"—not "design" or "designer," but "layout." That year, however, I "redesigned" *Interview* magazine at the request of Bob Colacello and Glenn O'Brien (who were the editors and ersatz "art director," respectively, and watched over me like hawks). If I do say so, my version was typographically cleaner than the handful of previous issues, which were grungy in the contemporary underground style.

When it premiered in 1969 at the Warhol Factory, high above Union Square in Manhattan (just blocks away from the legendary Max's Kansas City), *Interview* was Andy Warhol's very own DIY magazine before the term "Do It Yourself" became a fashion. It was his toy, but to be honest, Andy didn't really design or edit it himself—he had members of his entourage do it for him. In fact, I never even met him, but his spirit was pervasive, like a bewigged phantom peering through the clouds.

The first half dozen or so issues of *Interview* (with a logo that read: INTER/view) adhered to the slap-dash tradition of the late sixties underground newspapers, like the *East Village Other* and *Berkeley Barb*. I suppose it could have been influenced by George Maciunas' Fluxus periodicals—although I never heard any *Interview* editor mention *Fluxus* by name. I did, however, see the editors reading the so-called cheap-chic newsprint fashion magazine, *RAGS* (published by *Rolling Stone*'s Straight Arrow Publishing Co. and for which Barbara Kruger was a designer in her early years), which was somewhere between under- and middle-ground. John Wilcox's *Other Scenes*, a scrappy underground tabloid edited by one of the founders of the *Village Voice*, was also on the table. Hence early issues of *Interview* did not exhibit any uniquely exceptional design approaches.

As far as I could tell, Warhol rarely got his hands dirty with this rag. He ruled *Interview* many blocks from where I was, and was surprisingly listed as second on the masthead under coeditor and *Chelsea Girls* star Paul Morrissey. Not only had I never met Warhol, I was never even told whether he (or Morrissey) approved my redesign before it went to press. I still wonder whether they even read the publication.

At this time I was also art director and designer of *Rock*, a second-tier music tabloid, which, to make ends meet, rented typesetting services to *Interview* (and other publications), and included my "talents" as what in the retail business is called "a loss-leader" (something free to lure customers into the store). Actually I deserved a better title, since all the type and graphic choices for the redesign were mine. Instead, Colacello who selected all the photographs, in addition to writing and editing articles, saw himself as A.D. and O'Brien took that title for himself. They made choices they knew would please Andy, yet never dictated what typefaces I could use or prohibited me from using my then favorite two—Broadway and Busorama—which in retrospect was a big mistake.

I still cannot understand why Andy didn't vet my typography. Before becoming America's pioneering pop artist he was an accomplished graphic designer/illustrator (with a distinctive hand-lettering style) and should have been the first to realize that my pairing of art deco Broadway type for the nameplate *INTER/view* and the curvaceous Busorama typeface for the subtitle "Andy Warhol's Film Magazine" was one of the dumbest combinations ever. It was unsuitably retro and inappropriate for a progressive journal; moreover, the two faces lacked any harmony whatsoever. Add to that the heavy oxford rules I placed at the top and bottom of each page, and, if I were in charge I would have fired me. Still, no one uttered a displeased peep, and the magazine kept my logo for six issues, even after I voluntarily left for greener pastures (at *Screw Magazine*).

Mercifully for readers and staff, with Vol. 2 No. 10 the editors (or maybe Warhol himself) switched to a handwritten version that read *Andy Warhol's Interview*, and it has more or less stuck with that on the cover ever since. Soon after I left, of course, *Interview* became a herald of late-twentieth-century celebrity, glitz, and fashion, as well as a significant outlet for photography and graphic design. It is so iconic, that a few years ago an ambitious, limited edition, seven volume, thirty-five-year anniversary collection, *Andy Warhol's Interview: The Crystal Ball of Pop Culture* edited by Sandra J. Brant and Ingrid Sischy, was published by Karl Lagerfeld's 7L, Steidl Publishing. This mammoth boxed set only covered the first decade from 1969 to 1979.

Interview evolved into "the definitive guide to the most significant stars of today and tomorrow," say the reprint's editors, and it was the first magazine to employ a unique question-and-answer format to delve candidly into the minds of celebrities, artists, politicians, filmmakers, musicians, and literary figures. In many of the issues, celebrities interview other celebrities, which was a Warholian conceit that gave *Interview* such a deliciously voyeuristic appeal. Yet it is the visual persona, beginning with the haphazard original design, the pseudo-deco redesign that I perpetrated, and finally the introduction of mannered photo-illustration celebrity portrait covers by Richard Bernstein (1939 – 2002) that defined *Interview*'s graphic personality during the disco decade. Indeed, the latter marked a truly unique approach to editorial cover design.

Bernstein's covers owed much to 1960s fashion illustration; his heavily retouched photographs with paint, pencil, and pastel monumentalized subjects like nothing else in print. He exaggerated their already glamorous visages through colorful graphic enhancements that made each personality into a veritable mask that hid blemishes while accentuating their auras. He made "Superstars" into "Megastars" (which was also the title of his book of collected *Interview* covers)—fifteen minutes became weeks, months, and years.

The most memorable issue that I worked on was devoted to Luciano Visconti's film version of Thomas Mann's *Death in Venice* (Vol. II No. 4), and was filled with stunning film stills of Dirk Bogarde, Silvana Mangano, and Bjorn Anderesen. It was a startling issue, one of the last of *Interview* to use "handout" or publicity photos. *Interview* gradually shifted from publicity stock to its own photo-sessions with the eminences of celebrity and fashion photography—Robert Mapplethorpe, Barry McKinley, Francesco Scavullo, Herb Ritts, Ara Gallant, Peter Beard, Bruce Weber, Berry Berenson Perkins. These and others were given the freedom to create original work. Despite the continued use of yellowing newsprint, these photographs jumped off the pages.

Typographically, that first decade of *Interview* was comparatively staid. Compared to, say Fred Woodward's *Rolling Stone* of the same period, which expressed its typographic exuberance in so many ways, the interior format of *Interview* was fairly neutral, allowing the photographs to take center stage. It wasn't until the 1990s when Fabien Baron and later Tibor Kalman grabbed the design reins that the magazine's graphic attributes formed a dynamic fusion. During the 1970s, *Interview* was still uncertain whether it should hold to its avant-garde, alternative-culture persona or march from underground into fashionable mainstream. Of course, with Ingrid Sischy at the helm starting in 1990, after Warhol's demise in 1987, the magazine became more art, culture, and fashion oriented, and decidedly establishment in a chic/new wave sensibility. She brought in Kalman as creative director and designer, with whom she worked at *Art Forum*, and that's when die was cast. Although *Interview* has hit some rocks on the road of relevance, it continues to move—and groove.

Sgt. Pepper's Lonely Hearts Club Band

For the postwar generation that came of age in the 1960s there is no more influential band than the Beatles—they always groove. The most influential of their works, the 1967 *Sgt. Pepper's Lonely Hearts Club Band* album, forever altered the content and style of rock and pop music. Not coincidentally the album cover staged and designed by Peter Blake (b. 1932) and Jann Haworth, with photography by Michael Cooper, was the breakthrough that launched an extremely popular trend in "concept cover" art.

The Grammy Award-winning cover was created by art director Robert Fraser, collaborating with Paul McCartney. Blake and Haworth, his wife, were commissioned to produce an assemblage of life-sized cardboard models of famous people on the front of the album cover and lyrics printed on the back cover, which was something of a novelty at the time. Posing as the Sgt. Pepper band, the Beatles were dressed in brightly colored satin custom military-style uniforms, designed by Manuel Cuevas and replete with various medals and coats of arms.

Fraser was the proprietor of a gallery in London that focused on British modern art from the 1960s. Originally, McCartney wanted to use a painting titled *The Fool* for the album cover, but Fraser convinced McCartney to abandon it on the grounds it was inferior. Instead he proposed Blake, whose work was receiving acclaim at the time.

Blake once noted that the original concept was to create a scene that showed the Sgt. Pepper band performing in a beautiful, flower-bedecked setting, which evolved into the Beatles in uniform surrounded by an assortment of their heroes (as well as Madame Tussauds' wax work versions of their younger selves), made as life-sized, cut-out figures. The

word "Beatles" was spelled out in flowers simulating a gravesite, which led to speculation that this biographical tableau symbolized the transition from mop-tops to serious musician-composers.

The Beatles' songs were beginning to be scrutinized for hidden messages (like "Paul is dead") and this cover, with all of its iconic ephemera, triggered the ongoing rumors. The collage depicted more than 70 famous people, including writers, musicians, film stars, and Indian gurus. Some people refused to permit their images, including the former *Dead End Kid* film star, Leo Gorcey, who wanted to be paid. Mae West initially refused asking "What would I be doing in a lonely hearts club?" But she agreed after the Beatles pleaded in a personal missive. Mohandas Gandhi was also removed because the record label was uneasy about being disrespectful. The final tableau included Marlene Dietrich, W.C. Fields, Diana Dors, Bob Dylan, Marilyn Monroe, Karlheinz Stockhausen, Sigmund Freud, Aleister Crowley, Edgar Allan Poe, Karl Marx, Oscar Wilde, William S. Burroughs, Marlon Brando, Stan Laurel and Oliver Hardy, and Lenny Bruce. At John's insistence there was also an image of the original Beatles bass player, Stuart Sutcliffe. Adolf Hitler was requested by Lennon but was never used.

The package was a "gatefold" that opened to reveal a large color photo of the Beatles as Pepper in costume against a yellow background. Originally the recording was planned to fill two LPs and the designs had already been printed when it was clear there was enough material for only one LP. The album also came with a page of cut-outs of Sgt. Pepper regalia and gear.

The set was built during the last two weeks of March 1967 at the London studio of photographer Michael Cooper, who took the cover shots on March 30, 1967, in a three-hour evening session. The final bill for the cover was £2,868, a large sum for album art that, at the time, averaged in the hundreds, not thousands.

BOB BOOKER AND EARLE DOUD
PRESENT

THE FIRST FAMILY

FEATURING
VAUGHN MEADER

WITH

EARLE DOUD ~ NAOMI BROSSART ~ BOB BOOKER ~ NORMA MACMILLAN

The Last Loving Parody of the First Family

Becoming a design icon is not an intention but a by-product. It is also something that may relate to one generation and not another. There are many record albums that became icons owing to the context in which they were produced (and designed). This is one of them.

A long tradition exists in the United States for gentle parody of political leaders, yet over the past eight years satire aimed at the Bush Administration has been strident, if not also nasty. From the moment Bush was "selected" as President by the Supreme Court over the popular vote winner, Al Gore, the barbs targeted at Bush, Cheney, and their cabinet were sardonic at best and vicious at worst (or actually the other way around depending on where you sit on the red / blue color spectrum), and continued without interruption. Presidential humor has never been free from partisan prejudice, but during the brief Camelot era when JFK reigned (1960-63), satiric wit was respectfully meted out. Kennedy had his share of vehement detractors, but few were very funny. Political satire, which is normally designed to be harsh, was during the Kennedy era reduced to veritable love poems for the most popular President since the War. Even the various stand-up impersonators of JFK did not ridicule the man or the office. In fact, every comic with an ear for accents did Kennedy in endearing ways. The most hilarious of all parodies, *The First Family* album, managed not just to imitate his distinctive cadence but also to smartly poke fun of Camelot's quirks while rejecting the vitriol that was endemic to Jon Stewart's send-ups of Bush or, for that matter, the snarky *Lil' Bush* animated series on Comedy Central.

Vaughn Meader, a mid-level stand-up comic from New York, developed an excellent Kennedy impersonation style. His Boston / Harvard accent was pitch-perfect and even his look—hair, stance, and gestures—was spot on. By 1962, Kennedy had become such a public figure that he was fair game as entertainment. Meader struck gold with *The First Family* (co-written with Book Booker and Earle Doud), the fastest selling record ever with 7.5 million copies sold. He also won a Grammy Award, and appeared on *The Ed Sullivan Show* and *The Tonight Show*. The album's unprecedented popularity boosted Cadence Records' cash flow. While larger labels refused to produce the album, Cadence speculated that the nation was ready.

I was certainly ready. I was twelve, a dedicated Kennedyite (at ten I worked in his New York headquarters on 42nd Street running the movie projector while playing an incessant loop of Frank Sinatra singing "Vote for Kennedy" to the tune of "Rubber Tree Plant"), and a fanatical fan of the album. Meader was as big as The Beatles would become two years later and the album cover was every bit as iconic as *Meet The Beatles!*, with Meader standing next to a flawless Jackie look-alike and other characters on the White House lawn. Of course, this was before Photoshop, and the image looked too real to be retouched, so I figured JFK had given his approval (what a guy!). The typography on the front was all scrunched together, but back then what did I know about typography? The cover was flag, banner, and billboard for a fabulous age.

The routines were side-splitting and featured the talents of some of the best comedy writers and voice-actors of the day. One of them was Chuck McCann, known in New York for *The Chuck McCann Show* and *Chuck McCann's Laurel and Hardy Show*, where he brilliantly impersonated Oliver Hardy. My favorite skit, titled "Economy Lunch," was a dining room meeting presided over by JFK and included, among other world leaders, Nationalist Chinese president Chiang Kai-shek, who when asked whether he wanted mayo on his sandwich replied, "Please, not to mention that name!" It has stuck with me to this very day. Meader and company covered all the bases—rocking chairs, press conferences, Jackie's renovations, children, and Lyndon (who always played the fool).

Response to the album on both sides of the political aisle was favorable.

"Die-hard Republicans would say, 'I like the way you made fun of them Kennedys,'" Meader said in an interview before he died in 2004, immediately after launching a comeback attempt. "And die-hard Democrats would say, 'Gee, I like the way you did Jack.' Most of the reason for its success was that it transcended age and politics and just about everything."

Kennedy's assassination killed *The First Family* album and Meader's career too. No one would book the comedian who, almost as much as Lee Harvey Oswald, had come to symbolize the tragic end of Camelot. I didn't throw my copy of the album in the trash like so many people did, but I never played it again after November 22, 1963.

The Design of Necromancy

Death and taxes are two certainties in life. As a matter of fact, so are gravestones. While these monuments are not considered pop icons, a new generation of tombs and stones are becoming more iconic and, well, more popular.

In cemeteries, rows and rows of stone markers carved with essentially the same basic images and letter styles are rooted in the traditions of consecrating the dead dating back centuries, even millennia. But this venerable practice has, of late, been brought into the twenty-first century through new technologies. A generational shift in customs has also influenced the way death is now being memorialized. With baby-boomers approaching the twilight of "me" and "me-first" generations, death and its aftermath is more on the forefront of our minds, so new demands for personalized monuments are placed on both designers and manufacturers to break the classic molds.

Customizing memorials with personal graphics, including digital videos and expressive typefaces, mirror the quirks, eccentricities, and mythologies of the formerly sentient. However, this phenomenon is not altogether new. Take, for instance, the Egyptian Pyramids or Grant's Tomb, just two examples of how the superego played a historical role in the design of necromancy. Now, thanks to new laser and digital technologies, you don't need to be a pharaoh or president to have an unprecedented monument or effigy—or, for that matter, a monumental effigy.

Stipulating in wills how, where, and by whom monuments will be designed is increasingly more common, and these are not always traditional monuments. Before Paul Rand died in 1996 he asked (the now late) Swiss designer Fred Troller to design a headstone that rejected timeworn clichés while serving the requisite function.

The monument is comprised of two heavy stone cubes, with the top one sitting ajar, carved with Rand's name and dates in sans-serif letters, evocative of the modernist sensibility Rand was so totally immersed in. Although surrounded in his Connecticut cemetery by traditional tombstones, his stands out for its economical beauty, subtle ingenuity, and elegant typography. What's more, a layer of polished stones is placed around the base because Rand did not want just any old rock left on the gravestone, as prescribed by Jewish tradition to indicate someone had visited the site.

An increased awareness of design in most areas of commercial life has been comparatively slow to impact the funeral industry. Stones are routinely designed by monument companies or traditional lettercutters. The latter is, however, a dying breed in the United States, although the apprentice system is still alive in Europe. Still, some designers have become involved in the field out of commitment to the need for change.

In 1996 the *New York Times* published a story about a New York architect, Ali Weiss, who "turned tombstone designer" because she felt the American funeral industry depersonalized death. In an essay she wrote for *Tikkun* magazine she attacked the industry's "staggering lack of imagination" and "insensitivity to the demands of human spirit." She was appalled by the lack of aesthetics and abundance of commercialism. "I think baby boomers are going to take back control of the death-care industry," she told the *Times*, "the way they took back control of the childbirth experience—they are going to demand it be more meaningful." So she founded a company called Living Monuments and patented a process that features a 500-word biography of the deceased in 20-point type. The words are sandblasted onto a rotating component—oval, sphere, or rectangle—that is included as the integral part of the monument. Weiss' vision of the cemetery of the future is as a "library of past lives."

The trend to modernize gravestones using, among other things, images etched from photographs and artwork was covered in a 2005 *Boston Globe* story titled "Extreme Epitaphs." Comparing new approaches, reporter Douglas Belkin noted, "Tucked among the grim, gray headstones dating back 350 years in some New England cemeteries ... [a new breed are being erected]. .... Some depict a bit of whimsy. Others, a touch of irreverence. All are deeply personal tributes to the deceased." But not everyone in the industry feels this is a positive development. The problem with personalized headstones Robert Fells, general counsel for the International Cemetery and Funeral Association in Virginia, told Belkin, is that "one person's dream is another person's nightmare." With computer technology any image can be reproduced from any source, and some of those personal stones are adorned with Disney characters and Chevy trucks and all manner of typography, even the dread Comic Sans.

In 2004 a company called Vidstone began marketing "The Serenity Panel," a 7" solar-powered screen mounted on the front of a tombstone, which plays music and video about the deceased (they also market pet memorials). This high-tech version of the venerable enamel photograph of a late loved one has not, according to a 2007 CNN story titled "Death Goes Digital: The Electronic Tombstone," caught on yet. But CNN does note that more funeral homes are using LCD screens and multimedia tributes.

While monument and other funeral-industry companies are offering more variety than ever before, others argue that new trends in type and image design should still be governed by certain proprieties. Traditional serif faces are still the norm, but the computer has made the average consumer more familiar with various type "fonts" and so more likely to request novelty faces for their loved one's monuments. Where do we draw the line? Historically, certain gravestones have been ostentatious, yet shouldn't they still have an aura of solemnity? Can they veer too much from accepted norms? How do designers who work in this field mediate between old and new? Are there limits of taste?

I asked two tombstone designers to weigh in on how they practice their craft and their personal and imposed guidelines.

Ken Williams, a letter carver and design teacher from University of Georgia, Athens, began cutting letters out of his interest in history and maintains a sense of tradition in his work.

"Letter artists/calligraphers are always wondering why is this hand/font shaped as it is—obviously its antecedent has a great deal to do with its form," he said. "And so you keep chasing things back into the past until you run into a wall (Hadrian's) or Trajan's column. For the Western World this is where it all started, form-wise."

In the late '70s he found himself in southern Tuscany near a stone yard and a supplier, where he bought chisels and tried to cut his own letters. After eight summers he had mastered the craft.

"There's not much call for corner stones anymore," he said, "but as I got older more of my friends were dying and I started cutting their monuments."

Williams began his practice by replicating the classic Roman capital cut into stone from 2000 years ago. "It is almost impossible to beat. I will never master the nuances—you just keep noticing new things. I like to try to form the letters with a brush instead of copying a typeface.

And I like to contrast the caps with the chancery hand. They are both elegant, one more formal, one more organic. Stone and handcut letters from the Roman or Renaissance periods seem magical."

One of his favorite projects is sundials for two colleagues who had lost parents but wanted monuments in memorial gardens rather than cemeteries. They had shared times together in Italy, and it seemed appropriate to use stones from that region and, because they were to be sited in a garden, to use parts of St. Francis's canticle extolling Mother Earth, Sister Moon, and Brother Sun. (Unfortunately the canticle is shamelessly exploited for the tourist trade in Assisi). For the gnomon (the part of a sundial that casts the shadow), Williams had to figure out how to photo etch on both sides of a piece of brass. "If OSHA had only known what chemicals I was using in the university's darkrooms I would still be in jail," he said.

Williams notes that even in the arduous art of letter carving, he can do anything as long as the skill is there. But he has learned monument design is not a tabula rasa. He was once cutting in a stone shed in Elberton, Georgia, (granite capital of the south) when a truck delivered a number of huge weathered pieces of stone cut in strange semi-circles and triangles with sandblasted lettering all over them. He asked the guys who worked there, "What gives?" and they laughingly told him about the wacky doctor who designed his own monument, which looked like a spaceport for Martians. The doctor had died just a few days before, and the widow called the stone shed to come take down and haul away the embarrassing junk and cut the deceased a regular stone. "So I guess what you try not to do is make such an ungodly mess that the survivors [will] rip it out of the ground."

Drew Dernavich is probably best known by readers of the *New Yorker* for his dryly witty cartoons signed with an upper and lower case woodcut, Dd. But for years he has etched type and imagery into almost 1,000 gravestones.

His uncle owned a company that imported granite into the United States from India, China, and Africa, and sold it to monument shops and retailers. Unlike the lighter granites from North America, these stones were dark and richly colored when polished, and they were looking for somebody who could etch portraits and realistic scenes onto them. "Because I was out of college and looking to apply my art skills somewhere, my uncle gave me the opportunity to try it out," recalled Dernavich, who added that many if not most of the artists within the granite industry come from inside the industry itself.

He had done a fair amount of intaglio etching in college, so the approach of drawing white on black was familiar to him, although the specific tools were not. His tool of choice became the Dremel engraver, an electric tool that vibrates enough to carve a line into the surface of a stone while still allowing for a lot of control. "It was the easiest thing to use and to travel with, although it took a long time for it to feel as comfortable as a pencil did in my hand."

Creating imagery—the hand etching—used to be the only part of the stone carving process that was still done by hand. The stones are quarried and cut by machines, polished by machines, and carved and lettered by machines following programmed templates or rubber stencils. Dernavich noted there are probably more programmers in the business than stonecutters nowadays. And the etchings are following suit. Scanned images can be etched by laser onto stone very cheaply now. "The technology will undoubtedly change for the better, but these laser etchings tend to lack contrast and look flat and blurry, almost like a bad photocopy, except on a permanent piece of granite."

Dernavich worked for his uncle's company for a few years and also subcontracted with many other monument sellers in New England and New York, traveling to either their retail shops or manufacturer warehouses to do the work. By 1998 he had narrowed his clients down to six or seven dealers around Boston. "In many ways, this is an industry that's always at least a few years behind everybody else," he explained. "These businesses ran themselves without computers for years after they had become standard office equipment; one monument used rotary phones into the twenty-first century and some shops don't even have bathrooms. The majority of the places I etch at look virtually the same as they did thirty years ago. I never regarded this as … a bad thing. When people shop for a monument they're less concerned with technological advancements, and more concerned with how well established the owners are—who they know in town, how familiar they are with the way things run, and how their fathers went to the same grade school together." The only time this tradition-bound industry frustrates him is when, as someone who works mostly outside of the gravestone industry, he believes he can bring a new image or design idea into a particular work. "Much of the time the answer I get is 'it's never been done that way,' with the assumption being that people aren't looking for something like that. It's a little better now, though, and it depends on the particular business owner."

But there are clear parameters. What can be put on a stone is limited by the rules of the individual cemetery and tradition. Dernavich has etched logos of sports teams, album covers, cartoon characters, famous art works, restaurant facades, and beer insignias.

Recently cemeteries have battled with families and monument shops over what could or couldn't be portrayed on a stone, predominantly in Catholic-owned cemeteries, where grave lot owners were prohibited from featuring portraits, or non-religious scenery or phrases, or imagery exceeding a certain size. Frequently a family would ask the shop to sneak an image by the gatekeepers. So, where portraits were prohibited, Dernavich etched an angel that just so happened to bear the exact likeness of the deceased, subscribing to the idea that who could say what an angel really looked like?

"There were several ridiculous instances of measuring, in inches, the size of an etched car or house or pet Yorkshire terrier, to make sure that it was not bigger than the crucifix in the middle of the stone, and all of the petty wrangling that would occur if a bishop decided that the stone looked too 'secular,'" he explained. "I can remember doing a landscape scene that partly depicted somebody's house and car, and having to integrate a giant glowing cross into it to offset the worldliness of the picture. There is also a sunset scene I did where I was instructed to do the same thing, because apparently sunsets on their own are not reverent enough." In terms of the subject matter, Dernavich does mostly portraits, followed closely by religious (mainly Catholic) imagery, and then, what he calls "stuff," meaning cars, trucks, motorcycles, boats, etc., with that category moving into the number two position eventually.

When it comes to drawing portraits, there is a disconnect between artist and subject. "The process of copying an 8x10 glossy photo is a no-brainer, and I always tell customers that if they give me a good picture I can make it look 'just like the person,' but we're seeing two different things. I'm seeing a photo of someone I never knew, and they're seeing an image loaded with love, grief, history, meaning, and context, and so there have been instances where I've captured an exact likeness (in my eyes), only to have a family tell me that it looks nothing like the person." Dernavich has, however, had a good track record, and out of the hundreds he's done, only a few customers outright rejected portraits. When they have, it's because a family is too deep in grieving to be able to properly look at or communicate something, and it usually doesn't manifest itself until after the stone is finished.

New technologies and design attitudes may be apparent in more cemeteries today, but this is one craft where a greater widespread shift in typographic style and standards will be a hard rock to crack.

A Kodak Moment

From cemeteries to photo shops. The Kodak logo has been an icon for generations—a monument to progress (and hopefully not a headstone in the evolution of technologies, either). In the early 1920s Modernity was the spark that ignited the engine of an American consumer boom prior to the Great Depression. What was known as "commercial modernism" was a holy marriage of art and merchandising, and few corporations were more fervent about its application than the Eastman Kodak Company, the legendary film and camera company founded by George Eastman in Rochester, New York.

In 1928 Kodak commissioned industrial and advertising designer Walter Dorwin Teague (1883-1960) to design the art deco gift camera, an otherwise conventional box-camera with a colorful cubistic design on the lens side (the camera came in various color combinations and was reasonably priced). Teague's New York firm went on to design the Baby Brownie, Beau Brownie, Bantam Special, and Kodak Super 620, each one a modernistic gem.

Cubistic graphics on packages and point of purchase displays were all the rage in Paris at stores like Printemps, Bon Marché, and Galeries Lafayette. The advertising pioneer Earnest Elmo Calkins, who was the first in the United States. to champion modernistic veneers, wrote, "It is extremely 'new art' and some of it too bizarre, but it achieves a certain exciting harmony, and in detail is entertaining to a degree. [Everything is] arranged with an eye to display, a vast piece of consummate window dressing .... It is not always beautiful, but it is diabolically clever."

This cleverness—and aesthetic vigor—piqued the interest of designers like Teague, who at first simply applied a novel surface to otherwise antiquated shells, but ultimately transformed the core products as well. Like Calkins, Teague saw modernism as a tool for creating auras that mythologized products and used 'art' as a means to

trigger allure. As an advocate of the concept known as "styling the goods," Teague helped enliven the market (and created objects that defined their times). He also provided Kodak with a distinct visual personality through its products and packages.

Although some critics, including advertising man Claude Hopkins, argued that, "Fancy advertising images were elitist distractions, unresponsive to the tastes of ordinary consumers, and therefore doomed to fail," its promoters viewed Modern art as a democratizing force in terms of the middle classes, so-called "people of taste." And Teague, being one of the foremost industrial and product designers—known for his contributions to the 1939 New York World's Fair (The World of Tomorrow)—was a leading progenitor of the modern look.

Teague did not design the Cine-Kodak Eight, one of the early amateur movie cameras, but the modernistic design of the box in which it came (and was displayed on the shelves) was certainly based on his art deco gift camera. Although extremely popular, this deco gold, black, and white palette, modernistic lettering, and cubistic pattern lasted only for what amounted to a moment. It was supplanted by the yellow and red Kodak trademark and package design instituted around 1935 (which continues today). It was nonetheless a vivid mnemonic signaling the company's vision of the future—and its keen sense of style.

Take Me Out to the Old Yankee Stadium

We take our pop icons for granted until they are gone, or improved. Yankee baseball, and particularly Yankee Stadium, has long been a major cultural icon, which recently radically changed its design.

The seats of the old Yankee Stadium were hard, the floors sticky, and the directional signs confusing, but it was the perfect place to watch baseball, drink a cold one, and munch on deep-fried savories. The new Yankee stadium, however, like most retro stadiums, bears the burden of being faux—a recreation—like a Disney version of reality. It works and it doesn't.

The spanking new stone face and massive arches, suggesting the Roman Coliseum, makes this manufactured, vintage-style monument feel too fresh, too approximate. Over Gate 4 the Yankee Stadium inscription in large Roman capitals is too crisp, gold, and shiny. The eagle medallions on either side of these letters, reproductions of the original ones that hung on the 1923 stadium, are too pristine. The New York design firm C&G Partners, responsible for creating all the graphics, developed an enviable and ambitious sign and display system—twelve murals, 3,000 signs throughout the stadium, a scale model of the stadium, and a locker that visitors can personalize—but unlike the original stadium, where the few permanent displays were more or less tacked on, there is, for me, a sense that this is all too perfect—too designed. The house that Ruth built was a ballpark—this is an exhibition hall.

Environmental graphic design is supposed to make user experiences more pleasurable. And this system does. But must it be so corporate? The Yankee "brand" has long been a positive experience. And like Bombers' classic pinstripe uniforms that have eschewed the tacky, late-twentieth-century players' names emblazoned on the back above the number, the Yanks are ten times more sophisticated than all other teams. The new graphics are indeed quite elegant, yet possibly at the expense of the grit that is baseball—at least the way I want to experience the game.

Is it just me? What's wrong with cleaning up and making better the visual attributes of Yankee stadium? I asked Keith Helmetag, the C&G partner designer who led the four-person graphic design team, what motivated his signs, architectural design, museum, and retail graphics. First off, he called this three-year (and ongoing) design process "the project of a lifetime," and although he admitted to not being a baseball fan when he began, he's now steeped in the lore and traditions. He became a devoted Yankee and began the project with the realization that baseball is more than a game—it's a spectacle: "Today, there are more night games, which add drama. A contemporary sound system amplifies the pitch. The presence of screens (from jumbo to telephone) creates close-up to wide angle vantage points that make watching a contemporary game cinematic and visually layered," he said. So the environmental graphic flourishes are designed to underscore the idea of legacy and heighten the sense of monumentalism. "Unlike any other franchise, the Yankees fit the uniform of legacy and monumentality naturally," he added. "At the Stadium, presentation of legacy can be direct and unfettered with explanation, because the fans know the history, stats and facts."

Branding often involves inventing legacies. So how faithful is this historical recreation? According to Helmetag, the new Yankee Stadium lettering is based on 1923 archival photographs and architectural drawings that embrace the past, "but are expressed with contemporary lighting, materials and manner." And about the air of authenticity, he added, "Most of the murals and exhibits were developed by using baseball 'filters'—Most Valuable Players, World Championships, etc. Legendary past and current players immediately become intertwined. Old and new are always timelessly joined by a winning tradition." But more to the point, Helmetag, who is still working on the museum portion of the stadium, said the signs, murals, and exhibits are designed to "protect" the various Yankee brands—the interlocking NY, "hat & bat," and script as well as the dark blue, gray, and white—while giving the fans a visceral documentary experience they did not have in the old stadium.

The new stadium graphics do a fine job of branding the team and all it represents. The signs and banners provide visual consistency throughout the environment as never before at the old stadium. The design scheme does not overpower, but serves the essential goals of informing and wayfinding. What could be wrong with that? Yet as I sit in a much comfier seat than in the old park, the soles of my shoes free of sticky soft-drink residue, I have a nagging discomfort—something is wrong. There are too many offerings. I don't want to feel like I'm attending a corporate conference center. I don't want a high-tech experience. Frankly, I don't mind getting lost looking for my seat. I'm not as happy here. I miss the house that Ruth built and all its quirky design imperfections. If I were Steinbrenner, I'd have gone all the way with the retro idea and brought it back to the days before the corporate brand was more important than the simple joy of watching baseball.

Design Literacy

My first book of essays, coauthored in 1997 with Karen Pomeroy, was titled *Design Literacy: Understanding Graphic Design*. (I subsequently published two more editions without a collaborator.) The reason for insisting on "literacy" in the title was to tie together disparate strands of content under a single concept. The essays included in those volumes were all about objects or ideas that demanded a certain contextual positioning to appreciate their meaning. I referred to the book as a collection of "object lessons" and provided historical, biographical, and otherwise critical context for the objects addressed. Had I decided to compile a new *Design Literacy*, the essays in this section would certainly be included. Each represents interests I've explored since 2004, when the second edition of *Design Literacy* was published. I address my concern for studying design ephemera, including stencil typography, Hebrew type founding, textile trademarks, and press type (or transfer) lettering. Also covered are issues of design education, good and bad logos, and new tendencies in typographic ornament and decoration. Each story herein is a literacy lesson in the overall study of popular art and design.

Cult of the Squiggly

Graphic design is an amalgam of visual accents and dialects. Without fluency, designers could not be literate. Some are popular, others are not, and still others go in and out of fashion faster than you can shake a stick. Here's a recent cautionary tale.

Beware! Vines and tendrils have recently strangled designed surfaces and objects without mercy. Yet unlike almost all our other earthly woes, it has nothing to do with global warming—unless graphic designers are instinctively compensating for the depletion of the polar ice caps and degradation of the rainforest ecosystem by planting ornamental graphic vegetation on things. It may be in sympathy for the faltering environment. Or, more likely, it is a reaction to the perpetual dominance of sterile Modernism. You could argue that lush forests of typographic and imagistic embellishment are responses to a basic aesthetic need for—and under-abundance of—decoration in our basic design diet.

The cult of the squiggly, as we'll call this manifestation, was seeded by a few innovative form-givers, including Marian Bantjes, whose mastery of craft is unworldly, and Seb Lester, whose swirling lettering spirals joyously off the page. But now the trend is everywhere, like kudzu, multiplying and spreading in nonsensical uses to a terrifying degree. Think of Jack's beanstalk run amok, and the bloodthirsty plant, Audrey, from Little Shop of Horrors having mated with the nightmarish Invasion of the Body Snatcher pods. We have reached a point now, where the time has come to prune the invasive squigglies. But this is not the first time we've had to do so.

In a 1908 essay, "Ornament and Crime," Austrian architect Adolf Loos proclaimed, "The evolution of culture marches with the elimination of ornament from useful objects." Design was then, like now, in an ornamental quagmire. Eleven years after the initial blooming of art nouveau (Jugendstil, Vienna Secession, Stile Liberty, etc.), which began in

1896, forests of twisted stems and tendrils—what historians call floriated madness—covered everything from posters and typography to furniture and buildings. Loos' preference for "smooth and precious surfaces" derived from his belief that functional objects swathed in ornament were guaranteed instantaneous obsolescence. Loos'believed that superfluous design was not merely a waste of a designer's time, it was downright immoral.

Obsolescence was, therefore, a mortal sin. Yet barely twenty years later, just prior to the first Great Depression, the strategy known as "forced obsolescence" or what the innovative American adman Earnest Elmo Calkins referred to as "styling the goods" was being celebrated for having to some degree brought the United States economy back from stagnation to vibrancy—in large part by adding ornament (in this case art deco) onto products and structures like some sort of camouflage.

Visual austerity might be seen as a denial of aesthetic pleasure, a puritanical notion. For who would argue that an ornamented Persian miniature, with its complex graphic layering, or *The Book of Kells*, with the interlocking patterns and serpentine filigree that fill its pages, are not among the most beautiful (and in a sense, most functional) of graphic artifacts? How could baroque and rococo motifs in print or on edifices be pilloried for crimes against the eye or society in general, despite what they have come to symbolize?

William Morris, the late-nineteenth-century designer, printer, author, social critic, and founder of the Arts and Crafts movement, exalted in ornamentation as a high form of expression. His design for the Kelmscott Press edition of Chaucer's work, which marked the pinnacle of his career as a craftsman, reintroduced the medieval or gothic approach from its lavish ornamental borders to its decorative capitals and frames. But The Kelmscott Chaucer did more than simply revive an antique style. It was the realization of Morris's belief that a combination of modern printing techniques and traditional arts and crafts could counteract the corrosive impact of industrialization. Ornament was not merely a veil to hide ugly industrial machines and wares; it was an antidote to the perceived poisons spewing from factory chimneys—a prescient concept at that.

Ornamental embellishment is not inherently evil, even in excessive doses. In fact, sometimes excess is truly divine—take the psychedelic poster style, for instance. Nonetheless, passions are inflamed when the topic of ornamentation is injected into high-minded matters of design. The Bauhaus masters rejected ornamentation as symptomatic of a bourgeois aesthetic order. Followers of the Bauhaus and adherents of orthodox Modernism, even to this day, have maintained the belief that minimalism enables the clearest communication—purity is transcendent. They rail against what advertisers in the 1920s and '30s called frou frou and fight it in manifestos and essays about less being more. Yet there has long been a desire—indeed a compulsion—to inject complexity and even superfluity into design.

Ornament's startling, though predictable, comeback (see "The Decriminalization of Ornament," *Eye* 58) is as widespread and popular today as it was in the Victorian, art nouveau, and art deco eras. Decorative patterns, an offshoot of the current ornamental trend, are largely born out of the hip-hop and street-culture aesthetics rising in various media—from textiles to clothing to Web to print. Illustrated letterforms—not calligraphic in the classical sense nor illumination in the biblical context—have complimented these new decorative tendencies. Lettering—stitched, scrawled, scraped, carved, and more—has added an even more profound ornamental overlay to design of the twenty-first century. Sometime during the early 2000s, well over a decade after the computer became the primary design tool, squiggly serpentine, floral ornamentation was resurrected—with a vengeance—from its gilded age crypt.

The reasons? Rebellion against the blandness of template-driven computer-generated design has been one motivating factor. But more likely, the practical fact that once-difficult drafting processes are now much simpler with computer programs and have spawned a new enthusiasm for ornament.

The DIY movements of the mid-1990s contributed to the growth of digital foundries that offered scores of "novelty" faces made from countless nontraditional type materials, including such naturalistic ones as twigs, flowers, and trees. The use of leaves, stamens, and pistils today has been ubiquitous throughout the design world. In some instances, the plant is a perfect foil for Modernist austerity, but in others it is simply an opportunity to be overly fussy. Lettering made from branches and bark has a long history used both as a sign system for rustic homes and campsites as well as graphically illustrated lettering. One of the most popular nineteenth century novelty faces was Figgins' "Rustic" or "Log Cabin," made from -ogs. Current use is not much different, albeit more witty in purpose. When done well it can be surrealistically beautiful and comically engaging, like Stefan Sagmeister's poster for the School of Visual Arts where branches are transformed into words. When done poorly it's better off as kindling.

This decoflora (my coinage) resurgence also seems to have caught on because it animates so well. In the film *Yellow Submarine*, psychedelic plant life grew wild on the screen, rhythmically choreographed to follow the Beatles music—that was the beginning of the kinetic squigglies as practiced today on TV and computer screens. For HP printers, flora symbolizes color. For Bud Lite with Lime, vegetation suggests sweet hops. But florid arrangements are taking over so much more. Like ornamental psychedelic art in the 1960s, what began as a novel design approach was quickly co-opted by lesser talents for silly, exploitative purposes. Today, the Internet is full of clip art services engulfed with ornamental weeds. T-shirt entrepreneurs have developed repetitive patterns of flowers and vines. Recently Vodafone introduced a totally irrelevant floral motif in a card instructing their users how to make international calls.
A similarly gratuitous usage is the English edition book jacket design for Alex Ross' *The Rest is Noise*, in which squid-like tentacles flail across the image area—a prime example of inconsequence.

The squiggly approach is used, not to underscore the content of this fascinating book, but to fill up the negative space. And that's the problem: When ornament is profligate, design is made trivial. When ornament is misused, it just takes up space. This new floriated madness continues to engulf advertisements, magazine and book covers, textiles, t-shirts, package designs, and animations. Vines and other flora have crept onto pages, packages, and screens like bindweed after a summer rain. And like this everlasting pest, the new ornament is almost impossible to control without a lot of brush clearing. Prune now before it strangulates again and again and again.

When Bad Things Happen to Good Logos

Some logos are pruned, cut, and cleaned to appear blemish-free. Some simply attract blight for reasons beyond the designer's control.

When bad things happen, good design does not always help. Logos are judged good or bad by the deeds or policies they represent. Although inconceivable today, during the early twentieth century, the swastika or hooked cross—an ancient symbol of good fortune—was adopted as a commercial mark for such products as Good Luck Jar Rubbers, Fresh Deodorant, Swastika Fresh Fruit, Swastika Cigars, Swastika Matches, and even Coca-Cola. In 1922 it was, however, adopted by Adolf Hitler's National Socialist Workers' Party (the Nazis) and in 1935 was elevated to the national symbol of Nazi Germany. From that moment its symbolism went from benign to toxic. The possibility that the swastika can be cleansed of its dreadful connotations in Western culture is improbable for the foreseeable future.

This is the most extreme case of bad things happening to good logos, but the list goes on. Take the Enron "E" designed by Paul Rand. Prior to the massive corruption scandal that brought down the energy company and wiped out billions in employee pensions, the three horizontal bars on the "E" simply represented three pipelines meeting at a central distribution repository—an elegant way to represent the company's primary asset. While this was not necessarily Rand's best corporate logo, it was an effective mnemonic. Until, that is, the public learned of Enron's corporate malfeasance, which eventually brought its executives to trial, jail, and suicide. The "E" became a scarlet letter, the butt of stinging satire and vitriolic condemnation.

Rand warned that logos are like "rabbits' feet," imbued with mystical and magical properties not always rooted in the rational. He further noted that a logo is only as good as the entity it stands for. The Edsel automobile was a commercial failure, so the Edsel name and trademark became forever associated with folly. Recently, Circuit City, the big box electronics and appliance store, went belly-up, and I'd wager that red circular logos like theirs won't be repeated by other retailers in the near future lest they brand themselves a failure. Although the recession triggered Circuit City's demise, the logo will doubtless be blamed. The logo is the face of a company, institution, or state. It embodies the good, bad, and ugly aspects of what it brands. It is either lucky or unlucky, positive or negative, depending on the context in which it exists. Context is just about everything in logoland.

Much criticism has been heaped on the Arnell Group for its bland design of the Tropicana package and logo, which, following an unpredicted popular outcry, was returned to its previous, less generic state: the orange and candy-stripe straw motif. But few remember that, before the emblematic orange, the juice package was graced with a racially offensive trade character named Tropic-Ana. She was a slightly pot-bellied topless little girl in a skimpy grass skirt, carrying a basket of oranges on her head, a variation on the Minute Maid girl and Chiquita Banana lady. Cuteness was used in the same way one might view a baby bear. Innocent given the conventions of the times, Tropic-Ana symbolized a widespread view of superiority over indigenous peoples the world over (she was apparently a native to Florida) that underscored the colonialist/manifest destiny idea that "the natives" exist only to serve the American way of life.

Many trade characters have been retired over time for their offensive depictions. Around a score of such questionable characters are collected in the new book, *Ad Boy: Vintage Advertising with Character* (10 Speed Press) by Warren Dotz and Masud Husain. Included among the mostly benign, silly, and cute characters are the more tasteless: a sombrero/poncho-wearing hot dog for Tasty Pronto Pups; the Indian River maiden, an Indian "squaw" with the head of an orange and the va-va-voom body of a femme fatale; and of course, the Frito Bandito, the Mexican bandito (as if all Mexicans were outlaws) who is always pilfering corn chips. Analysis is not necessary because these characters speak for themselves—we know they're wrong when we see them. Racist trademarks were once copious on labels and advertisements for American products (and many foreign ones too), in part because minorities had little or no voice in mainstream society, and their otherness gave them curiosity value. Some of these characterizations still exist, however, in the sports field. Others, including Aunt Jemima, Uncle Ben, and the Cream of Wheat chef, were so positively ingrained in the public's consciousness (in the trade press they were referred to as "friendly characters" that housewives welcomed into their homes) that, rather than retire them, they were refined to reflect the times. Aunt Jemima, who in the late nineteenth century was actually a real-life African-American pitchwoman who performed around the country, was transformed from a plantation house slave into a benign aunty. Uncle Ben, the happy house servant, has not changed much to this day (incidentally, the product was originally produced by an African-American entrepreneur, Gordon L. Harwell).

A logo is designed to activate positive recognition. There's nothing worse than a logo that sparks indifference, except perhaps one that has no redeeming value at all. Failure—a product that fails to appeal—is one such valueless attribute. Designers who have created logos for failed or sluggish businesses are wise to remove such work from their portfolios. On some occasions, logos are more than marks of failure or malfeasance; sometimes they unintentionally illustrate the foibles or folly of a company or institution all too vividly. Take the Archdiocesan Youth Commission logo from 1974, designed three decades before the sex abuse scandal broke out in the Catholic Church. The unfortunate pictorial relationship between the priest and the child, given our collective awareness in 2009, suggests a much too ironic interpretation. It's a challenge to see what this positive/ negative image once suggested, a guardian protecting the innocent, since the subject is no longer black and white. When a good design signifies bad deeds, the result is, well, a really terrible logo.

HI-NARCO

HIPI-HAPA

HI-SPOT

Hobby Brand

HOCKANUM

HODAR

Hoffman
California FABRICS

Hoffman
California
WOOLENS

hofi

HOLBROOK

HOLLAS

HOLLOW ROY

Holly Huck

HI-NARCO Ser. no. 456,243. North American Rayon Corp., New York. Filed Oct. 16, 1942. For thread and yarn of artificial origin. Claims use since Sept. 29, 1942.

HIPI-HAPA Ser. no. 410,273. Southbridge Finishing Co., Southbridge, Mass. Filed Sept. 3, 1938. For cotton piece goods. Claims use since April, 1938.

HI-SPOT Ser. no. 356,579. Crown Fabrics Corp., New York. Filed Sept. 29, 1934. For rayon and cotton goods in the piece. Claims use since Sept. 7, 1934.

HI-TYME Ser. no. 460,572. Lankenau Co., New York. Filed May 12, 1943. For silk, rayon, woolen, and worsted piece goods. Claims use since Jan. 25, 1942.

HOBBY BRAND Ser. no. 424,807. Fraser Manufacturing Co., Inc., New York. Filed Oct. 23, 1939. For gimp yarn. Claims use since Oct. 9, 1939.

HOCKANUM Ser. no. 361,132. M. T. Stevens and Sons Co., North Andover, Mass. Filed Feb. 6, 1935. For woolen and worsted piece goods. Claims use since 1938.

HODAR Ser. no. 415,316. (Class 42. Knitted, netted, and textile fabrics.) Brown Bros., Utica, N. Y. Filed Jan. 27, 1939. For blankets, sheets, pillowcases, bedspreads, silk and lace curtains, linen sets, linens of all kinds, lace tablecloths. Claims use since Nov. 1, 1938.

HOFFMAN CALIFORNIA FABRICS Ser. no. 470,532. (Class 42. Knitted, netted, and textile fabrics.) Rube P. Hoffman, Los Angeles, Calif. Filed May 23, 1944. For piece goods of wool, cotton, silk, and rayon and of mixtures thereof. Claims use since Dec. 1, 1943.

HOFFMAN CALIFORNIA WOOLENS Ser. no. 476,765. (Class 42. Knitted, netted, and textile fabrics.) Rube P. Hoffman, Los Angeles, Calif. Filed Nov. 22, 1944. For piece goods — namely, woolens and mixtures of woolens with cotton and rayon. Claims use since Feb. 1, 1944.

HOFI Ser. no. 403,947. Hodges Carpet Co., Indian Orchard, Mass. Filed Mar. 11, 1938. For woven fiber fabrics — viz., piece goods, the yarns of which are of twisted paper, rayon, cellophane, and the like. Claims use since Jan. 1, 1938.

HOLBROOK Ser. no. 325,566. (Class 42. Knitted, netted, and textile fabrics.) Bigelow-Sanford Carpet Co., Inc., Thompsonville, Conn. Filed Mar. 7, 1934. Ser. no. 348,265. For woven textile rugs and carpets. Claims use since Feb. 10, 1934.

HOLLAS Ser. no. 485,704. Terhune, Yereance & Wolff, Inc., New York. Filed July 11, 1945. For woolen and worsted fabrics in the piece. Claims use since June 28, 1945.

HOLLOW ROY Ser. no. 447,389. Crompton Co., West Warwick, R. I. Filed Sept. 29, 1941. For fabrics in the piece, made of cotton, silk, rayon, wool, linen, or mixtures thereof. Claims use since Sept. 10, 1941.

HOLLY HUCK Ser. no. 406,113. Bloomingdale Bros., Inc., New York. Filed May 9, 1938. For towels. Claims use since April 8, 1938.

A Good Trademark: A Historical Perspective

Trademarks are made, not born. In other words it is not nature, but nurture that insures a trademark is a useful tool. Here are some examples. "The significance of trademarks in the textile industry is, perhaps, greater than in any other industry of equal magnitude," wrote V. Alexander Scher (no relation to Paula or Jeff) of Richards & Geier, patent and trademark attorneys, New York City. He was writing in a now forgotten book titled *Textile Brand Names Dictionary*, which was published in 1947; it was designed "to be of daily service in identifying the names already in use, thereby facilitating the choice and registering of new names and marks," asserted the editor at the Textile Book Publishers Inc. Included were more than 4,000 names of fibers, yarns, fabrics, and garments registered with the United States Patent Office between 1934 and 1947. 4,000!!! That's a lot of 7th Avenue brainstorming to devise names like Devogue, Denicron, Glytone, Glossitwist, Ma-Tex, Perma-Fluff, Permacrisp, Perma glaze, Permaglo, Perma-Seal, Permaset, Perma-Shade, and Permoflex, to name a few (today they could double as rock band or design firm names).

Naming products is a craft as old as the marketing of consumer products, beginning just prior to the twentieth century and continuing to this day. As Mr. Scher notes, "Trademarks are indispensable not only to manufacturers ... but also to merchants in the advertising of their goods." Of course, we all know this simple truth, but in 1947 "branding" was barely even considered a pseudo-science, much less a major industry. Scher, however, correctly predicted, "Trademarks will continue to gain importance in the years to come." This book was possibly the first

American primer on how to "select" a successful mark. So, in the spirit of advancing design history, it is instructive to read what our ancestors believed were the ideal trademarks. In the words of Mr. Scher, "A new trademark should be selected with great care." Well, that makes sense. But here's the real take-away, which was still novel in its day: "A good trademark should consist of some short and expressive term which must be sufficiently striking to linger in the memory of the purchaser. When selecting an appropriate trademark, it is most important to take into consideration the character of the potential purchaser as well as the nature of the merchandise itself." Can you guess who names like Kinkitone, Lookool, Old Standby, Strutter, Strawberry Blonde, and Yippee were aimed at?

Marks not only defined the respective companies but the ultimate users; it was necessary to have intimacy yet not informality. Scher advised, "It is preferable to choose a mark which consists of a coined word or words, symbol or symbols, or a combination of the two, since coined words or symbols will unfailingly become associated with their owners .... On the other hand, a word which is descriptive of the nature and quality of the merchandise is not a good trademark since it does not distinguish the goods from the products of another. Similarly, proper names or geographical terms are not, as a rule, good trademarks, since it is only after long use that they acquire distinctive character and thus become capable of properly identifying their owners." This latter word to the wise has its exceptions—i.e. Canada Dry and U.S. Steel seem to have worked, but they are not textiles. With the notable exceptions of Grenfell of Labrador and NY-Tee I did not find another geographical locale as brand name.

Much of Mr. Scher's advisory focused on the meat 'n' potatoes—registration, specifically the Lanham Act instituted on July 5, 1947. Protection under this Act was broader than previous mandates. "The Act makes registration incontestable by another party after five years of continuous use following registration, unless certain specific causes for cancellation exist." So, I wonder whatever happened to the original Tropicana, which was registered in 1936 to S.J. Aronsohn, New York, who produced rayon and silk fabrics.

This directory vividly underscores the principle of don't mess with success: The most common prefixes (like Gold—Gold Crest, Gold Medal, Gold Rose, Gold Seal, Gold Spun, Gold Star, Golden Fleece, Golden Fleet, or Doebara, Doelene, Doepac, Doesheen, Doeskin, Doe-Suede, Doevel, Doe-Vella) were repeated in different forms for many brands.

Certain suffixes also dominated like, Spun, Tex, Lastic, and Net. And of course, French sounding names were high on the overused list, like those with "ette" (i.e. Blancette, Dem-Ettes) or "elle" (i.e. Corsetelle) at the end or these: Calais, Cale, and Calide. This was also the era when SMS expressive spelling came into its own as with Everstai-Dri, Fash-un-Sho or Ev-R-So. Alliteration was also popular, like Kameo, Kandoo, Kant-Fade, and Kook-Kist. Yet among these 4,000 few brands actually continued for these many years, notably Celanese. So if you're in the market for a name, this book is for you.

Design Patois

Design literacy is as verbal as it is visual. A smart designer can speak as eloquently as she designs. But it's sometimes embarrassing the way that designers prostrate themselves—and the English language—in their promotional material describing in words what they do, as though their designs alone aren't enough to tell the story. It may be true that some clients (or prospective clients) don't have a good grasp of what design is, but most have eyes and can intuit. During the nascent period of graphic design (somewhere around the mid-1920s) all that a commercial artist advertising in one of the many promotional annuals had to say was, "Jeanne Doe, calligraphy, layout, illustration," and the point was made (in part because the services were being bought by agencies or art directors, not directly by clients). Today, with non-design clients being more active in the hiring process, something called design philosophy has become the basis of a new patois. Philosophy is not pejorative, but when it turns to sophistry—beware!

"When there is a gap between one's real and one's declared aims, one turns as it were instinctively to long words and exhausted idioms, like cuttlefish squirting out ink."—George Orwell

For at least the past decade designers have tried to position themselves as legitimate professionals. Inherent in this quest is an attempt to squelch the myth that visual people are ostensibly illiterate. Where the myth started is anyone's guess. After all, the first, what one might call, literate people—those who developed the earliest codified languages—were image makers. The first alphabets were comprised of images. Early scripture was illuminated by scribes who made pictures as well as words. The first typefaces were designed by artists. The first books were designed by artist/writers. So, traditionally, designers have been a very literate people. Then where and when did the distinction begin? Maybe it came with the onset of commercial printing, when publicity was churned out, not designed—when its makers began providing service, not art. Not all commercial printers or commercial artists were enemies of the word, yet the impact of those who were has had a detrimental effect, ultimately leading in the early twentieth century to the schism between copywriters and designers.

During the 1950s these distinctions in the advertising world started to blur, but graphic designers were still suffering from the effects of negative stereotypes. Ever since graphic designers began adding terms like "marketing" and "communications" to their billheads, the accepted notion that having a codified philosophy would undo those negative stereotypes has resulted in design firms issuing promotional materials replete with weighty (and sometimes dramatic) mission statements that read either like legal briefs or epic poems, like this one:

Communications: Visual plays leading to emotional involvement.
Communications: Creativity at levels that make the experience.
Communications: Materials that desire to be collected for keeps.
Communications: Turn the target. Flip the crowd.
Communications: Translate the message into action to your advantage.
Communications: Manage the trains of thought and the rest will come to
                you for yours.

Without any disrespect intended, is what you just read substance or hype? Did it describe or confuse? Think about the selling (flap or ad) copy on a book or the liner notes on a record. In both cases the best of these titillate, if not illuminate. What does this copy tell us? Visual plays? A rather strained metaphor. Emotional involvement? A lot to hope for from a piece of paper. Collected for keeps? Hold on! Even the best publicity has a limited shelf life. Manage the trains of thought? Hey, did anyone copy-edit this?

"If language be not in accordance with the truth of things, affairs cannot be carried on to success." —Confucius

As hyperbolic as it is, the "visual plays" copy is at least somewhat creative compared to the rest of the conventional fare. Indeed, with few welcome exceptions when designers, especially firms, extol their own virtues, the results are dry, platitudinous, and repetitive, with buzzwords reminiscent of police accounts like the ones one hears uttered on the TV news by rookie cops: "The perp, a Caucasian, white female, was apprehended and subdued by two pursuing, uniformed officers, while proceeding to gain unlawful access to the abode of the victim..."

To a teacher of languages there comes a time when the world is but a place of many words and man appears a mere talking animal not more wonderful than a parrot. —Joseph Conrad

Like cadets parroting the phrases in Jargon 101 at any police academy, most designers learn—Lord knows from where—that to gain respect in the outside world it is imperative to use officious language they would never normally use. No school exists to teach this stuff, yet take virtually any promotional brochure for a design firm, scratch the surface, and you will find variations of the following platitudes:

• Design is a tool for achieving specific results. Being responsive, we begin each project by learning exactly what results our client expects. This then becomes our communications goal.

• Establishing an appropriate, positive emphasis is the key. This, in conjunction with good graphic design, is our special skill.

• Our work exhibits a great diversity of styles and imagery. In an era of design specialists, we invariably believe that as varied as the messages are, so should the means of conveying them.

These statements by three very different design firms are not inherently disingenuous, but when viewed as representative of most promo copy they are formulaic. Should all selling copy sound alike? Imagine what the prospective client who gets pitched by many designers must think after reading the same phrases and sentiments over and over. Probably he or she must think that they've all read the same copy of *How To Succeed In Business Without Really Trying*, or at least have hired the same PR firm. To further the point, despite the remarkable diversity among design firms today, their hype comes from the same copy of *Bartlett's Familiar Design Firm Promotions*.

The following phrases have been culled from a variety of sources. In fact, virtually no two design firms represented by these unattributed statements do the same kind of work. For purposes of clarity they are categorized according to the seven major thematic categories.

1. Happiness Is a Warm Client

- The process begins with analysis, immersion into the client's situation in order to define the true problem.

- Our primary concern is with our clients' success in their business.

- The basic need of most clients who come to us is to fulfill a business function.

- Our primary concern is to solve the client's communications objective.

- Our goal is to meet our clients' visual communications needs by applying an approach based on discipline, appropriateness, and ambiguity. [huh?]

- We carefully analyze our client's needs, and if necessary, reinterpret them in a more profound way than the client can do.

- A key element to our approach is that we uniquely tailor each project to a particular client's needs.

- We will not begin a project without a clear understanding of the spoken and unspoken client needs.

- Today, we bring to our clients a rich, ever-expanding base of knowledge and experience.

- Our main concern is understanding and working closely with our clients to carefully think through and define the problem at hand.

- No matter how well we prepare ourselves with information, the client's knowledge far exceeds ours.

2. Style? We Don't Have No Stinkin' Style

- Our approach to design has always been concept-oriented. We feel that a good concept is the single most important aspect of any project. Along with effective design and attention to detail, a strong concept has always made the difference between a good solution and a great one.

- The diversity of our work provides us with the experience and ability to approach a range of design problems in a fresh way.

- Design is the solution of problems, incorporating ideas in relation to the given problem, rather than the arbitrary application of fashionable styles.

- We produce design that goes against the jarring nature of our times.

- We're interested in producing contemporary design, design that's straightforward looking and appropriate for each client.

- Our belief is that any one visual problem has an infinite number of solutions.

- We don't have a style or philosophical framework. We simply want to understand, then solve the problem.

- We do not have a house style, but favor designs that are crisp and simple enough to stand out among today's cluttered communications.

3. Meaningful Relationships

- Our professional ability has been developed and tested for 20 years in a highly competitive environment and has been the basis of many enduring relationships.

- We pay special attention to creating strong working relationships among members of the project team. That our approach works has been proven by the unusual amount of repeat business our clients have offered us.

- Recognizing that team effort is required to create successful design, we define our role as a collaborative one.

- We thrive on long-term client relationships, having many major corporate clients for years.

- We nurture the client from beginning to end.

4. Diversified Meaningful Relationships

- We've maintained variety in the types of projects and clients that we handle; this has given us the opportunity to develop a diversified portfolio of work.

- Because of our diversity we've attracted a wonderful group of multi-talented designers, and we are very proud of them.

5 Touchy-Feely-Squeezy

- Graphic design should touch the viewer as well as inform.

- Imagination and sensibility create the most potent visual communication.

- It's not that we don't believe in a structure or grid; we just believe they should be felt instead of seen.

- We try to balance our own personal insight with the client's particular needs—design is a magical balance.

6. Today Is the First Day of the Rest of Our Lives

- Every client, project, and problem is unpredictable. Each is unique. Our mission as a group is to solve the unique problem, manage the unusual project, and serve our wary client the best quality design available.

- We welcome the challenge of different business involvements.

- Our experience allows us to approach a range of design problems in a fresh way.

7. How Do I Love Me?

- We take great pride in a body of work that has received national recognition for excellence, and in the roster of prestigious clients who hired us to create it.

One has to wonder whether these designers and firms read each other's promotions or whether these pearls just develop over time in their own hermetically sealed environments. Design firms tend to stink of their own perfume. In fact, virtually all of the designers represented by the statements above are fluid and literate when talking about their work. But put them in front of a keyboard and they choke up.

Of course, there are those who eschew the conventions of promo writing. Some designers have gone overboard in the other direction emphasizing human, rather than business, values like this one: "During our day, we encourage pride but not possessiveness. Rarely, in an open-office environment can an idea emerge and evolve without being 'touched' by more than one person. And this interaction is what tests the idea to make sure of its rightfulness." Others prefer wit and humor, like this send-up of a famous quote: When I hear the words "design philosophy" I reach for my X-Acto. (The reference is to Hermann Goring, who said, "When I hear the word culture, I reach for my revolver.")

But the most understated and curiously poetic piece that this writer ever read can be attributed to Henry Wolf in the book *New York Design*: "My firm is not unique but it combines the facilities of photography and design under one roof. I photograph for my own concepts." Though a masterpiece of clarity and concision, one might nevertheless wonder, does he get much work?

The Return of Stencil Lettering

Typographic literacy is perhaps the single-most important attribute a designer can possess. It's important to know how to use all kinds of type, even those that may seem unsophisticated. The stencil is just such a type style, but it should not be prejudiced against.

In a just world, a Baltimore elementary school teacher, Ruth Libauer Hormats, along with her brother, Robert Libauer, should have been elevated into the type design pantheon. In the 1940s the former invented and the latter marketed a handy stencil letter drawing system for the do-it-yourselfer, making ad hoc lettering for signs, posters, and displays much easier. Although Hormats did not invent the stencil per se, her Stenso guide sheets on heavy cardboard were state of the art for decades before the computer. They came in various sizes and type families, including Gothic, Old English, Frontier, Modern Script, Art Deco, and even Hebrew. Although it was a significant departure from the standard brass stencils once used for marking crates, packages, and bales of all kinds dating back to the eighteenth century and before, Stenso was to type design as military music is to music—decidedly functional yet not nuanced and, by fine typographic standards, comparatively unattractive, even crass. Nonetheless, in the same way that booming marshal rhythms have been incorporated into classical and popular music, stencil-lettering style has long influenced sophisticated typography and graphic design.

Stencil lettering, characterized by breaks of negative space between portions of each letter, never really went out of fashion (if you consider fashion to be "Post No Bills" signs, military labels, parking garage directional signs, and even the Boston Police and Fire department logos) yet for the past few years it has been coming back into style. The most visible examples lately are found on the sides of New York City buses

where the stencil logos for the Broadway revival of *West Side Story* and the new sci-fi film *District 9* are writ large. The stencil style is commonly used to signify something raw or dirty. The *West Side Story* logo, with its silhouetted fire escapes, originally designed in the 1950s by Saul Bass, evokes the look of a tenement; the sullied stencil letters suggest the torn posters found on many such buildings. (Bass also designed the stenciled logo for *Exodus* to suggest the Israeli armed struggle.) *West Side Story* is also the inspiration for the trademark of yet another urban musical, RENT. This logo, designed by Drew Hodges, aesthetically telegraphs the graffiti-layered Lower East Side, once a ghetto for the alternative culture. The logo for *District 9* implies a ghetto of a different kind—this one an off-limits refugee camp for extraterrestrials who had the ironic misfortune to land in post apartheid South Africa. These examples represent what I call "typography parlant," in which typefaces conjure or speak to the essence of what the word or words mean—like the word ICE with icicles hanging from it. When it is not evoking a military mood, stencil lettering shouts commands like "danger," "keep out," or "no parking."

But not all stencil typefaces are so grittily authoritarian. About every year, type designers produce one or two new stencil fonts continuing an urbane typographic tradition started in the early twentieth century by such devout modernists as Paul Renner, who designed the landmark Futura typeface and its stencil cousin, Futura Black, or the Bauhausler Josef Albers, who constructed an avant-garde geometric stencil face, or the American logo-meister Paul Rand, who introduced a stencil logo for El Producto cigars. Arguably, Rand's stripped IBM logo is a kind of stencil too.

Stencil fonts can be either high or low typographic art, sometimes both at once. Milton Glaser's "Glaser Stencil," a very clean, contemporary geometric sans serif, has been used on everything from posters advertising a jazz record label to a series of art books, and is a popular seller on the Web site "My Fonts" (where customers can "test drive" fonts by setting their own words to see how they look). Matt Desmond's "Bandoleer," so titled because the face evokes martial might, is not as pristine as Glaser's but evokes an alluring coolness. The negative space between the letters also makes "Bandoleer" seem kinetic, which increases its intrinsic eye-catchiness. Eben Sorkin's "No Step," featured on the Typophile blog (where type fanatics critique one another's work), is another of the many entries into the crowded stencil field, inspired by lettering he had seen on an airplane wing (indeed many new typefaces are inspired by the vernacular and adapted as formal alphabets). Where to place the negative space is often the difference between a boring stencil and a vibrant one, and the extra spaces in Sorkin's Os, Cs, and Us add "color" to the type.

Although the majority of stencil faces are sans serif, even venerable and classic serif faces, like Caslon and Garamond have been adapted as stencils, albeit poorly. An authentic stencil is usually a little rough around the edges, but owing to the precision of computer font-making programs current stencils are flawless (unless not intended to be). My favorite, and not just for its name, is called Der Wiener Stenzel (available through Font Bros), which comes in all caps, and is frankfurter shaped characters cut into pieces with perfect vertical lines. Maybe that's the next direction for stencil faces—type and food. Delicious. I wonder whether Ruth Libauer Hormats would approve?

AAAAA BC
CDDEEEEE"
EEFFGGXX
XIIIIIJKLLL
MMMNNNN
OOOOPPQ
RRRRSSS
STTTTTU
UUUWXY:
ZÆŒŒ(Ø;
%&£.$¢&:
/Qu?[];()
≡≡ ‑‑‑‑‑ ‹‹››
∎∎∎ ∙∙∙∙∙ ○○
890 ‹‹›› +×
II234567"

a a aaccc;
eeeeeeeeen
mmmnnnn
o o o rrr
ssss suuu
uwxzzsø"
bddfhhh
iiii kllll
tttttttzz"
99ppqyj
œœœesn;
ſſſſſſſſſſſ
ſsſsllchck
/ßßtßſ¢()
§‹‹›› ‑‑‑‑‑
∙∙∙ ∙∙∙∙∙ ○○
890%&?[]
II23456?

Velvet Touch Lettering Redux

Speaking of unsophisticated, it's all in the eye, or hand, of the beholder. It was the wee hours of Sunday morning some months back when my computer died while I was designing a brochure that had to be shipped later that day. Without a computer what could I do? Despite my typographic literacy, dependency on technology is a horrible thing. But rather than self-indulgently lament my misfortune, I walked over to a flat file where I stored dozens of old press type sheets—it had not been opened for a decade. Although I hadn't worked with pressure sensitive materials since 1988 B.C. (before computer), I still knew how to use the burnishing tool (it's like riding a bike, you never ever forget) and began to look for any face I could find that included a full alphabet. The one that came closest to what I needed was Compacta Light (120pt).

I know this was a bit rash. A few hours later my office building would be open and I could use the computer there. But the intense and obsessive anxiety of missing a deadline drove me to do the imponderable—return to those primitive, time-consuming methods when many like me spent hours making comps from Letraset, Formatt, Normatype, Letragraphica, and Chartpak Velvet Touch lettering.

I was so happy to forget that process. But you know what? The press down experience wasn't half as bad as I remembered it. In fact it was kind of a Zen-like pleasure to revisit the old velum sheets of black-and-white letters I once so delicately placed on illustration board when metal or phototype was unavailable (or too expensive).

Most young designers will never know how difficult it was to set type, unless you leased your own Compugraphic or PhotoTypositor. It took hours, sometimes days to spec and then get back galleys. Today it is as easy as opening a suitcase. So during the B.C. era, press type was the poor-man/woman's best means of hastily and cheaply composing display type. And it took real skill too. Pity those whose hands were unsteady. Expert burnish-people were worth their weight in gold, although they usually earned minimum wage.

I recall the first time I was introduced to Letraset's revolutionary "Spacematic," a system of broken lines that when matched up served as a baseline. I thought I had found God—the results were so seemingly precise that even I could do it (or that's what I told myself). When I looked at the type I set in this manner, I easily found many flaws. So I decided to make a virtue out of failure and proceeded to copy Dada typography with multiple styles used in a single line or word. It's easy to become good when you start with mistakes as the standard.

Recently, while throwing things out, I found yet another cache of my ancient "instant lettering." There was not a single sheet that was not missing a few letters, and some were more decimated than others. The sheets serve as a mini-history of typographic style, and personal proclivity. At least a dozen sheets of Avant Garde (med. 36pt) were in the folder, but with the exception of the AV combo, I never touched those dreadful ligatures. Other faces I remember using were Neon (I once composed an entire 200-word story at 24pt), Circus (there was something that said loving when using this face), Horatio Light (whatever came over me?), Delfin (pressure-sensitive elegance), and Welt Extra Bold (a replacement for all those News Gothics). Of course, there were standard faces too: The first time I ever used Univers 45 + 75 was in this format. And my introduction to Helvetica, though it was called Geneva, was thanks to press type.

I can't bear to throw these sheets away. Someday (if not today) they may be seen as valuable artifacts from that interregnum between hot and cold type, and between photo and digital composition. The computer put pressure on the pressure-sensitive type companies to find alternatives (or go out of business). But there is something to be said for working with type in this way. As for me, I finished the brochure using Compacta Light and it looked wretched. So I went into the office early and redid the job.

Clipping Art, One Engraving at a Time

To be literate meant understanding how to apply distinct art of clip art. Mastering its mysteries was one way to make great, or merely passable, illustration.

While thinning out my unwieldy design library recently, I came across a dusty collection of books that had not been opened in many, many years. Yet as I began turning the dog-eared, torn, and cut-up pages, vivid memories flew out and landed on me like flies on a heifer. These books, universally known as clip art books, some edited by Dick Sutphen and many others published by Dover and Chelsea House, were owned by almost every American illustrator, designer, and art director who found solace in them when an idea was needed but their imaginations were not entirely up to the task. I know: I was certainly one of the needy ones. The engravings, drawings, and assorted decorative devices that filled the voluminous volumes were more than mere mainstays of the editorial and advertising art fields—the word bible comes to mind. Although currently "copyright free art" is digitally available on CD or the Web, in book form these are becoming increasingly scarce. This is a personal remembrance and homage to them.

I don't know who coined the term "clip art" but it is the universal moniker for permission-free imagery. The concept dates back to decoupage in the late nineteenth century, but became a formal anti-art art in the twentieth with the Dadas in Zurich and Berlin, who freely clipped printer's cuts found in commercial catalogues and samplers for use in their ersatz advertisement and periodical layouts. It was further fine-tuned by, among others, Max Ernst in his 1934 proto- "graphic novel" *Une Semaine De Bonté* (*A Week of Kindness*), which usurps and converts nineteenth-century steel engravings for his quirky surreal narrative. To say the preoccupation with old engravings and printer's fragments pre-dates psychedelic, punk, and grunge is a cliché. Nonetheless it did; each style used clip art. While influenced by dada and surrealism, it was also a cheap and facile way to make something that had all the characteristics of professional art but none of the muss. All one needed were scissors, X-Acto, glue (or wax), and a meager sense of the absurd. The funny thing about clip art is it kind of composed itself. There were (and are) so many variations on so many visual themes, that one had to be blind as a mole not to find a way to make graphic connections. In other words, if one could not employ clip art to great advantage one should look for another line of less demanding work.

Paging through my old books was a trip down desperation lane. I was reminded of literally scores of collage illustrations I made on numerous occasions for a couple publications just when deadline time was running out. My biggest outlet was the *New York Times* Letters to the Editor page back in the '70s, which I art directed back in the day. In fact, I actually remember many of the specific briefs I was illustrating and the various cuts I played with until coming up with the finished mechanical. Usually, these things took less than an hour to make, and as long as I stuck tangentially to the text, the image did its job. For an image I once made titled "Meditations From the Countryside," I found cuts of dancers prancing, a Lincoln log cabin, and variations of bulrushes a-growin' (all in the same book) that I photostated in three different sizes, cut, and pasted into a seemingly seamless whole. It was a pleasurable feeling to make the puzzle work out. I also loved Oxford rule boarder tape that gave the image a more vintage patina. Voila! Instant art! And free too! Yet how embarrassing it was to find other collagists using the same imagery, doubtless from the same source, for totally different concepts.

That was one major problem with clip art: The curious phenomenon that most of us who used it used the same basic 100 or so cuts. Aside from the typical tropes—flags, Uncle Sam's, Santa, donkeys and elephants, variations on Venus and David, Model T cars, etc.—pointing fingers were biggest favorites. It is incredible how many editorial problems could be solved simply with a pointing finger—they were everywhere. But one image that for some inexplicable reason was the most commonly and annoyingly employed was the one of a crazed old man in a nightshirt frolicking, hand-in-hand with a young barefoot nymph. It is on the cover of *Old Engravings & Illustrations* just beside the famous Gibson Girl (the number one icon of the Gilded Age), and could be found in countless layouts, almost as though it was the sign of some cult and all the members conspired to fill the media with it.

Eventually, I weaned myself of clip art. The style had become too familiar and out-of-date. What's more, getting illustrators to do original work was far more satisfying. There were still a number of illustrators, however, using clip art in their own work and after a while I forbade any such being used in the work I assigned for the *Times*. Of course, in the age of Photoshop and digital tomfoolery, an entirely new clip art aesthetic has emerged that some art directors I know have begun to reject. I wonder as the style wheel turns, whether the new generation will return to the old clip art tradition. Let's hope not. I prefer it as a memory.

H. BERTHOLD

SCHRIFTGIESSEREIEN
UND MESSINGLINIEN-FABRIKEN
AKTIEN-GESELLSCHAFT

BERLIN SW 61
LEIPZIG, STUTTGART, WIEN UND RIGA

Berthold's 1924 *Hebrew Type Catalogue*

Type comes in many different languages. Learning how to design non-Roman type is part of the literacy challenge.

Hebrew is one of those difficult languages to master. Hebrew was prohibited in Russia after the 1917 Bolshevik Revolution, effectively curtailing a rich tradition of Jewish publishing. As a result those scholars and authors who could emigrated to England, France, and the United States, while a particularly larger number also resettled in Germany (in part owing to the shared linguistics of German and Yiddish). As Berlin's Jewish community swelled in the 1920s, the city became a wellspring for Jewish book and periodical publishing with various ambitious endeavors—notably the eight-volume *Encyclopedia Judaica*, the last volume of which was published in 1933, the year Hitler was appointed German Chancellor. Another impressive series, the 12-volume *Weltgeschichte des Jüdischen Volkes*, sold over 100,000 copies. In 1931 Salman Schocken founded the prestigious Schocken Verlag, a leading Jewish publisher that produced fiction and nonfiction books, as well as an acclaimed annual Almanach of Jewish literature. The firm released over 225 titles until 1938 when forced into exile after the *Kristallnacht pogrom* (night of broken glass). Salman had already left Germany in 1934 for a new life in Palestine, leaving his manager in charge until they could publish no longer. Later in the 1980s, over twenty years after Salman died, Schocken became an imprint of the American publisher, Pantheon Books.

With this critical mass of Jewish culture emerging during the post-Russian Revolution and post-World War I years, it made sense that one of Germany's most venerable and largest type foundries, H. Berthold AG (founded in Berlin in 1858, with outlets in Leipzig, Stuttgart, Vienna, and Riga), would rigorously develop, produce, and market a relatively wide selection of Hebrew typefaces and ornaments designed both for secular and religious applications. By the late 1910s, Berthold had already adopted standard fonts used for text and display based on original "Shephardic" faces cut in the sixteenth century by French punch-cutter Guillaume Le Bé (known for a keen interest in Hebrew and Arabic lettering). It also offered latter-day variations: Frank Rühl (designed by Cantor Rafael Frank in 1909 for CF Rühl Schriftgießerei in Leipzig, which was bought by Berthold in 1918), Meruba, Margalit, Rashi, and Miriam. Berthold also seriously invested in the production of new faces in the European, or Ashkenazi, style, including Stam, Stam Book, Rahel, and Rambam (all with and without vowels), which were commonly used in European and American commercial, book, and newspaper printing. These types were made available in various weights through general Berthold specimen catalogues, which also featured other non-western alphabets. But in 1924 a dedicated Hebrew catalogue was produced that perfectly complimented Berthold's routine promotional materials for sheer precision and graphic splendor. In hindsight, knowing that barely eleven years later, Jews would be ostracized and the so-called "Jewish lettering" be outlawed by the Nazi state, makes this catalogue all the more poignant.

At the time of what some have called the "Hebrew Renaissance" in Germany, which took hold throughout Central and Eastern Europe, the catalogue was nothing less than a joyous celebration of Hebrew and Yiddish culture. The specimens were vibrantly rendered in the dominant art nouveau and art moderne (deco) graphic mannerisms used by European printers for all kinds of commercial purposes. Yet these graphics also exuded a decidedly Jewish style. The man responsible for the catalogue's creation, Joseph Tscherkassky, was the Manager of the Oriental Department of H Berthold AG. The department was to cater to the growing printing market in Europe and abroad. Born in the Ukraine in 1879, Tscherkassky was proprietor of his own self-named foundry in Kiev, where he created Hebrew fonts for secular use. Yet little is known about his early life, the success or failure of his foundry, or when, in fact, he immigrated to Germany—although his reasons must have been tied to the fortunes (or misfortunes) of the Revolution. Type historian Stephen Lubell, author of *Joseph Tscherkassky: Orientalist and Typefounder*, published in Gutenberg-Jahrbuch in 1996, writes that Tscherkassky was interested in the traditions of both Hebrew and Arabic types. This interest and research resulted later on in an equally exquisite Berthold companion catalogue dedicated to Arabic faces.

"Tscherkassky attempted to give the type specimens a very oriental character combined with his visions of the new Hebrew typography," writes Lubell about the man who might arguably be called the Jan Tschichold of Jewish type. How many typefaces he commissioned, designed, or whether he even designed the complete type catalogue is not categorically known. But it is certain that Tscherkassky, at the behest of Berthold's directors, Dr. Oskar Jolles and Erwin Graumann, was responsible for providing Jewish publishers and cultural organizations with a well-stocked library of fine types.

Nothing was spared in the production of the catalogue, which opens both right to left (with text set in Roman) and left to right (with text set in Hebrew). In addition to its intricately embossed reddish-brown covers with hints of gold leaf printing (actually quite biblical in appearance), the endpapers are a cleverly repeating pattern of interlocking Stars of David with the Berthold logo in Hebrew. Inside, the bountiful offerings include numerous examples of calligraphic text and display faces along with assortments, decorative initial capitals, dingbats, fleurons, and borders. The typefaces are mostly printed in black, yet the ornaments and a major section devoted to especially designed applications is saturated in vibrant colors. A few spreads of sample book title pages show the blend of classical and modern influences, while the majority of customized designed samples, including menus, theatre programs, and letter and billheads, are illuminated as though they were contemporary Medieval manuscripts. There is also a noticeable Arts and Crafts influence in some Pre-Raphaelite illuminated initials. But the over-arching stylistic trope is streamlined Egyptian borrowed from the Pharaoh's tombs. One of the specimens features a quotation from Martin Luther about the ancient Hebrew language, which Lubell correctly observes is "a curious and somewhat disconcerting quotation given Martin Luther's other statements about Jews."

"This catalogue of Hebrew and Jewish Types," writes Tscherkassky in his seven-language (including Arabic) preface, "the first of its kind should redress a great deficiency hitherto existing in Hebrew printing matters." This correctly presumed great interest on the part of publishing houses and bibliographic societies to preserve and propagate the Hebrew alphabet and language. "During my long years as owner of the typefoundry Joseph Tscherkassky in Kiew [Kiev] I had no chance of carrying out the long-entertained idea of perfecting the Hebrew types," he adds.

"Only by assistance on the part of the firm H Berthold AG, the largest type-foundry in Germany, I was able to realize my plans to this great extent." He continues in a salutary tone, "It took 'long years' toilsome preparatory work to examine the Berthold stocks of Hebrew types with the aid of leading Jewish type experts and typographers, and I hope I have found the best and most perfect as regards to form, shape, and technical make." He ends by dedicating the catalogue to Dr. Jolles on the celebration of his twenty-fifth jubilee as director. Incidentally, Dr. Jolles, though trained as an economist and banker, was an avid Jewish bibliophile, the force behind Berthold-Druck private press monographs used for publishing work of Hebrew type designers and other type matters—and so the perfect advocate for Tscherkassky's work.

The Berthold Hebrew catalogue was largely responsible for spreading the gospel of type throughout central Europe, but it was not the only vehicle. Also in 1924, Berthold produced a booklet of Hebrew types designed by Leopold Kurzböck and Anton Schmid, according to Lubell. And in 1925 Berthold also printed a limited edition of ten verses from the Book of Ecclesiasticus. Still, Tscherkassky's catalogue was the flagship for Hebrew lettering for many years. Although he was not able in 1924 to predict the campaign to rid Europe of Jewish culture (even though Hitler's beer hall anti-Semitism was audible), he predicted a resurgence of Yiddish in everyday life, thus a growing market for books and other commercial

printing. 1924 also marked the founding of The Soncino-Gesellschaft (the Society for the Friends of Jewish Books) in Germany, which, according to Lubell, was critical of the catalogue in its official newsletter. Although grateful to Berthold for making the effort, the society took issue with the nuances of its design. "Yet once again one must add with regret, that the creation of a completely satisfactory, well-conceived and classical Hebrew type has not yet been achieved," wrote a reviewer. Similar sighs of classical angst were also heard when in 1925 Tschichold edited an issue of the magazine *TM*, devoted to radical modern "Elementare Typographie." Tscherkassky was understandably disappointed by the response.

While Tscherkassky's contribution was considerable, the market for commercial Hebrew type did not grow as rapidly as anticipated. This may have been one reason why in 1930 he moved to South America to manage a Berthold branch in Brazil. Lubell assumes he was demoted from his position in Berlin, but nonetheless the move saved his life. Three years later in 1933 he was fired in a move that prefigured the widespread dismissals of Jews from German professions. He started a new printing company, which became the largest packaging printer in South America. Although Joseph Tscherkassky seemed to have abandoned his overt interests in Hebrew types, Berthold's 1924 *Hebrew Type Catalogue*—while rare today—is a crucial historical document in light of the fate that befell the Jews (and so-called Jewish lettering) of Europe.

A.TOLMER

M I S E

THEORY
PRACTICE
PAST...
PRESENT
ART...
DRAUGHTSMAN
PAINTING
ARCHITECTURE
DECORATION
GEOMETRY
IMAGES
THE BOOK
PUBLICITY
PRECEDENT
WRITING
PRINTING
TYPOGRAPHY
SLOGANS
PHOTOS
BLACK AND
FORM
ESPRIT
STYLE
SIMPLICITY
DARING
BALANCE
AVANT-GARDE
MASS

EN

the theory and
practice of lay-out

PAGE

THE STUDIO LTD

First on Deco

There are many manuals that teach designers literacy. During the nascent years of modernism in the early 1920a and 1930s, certain eminent designers in Europe and the United States delighted in telling other designers how, and what, to design. These self-appointed prophets were so convinced they had discovered graphic design's holy grail—rightness of form—they wanted everyone in eye and earshot to revel in their revelations. To spread the Word (and image), they frequently issued sermons from the mount in the form of verbose manifestos and detailed manuals. Most proved inconsequential; a few, such as W.A. Dwiggins' *Layout in Advertising* and Jan Tschichold's *Die Neue Typographie (The New Typography)*, both published in 1928, endured. The former laid out rigid rules of contemporary advertising design, while the latter foretold progressive mannerisms and styles that did, in fact, take hold.

But it was another, more commercially oriented book, appearing a few years later, that defined the new mainstream aesthetic of the period and became, arguably, the design bible of all design bibles. Alfred Tolmer's *Mise en Page: The Theory and Practice of Layout*, published in 1932 in separate English and French editions (Dwiggins' and Tschichold's books at that time were published only in English in the United States and in German in Germany, respectively), codified the most widely practiced of all the early twentieth-century design styles. Advertised in the leading design journals and sought after by European and American advertising artists, *Mise en Page* (the French term for layout) was a lavishly printed primer of that strain of design then called moderne, and subsequently dubbed art deco.

Tolmer's tome was an ambitious and alluring treatise on contemporary style. His goal was to position deco in history and provide formal guidelines, while at the same time encouraging opportunities for inventive design options, thus luring some business to his firm. With

The real and the imaginary, true and the false, the object the interpretation of the obj get on very well together

The starting point of an advertising campaign may either artistic and literary, or severely commercial humorous, according to the public aimed at. From starting point to the supporting arguments, from first shout of the slogan to the clinching explanat from the picture which brutally exposes the worst that which demonstrates the best, from that which sugg a good thing to do to that which explains how to do every element of publicity can be brought into play w an infinite diversity of effect. There may be symb elements, anecdotic elements, schematized eleme varying in artistic form according to the nature of the ticular problem. This form will decide what processe

slip-sheets, tip-ons, embossed and debossed pages, and fold-outs, the book itself was a model of eclectic mastery, a template for all designers who wanted to be on the crest of a stylish wave.

In *Mise en Page*, Tolmer co-opted fundamental aspects of apolitical modernism for commercial application. Photomontage, then considered the foremost progressive design conceit (Moholy-Nagy called it "mechanical art for a mechanical age"), is given considerable attention in Tolmer's hierarchy. "Photography gives concrete form to the subtlest thoughts," he wrote. "It has the gift of imparting the dullest, most mechanical, and impersonal things the sensitiveness and poetry

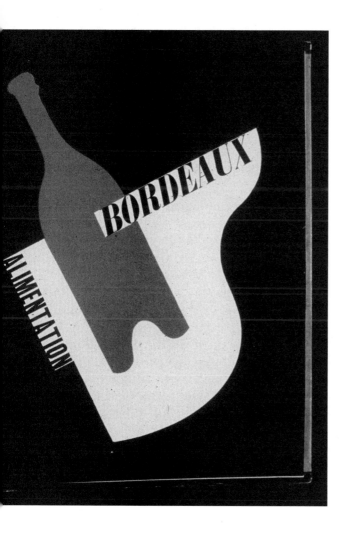

which admits them into our dreams." These words may be more flowery than those found in the typical modernist manifesto, but they are no less committed to a cause. And they exemplify how Tolmer fervently and single-handedly smoothed the edges off orthodox modernism, making once radical design concepts palatable for business and the masses.

Tolmer, who died in 1957, is not as well known today as Dwiggins or Tschichold, but he played a significant role in the French printing and advertising industries. He was the third generation of the prestigious Parisian printing house Maison Tolmer, which produced some of the most stylish graphics in France for luxe publications and packaging, fashioning a diverse array of exquisitely conceived printed commercial products, from elegant boxes to advertising posters and publicity brochures. In addition to overseeing the output of his family's firm, Tolmer edited art books and catalogues, and illustrated covers for magazines and children's books: a true design auteur.

While his writing was a bit strained (maybe a result of bad French to English translation), he did his utmost to present solid intellectual arguments for why modern/moderne design was the perfect form for the age. Tolmer began by posing the idea that writing and design were one and the same. "The art of layout," he wrote, "is born at the moment when man feels the urge to arrange in an orderly fashion the expression of his thoughts. The first writing is a decorative setting in itself, a symbolic décor closely connected with the décor that is purely ornamental."

This vivid presentation of moderne design appeared at exactly the right moment. The visual genre was introduced to the world in Paris at the Exposition Internationale des Arts Decoratifs et Industriels Modernes in 1925, and the new, ornamental sensibility quickly became en vogue for all the applied arts throughout the industrialized and commercialized world. A style of affluence at the outset, deco trickled down to the bourgeoisie, skirting the ideological overlays of its mingled modernist traits. Cubist, Futurist, Constructivist, De Stijl, even Bauhaus elements were absorbed by moderne; rectilinear geometries and sans-serif typefaces combined with stark ornamental patterns such as sunrays, lightning bolts, motion lines, and other symbols of Machine Age progress.

Between the world wars, design entrepreneurs like Tolmer understood that given the ebbs and flows in European and American consumption brought about by the financial roller-coaster of the world markets, this kind of high style was needed to position goods. Styling was touted by marketing and advertising experts as a tool of allure that encouraged sales in everything consumable.

For all its popularity, *Mise en Page* was not always easy to obtain. The book earned a reputation that far exceeded its initial French edition printing of 1,500 and a comparable number of English language editions simultaneously published by prestigious London design publisher Studio Books and New York-based William Rudge (the publisher of the original *PRINT*). Each edition reportedly sold out within three months of release, but designers who never laid their hands on the original were given some access to it through excerpts in leading trade magazines like the German *Gebrausgraphik* and French *Arts et Métiers Graphiques*.

Mise en Page's astute sampling of modernistic methodologies convinced contemporary designers they were essential: With Tolmer's boost, deco lasted more or less until the outbreak of World War II, when an austerity binge hit Europe. Elements of deco were incorporated into subsequent styles, but for the most part simplicity ruled design. In 1966, following a retrospective exhibition, *Les Années '25'*, held at the Musée des Arts Décoratifs in Paris, the allure of deco artifacts triggered a rash of pastiche. Today the original artifacts are treasured as mid-century gems in exhibitions (like one in 2003 at the Victoria & Albert Museum that traveled to the Museum of Fine Arts in Boston in 2004) and updated versions of this stunning decorative mannerism are routinely injected into contemporary design.

The Missing Link: Graphic Design Trade Magazines and the Modern Avant Garde

In addition to manuals, trade magazines taught literacy. Graphic design evolved during the late nineteenth century from a sideline of the printing industry into an autonomous field with its own lore, icons, and personalities. The missing link in this evolutionary process is trade magazines. Initially they established professional standards for printing, typesetting, and bookbinding yet viewed ornamental design as ephemeral. However, by the turn of the century, when businesses demanded printers provide more sophisticated layout and typography, trade magazine editors were forced to analyze and critique new advances, which in turn gave weight to an art of graphic design. These magazines did not just reflexively report the current trends. Instead some aggressively codified key methods and mannerisms that in turn defined a profession no longer at the mercy of ad hoc taste but rather supported by a received canon.

Trade periodicals also cautiously tweaked the status quo. Indeed most of the early ones were neutral but occasionally contained articles about novel design mannerisms—like in the late 1890s when *The Inland Printer* introduced a variant of French art nouveau to America. This unconventional curvilinear style challenged accepted taste but made posters and handbills ten times more eye-catching than predictable fare.

The Inland Printer became the clarion for American art nouveau in the same way that a hundred years later *Emigre* was the clarion for digital postmodernism.

Developments in European art could not be ignored because impressionism, expressionism, and later cubism influenced the design of letterforms and illustrations, and ultimately late-nineteenth-century poster designers in France, Germany, and England (where radical styles were practiced by a new breed of artist/designer) adopted modern concepts of space, composition, perspective, and color.

Maîtres de l'Affiche (1895-1900) was the first periodical devoted to the late nineteenth century French poster art. With portfolios generously filled with poster miniatures printed in color on one side of each page, *Maîtres* was a model of how trade magazines could integrate art, commerce, and aesthetics into a single editorial entity. Consequently, the advertising poster was an ideal theme on which to build a trade magazine, because it integrated art and craft, which could elicit stories about type, image, and message applicable to all graphic design genres. Subsequent early-twentieth-century magazines, such as the separate editions of *The Poster* in England and the United States, sprang up as the advertising industry became a more integral part of business. Although most were not as conscientious about the quality of their reproductions as *Maîtres*, there was one magazine, the Berlin-based *Das Plakat* (*The Poster*), that, given its focus on conventional and avant garde sensibilities, emerged as a more historically influential review than any of the others.

Founded in 1910 by Hans Josef Sachs, a chemist by training, dentist by profession, and poster collector by preference, *Das Plakat* was the official journal of the Verein der Plakatfreunde (The Society for Friends of the Poster). Its purpose was to champion art poster collecting, increase scholarship among amateurs and professionals, and promote the advantages of poster art to would-be clients. In the process it covered the poster scene by raising aesthetic, cultural, and legal issues. As a survey of significant German (and ultimately international) work, the magazine addressed plagiarism and originality, design in the service of politics and propaganda, and representation versus abstraction, raising the discourse of poster art from purely trade to cultural. Through the years its influence on designers increased, as did its circulation, from an initial print run of 200 copies to over 10,000.

Sachs was inspired by a progressive group of German advertising artists known as the Berliner Plakat who practiced a new style called the sachplakat (object poster) that transformed the bold linearity of German

Jugenstil into a reductive graphic language. In 1906, Lucian Bernhard "invented" this objective method when he submitted a starkly simple poster to a prestigious competition. The poster for Priester Matches showing only two large, wooden matches on a solid maroon background became the hallmark of sachplakat characterized by the rejection of ornament in favor of an unambiguous focal image of the product with only the brand-name as headline. Sachplakat monumentalized the ordinary, whether a pair of matches, typewriter, shoes, or light bulb.

Das Plakat favored sachplakat because Bernhard, who Sachs invited to design the Society's logo and stationery and join its board, had strong ties to the Berlin advertising and printing firm, Hollerbaum and Schmidt, which built its reputation on the popular style and took out many advertising pages in the magazine. But quid pro quo aside, sachplakat was not the only style represented in the magazine. Its cover images were designed by many different artists in various graphic mannerisms and the nameplate of each bi-monthly *Das Plakat* was routinely changed to fit the style of the cover. Most covers were printed on a heavy, uncoated paper allowing for concentrated color saturation, and occasionally special metallic ink was used. The interior layout and typefaces were fairly consistent (Antiqua designed by Bernhard) and the illustrations of graphic works were frequently mortised out of the columns and framed inside black borders. This and a generous number of color plate, tip-in facsimiles made *Das Plakat* the most awesome trade magazine of its time.

During World War I *Das Plakat* featured articles on the design of war bonds, stamps, and posters produced by allied and belligerent nations. After the war, Sachs published a supplement exclusively devoted to political posters and turned the magazine's attention towards media other than posters, such as trademarks and typefaces, which made it even more professionally oriented than when it began.

Sachs acknowledged the European modern avant garde but never wholeheartedly embraced its more radical tendencies. Yet by *Das Plakat*'s demise in 1921, commercial artists and typographers were indeed influenced by futurism, de stijl, constructivism, and dada, and some of the keepers of tradition gradually began to apply these methods to their quotidian work. Nonetheless, it took an acute visionary to truly see how avant garde ideas could be efficiently applied to commerce, therefore, it was not until 1925 that a mainstream printing and design trade magazine, *Typographische Mitteilungen*, the monthly organ of the German Printer's Association in Leipzig, shocked the professional nervous system by sanctioning the most radical approaches.

Under the guest editorship of the typographic prodigy Jan Tschichold, *Typographische Mitteilungen* showcased graphic design and typography from the Bauhaus, de stijl, and constructivism as functional for use among the widespread profession. It was the first time that the German printing and graphics industry was offered a full dose of the type and layout, later known as the New Typography, produced by what was largely thought of, if considered in mainstream circles at all, as an aesthetic fringe with socialist political implications.

Nonetheless, *TM*, founded in 1903, did not intend to radicalize design. The magazine's regular editorial policy was fairly restrained when it came to promoting experimental work and showed little regard for radical schools or movements. The magazine's basic style menu included conventional German Black Letter typography with occasional moderne examples of letterheads, logos, and book covers sprinkled through its monthly issues. While *TM*'s responsibility was to report on the status quo, it nonetheless allowed Tschichold an unprecedented opportunity in his issue titled "Elementary Typography" to showcase form-givers El Lissitzky, Kurt Schwitters, Theo Van Doesburg, Karel Teige, among others, and totally redesign the entire format and masthead of the magazine in their manner.

Tschichold's October 1925 issue was a kind of October revolution in its own right, given the strong dose of avant garde dissonance and asymmetry injected into the otherwise straight-laced, central-axis commercial advertising of the time. Yet though *TM* inadvertently made history, the very next month it returned to its regular staid layouts. Still, the deed was done and it inspired other trade magazines of the period to be more open. In fact, German journals like *Gebrauchsgraphik*, *Reklame*, and *Archiv* devoted considerable space to avant garde and avant garde-inspired approaches which effectively mainstreamed these ideas until the rise of Nazism in 1933 and its prohibitions against modernism.

Of these assorted trade magazines the most cosmopolitan and far-reaching was Berlin-based *Gebrauchsgraphik*, founded and edited by Dr. H.K. Frenzel in 1923, just as the chaos caused by devastating postwar economic inflation was causing severe privations. *Gebrauchsgraphik* was a bi-lingual (English and German) chronicle of "new" international graphic art styles and techniques, yet it was truly distinguished by the guiding editorial notion that advertising art was a force for good in the world. Frenzel held the idealistic belief that commercial art educated the public because, "He saw advertising as the great mediator between peoples, the facilitator of world understanding, and through that understanding, world peace," author Virginia Smith explains in *The Funny Little Man* (Van Nostrand Reinhold, New York, 1996). Frenzel was a free thinker and *Gebrauchsgraphik* had no direct or subordinate ties to any ideological, political, or philosophical movements.

Despite his social idealism, Frenzel was professionally pragmatic enough to balance traditional and progressive aspects of contemporary design in his magazine. He also understood the psychology of the mass mind, knowing that stimulation would be achieved through novel, sometimes challenging visual approaches. So he used the Bauhaus ideal as a model for integrating graphic and other design disciplines into one overarching practice and promoted designers who exemplified this ideal, like Herbert Bayer who was showcased in *Gebrauchsgraphik*'s portfolios and on covers. However, compared to Jan Tschichold's *Typographische Mitteilungen*, Frenzel's magazine was a much more conservative graphic environment.

Frenzel's advocacy for the new stopped short of making Modern design himself. His magazine visually toed the line between what the public would find acceptable and unacceptable experimental progressive principles regarding legibility. Perhaps for this reason *Gebrauchsgraphik* survived through the early years of the Third Reich more or less unscathed. Yet Nazi dictates ultimately transformed the magazine by forcing out unsanctioned "degenerate" modern design. After Frenzel's death in 1937 (purportedly a suicide) *Gebrauchsgraphik*'s new editors cautioned gebrauchsgraphikers to "avoid Impressionism, Expressionism, Cubism, and Futurism," thus severing those ties to the avant garde that Frenzel had proudly established.

In the United States during the early 1930s, avant garde graphic design was promoted by the trade press only once the dust had settled in Europe. England's premier journal, *Commercial Art* (and later *Art and Industry*) was far ahead of America in its embrace of the avant garde, and provided one of the earliest English language introductions to the Bauhaus and its affinities. In America during the 1920s the advertising industry was surprisingly cautious about changing its time-tested methods of selling products through clever slogans, headlines, and tag- lines, more so than images alone. Few American design pundits were so bold as to advocate advertising or commercial art as utopian—it was realistically viewed as a capitalist tool. Nonetheless, two magazines that were often favorably compared to *Gebrauchsgraphik*, *Advertising Arts*, and *PM* (later renamed *AD*) advanced the practice of progressive graphic design that had been brought to America, in part, by émigré European designers and influenced by native born modernists.

The premiere issue of *Advertising Arts* on January 8, 1930, was the first mainstream attempt to integrate modern art into an admittedly antiquated commercial culture. Although dada and surrealist art journals had published in the United States in the 1920s, this perfect-bound monthly supplement of the weekly trade magazine, *Advertising and Selling*, offered ways to institute design programs in everyday practice that it noted was "adopted by radicals." The magazine became a vortex for progressive American graphic and (the newly christened field) industrial design. Yet *Advertising Arts* is not to be confused with the radical European design manifestoes that introduced the New Typography. The modernistic design (i.e. modernism with the edges dulled) proffered in its pages was a tool of the capitalist concept known as style obsolescence. As devised by advertising man Earnest Elmo Calkins, this notion of programmed obsolescence was a means of exploiting "modern art" to encourage consumers to "move the goods" and sell, sell, sell.

Advertising Arts debuted during the throes of the Great Depression, when the economy was at its nadir and desperation was at its zenith. Design was a weapon in the war against stagnation. Editors Frederick C. Kendall and Ruth Fleischer had a mission—to encourage innovation while celebrating advertising designers who manipulated consumers to consume. So rather than publish the usual diet of trade gossip and technical notices, Kendall and Fleischer made their magazine into a blueprint for the marketing of modernity. Its writers, including influential graphic and industrial artists such as Lucian Bernhard, Rene Clark Clarence P. Hornung, Paul Hollister, Norman Bel Geddes, and Rockwell Kent, passionately advocated contemporary art as industry's foremost savior. In *Modern Layouts Must Sell Rather Than Startle*, author Frank H. Young summed up *Advertising Arts'* ethos this way: "Daring originality in the use of new forms, new patterns, new methods of organization, and bizarre color effects is the keynote of modern layout and is achieving the startling results we see today." At the same time, *Advertising Arts* also cautioned against flagrant excess: "In some instances enthusiasm for modernism has overshadowed good judgment and the all-import selling message is completely destroyed," continued Young. The design of the magazine itself lived up to his words, for each issue had a striking cover by a contemporary designer, illustrator, or photographer that signaled rejection of the old.

Advertising Arts promulgated a uniquely American design

style called streamline. Compared to the elegant austerity of the Bauhaus, streamline was a bluntly futuristic mannerism based on sleek aerodynamic design born of science and technology that included ornamental flourishes symbolizing speed. Rather than the right angles of European modernism, streamline was characterized by aerodynamic curves. Planes, trains, and cars were given the swooped-back appearance that both symbolized and physically accelerated velocity. Consequently, type and image were designed to echo that sensibility. The airbrush was the graphic medium of choice, and all futuristic visual conceits, practical or symbolic, were encouraged.

PM (*Production Manager*) later re-christened *AD* (*Art Director*) did not advocate the streamline aesthetic with the same fervency as *Advertising Arts* but did champion both modern and modernistic methods. Founded in 1934 by Dr. Robert Leslie, a medical doctor by training, type aficionado by choice, and co-founder of the Composing Room Inc, a leading New York type house, *PM* was a trade magazine imbued with missionary zeal. Leslie and co-editor Percy Seitlin committed to explore design with a blind eye towards style or ideology and gave progressive designers a platform that underscored the viability of the New Typography in American advertising and graphic design. The small 6" x 8" bi-monthly journal explored a variety of print media, covered industry news, and often celebrated the virtues of asymmetric typography and design. It was also the first American journal to showcase émigrés Herbert Bayer, Will Burtin, Gustav Jensen, Joseph Binder, M.F. Agha, as well as native-grown Mmderns Lester Beall, Joseph Sinel, E. McKnight Kauffer, and Paul Rand. Like Das Plakat, et al, PM/AD's covers were each original and unique. Kauffer's, for example, was characteristically cubistic. Bayer's was objective, and Rand's was playfully modern. Matthew Leibowitz's prefigured new wave in its dada-inspired juxtaposition of discordant decorative old wood types.

Three years after starting *PM* Leslie opened a small room in The Composing Room office as the *PM* Gallery, the first exhibition space in New York seriously devoted to graphic design and typography. The magazine and gallery had a symbiotic relationship; often a feature in the magazine would lead to an exhibition in the gallery or vice versa. Thanks to these additional events, the magazine's own following grew and with it emerged a lively appreciation for an avant garde that by 1942 was effectively adopted by mainstream businesses.

By the April-May 1942 issue, with World War II then in full throttle, the editors ran this solemn note: "AD is such a small segment of this wartime world that it is almost with embarrassment, and certainly with humility, that we announce the suspension of its publication...for the duration. The reasons are easy to understand: shortage of men and materials, shrinkage of the advertising business whose professional workers AD has served, and all-out digging in for Victory." The magazine did not resume publishing after the war but left a documentary record of how American and European designers forged a universal design language in the service of business. World War II ended the idealistic stage of avant garde design. *PM/AD* helped to define a commercial stage that continued well into the 1950s.

After World War II graphic design was intensely covered in dozens of trade magazines published in countries where industry and design were integral bedfellows. But the most significant of the postwar graphic design clarions was *Graphis*. This Zurich-based, multi-lingual, international magazine founded in 1946 by poster designer Walter Herdeg was an outlet for iconoclastic designers and illustrators from around the world, especially from Soviet Eastern European countries, which he believed were the seat of a new underground avant garde. *Graphis* was a newly opened window on the design world's most ambitious emerging movements and individuals, in addition to a handful of significant design and typography magazines published from the late 1940s through the early 1950s that emphasized art, commerce, and indigenous trends—including *Word & Image* in England, *Print* and *CA* in the United States, and *Graphik* and *Novum Gebrauchsgraphik* in West Germany. But the most groundbreaking, *Portfolio* (from 1949–51), truly celebrated interdisciplinary design serving as a direct link to postwar avant garde thinking.

Edited for three issues by Frank Zachary and designed by Alexey Brodovitch, *Portfolio* defined a late-modern sensibility that viewed the concept of good design as weaving throughout culture as a whole. Portfolio leveled the field between high and low art and so doing changed the fundamental definition of a trade journal. *Portfolio* was not merely a professional organ but a mainstream design magazine with its roots firmly planted in culture. Much has been written about *Portfolio* so suffice it to say, it markedly influenced the 1950s and 1960s magazines *Neue Grafik* in Switzerland, *Typographica* in England, and even *U&lc* in the United States. which are the forbears of *Emigre*, *Eye*, and *Baseline* today.

Early graphic design trade magazines are missing links in the development of styles, propagation of standards, and canonization of the profession. Although current periodicals have come a long way since the late-nineteenth-century periodicals, the common editorial mandate to analyze, critique, and showcase contemporary and avant garde achievement is what makes these journals integral to graphic design history.

arts & architecture

PRICE 50 CENTS

FEBRUA
1 9 4

Better than Real: Graphic Design Facsimiles Steal the Stage

Paging through vintage dada journals, El Lissitzky's *For the Voice*, or Depero's bolted book should provide more than vicarious design thrills. Hands-on contact with important graphic design artifacts such as these can influence how a design scholar views a body of work or inspire a graphic designer to practice his craft in new ways. The photographic reproductions of rare design pieces that appear in history books and magazines provide a glimmer of insight, but to truly appreciate—and savor—historic design objects one must understand nuances of form and structure. This derives from scrutiny. Yet such relics are not so easy to scrutinize since many of them from the late nineteenth and early twentieth centuries are so fragile that turning their pages can be risky. Librarians and curators are justifiably reluctant to let even the most serious scholar finger through these valuables lest they get damaged or destroyed.

But there is an alternative. Near perfect duplications of originals are almost as good as the real thing. And don't let any stuffy bibliophile tell you otherwise. Facsimiles are more practical research tools for historians and connoisseurs. In fact, many limited edition facsimiles (and all of them are usually published in limited quantities) are often as valuable as those precious originals. A facsimile is a document incarnate—an artifact reborn. The best of them are produced by master printers who capture the nuanced details of the original, from the coverage of ink to the texture of paper. A photographic reproduction

records a particular version of the document—imperfections and all—but a facsimile preserves the essence of the original, as though it just came off the press. Depero Futurista, known as "the bolted book" (libro bullonato), originally published in 1927 by Dinamo-Azari editions of Milan, was a catalogue of paintings, advertisements, and typography by Fortunato Depero, bound by industrial bolts, that is today a bible of late futurist typographic innovation. In 1987 Studio Edizioni Scelte (SPES) in Florence pristinely recreated this masterpiece of futurist adventurism as part of its extensive series of futurist books and manifesti. Each page is a precise echo of the original, retouched to give a mint appearance (nonetheless since publication, the paper has turned yellow with age

giving it an even more authentic patina). The original, which was published in an edition of less than 1,000 copies, and is currently priced as high as $30,000 (*Ars Libri Catalog* 147), is often too delicate to handle. Yet the facsimile can be perused without concern for wear and tear.

This facsimile was relatively expensive because of all the handwork that went into insuring its verisimilitude. Likewise most facsimile publishers pride themselves on how close they come to making flawless copies. In the late 1950s the state-run Zentralantiquariat der DDR began publishing and distributing facsimiles of key avant garde books and journals, many of which had been labeled degenerate by the Nazis. Among the most valued were publications issued through the leftwing publisher Malik Verlag. Original Malik books and periodicals were not always flawlessly printed, but even capturing the fundamental flaws is important to insure an overall gestalt. Facsimiles of the 1925 *Kleine Malik Bücherei*, (Little Malik Library), their inexpensive line targeted to the masses, which includes essential texts by leftist authors and graphics and covers by George Grosz and John Heartfield, are now the primary source material for many scholars of art, design, and politics during the Weimar period. In the early1960s Edition Leipzig in the DDR launched an even more extensive facsimile program that proved a boon for scholars denied access to original documents.

Although facsimiles should not be confused with originals, they do provide a unique virtual experience. In recent years facsimiles have brought publications like the San Francisco Oracle (Regent Press) from 1966-1968 and Andy Warhol's Interview (Edition 7L) from the 1970s back to life. Hundreds of other documentary materials would otherwise be too costly to preserve if not made available through facsimiles. And, while often expensive to produce, facsimiles are high on the agenda of publishers with a historical focus.

The latest batch of facsimiles include two significant periodicals: *Zenit*, the journal of the avant garde movement known as Zenitism, formed in Zagreb during the 1920s, and *Art & Architecture* (1945 -1954), the progressive design magazine that helped put California modernism on the map, edited by John D. Entenza, with original covers by Saul Bass, Gyorgy Kepes, Alvin Lustig, Herbert Matter, and others. Both hold to ambitious production standards.

Ranko Horetzky, a designer in Zagreb, published the boxed collection of individual copies of *Zenit* (originally edited by Ljubomir Micić), which began in 1921. It took him more than 2,000 working hours and more than two years of preparation. "My previous experience with printing posters and graphics in silkscreen helped me a lot with it," Horetzky told me, referring to the many original issues that were in such bad condition he had to make separate scans for each page to be able to make a final completed "reconstruction." The most painstaking part of the work, he said, "was how to find and choose the adequate sorts of papers, similar to the original papers from 1920s. From the beginning I had an idea to make the reprints with the highest possible quality; tactile and visual, free of patina and marks of time and/or use."

The original *Zenit* issues came from mostly from the library and the collections of the Museum of Contemporary Art in Zagreb, and some issues are from private collections in Belgrade and Ljubljana. Difficulty in procuring them was the main reason for producing this edition; he wanted to make issues available to scholars and designers who have had no opportunity to touch them. "I was much more interested in visual than in literal aspect of the content," he added, "as well as the connections and influences between domestic and international avant-garde scene. I also wanted to present not only *Zenit*, but other magazines from that period published by the collaborators of *Zenit*." In addition to the complete run of Zenit he also produced pristine facsimiles of the rare Croatian journals *DaDa* and *Tank*.

The *Zenit* portfolio is impressive, but few facsimiles are as elaborate as *Art & Architecture*, published in 2008 by Taschen Books. Having long been an admirer of California modern, publisher Benedikt Taschen coveted the complete run of this influential wellspring for a small but dynamic group of modern designers in California after World War II. In its pages the celebrated Case Study House program was launched and the progressive California style was born. Although an earlier volume, *Arts and Architecture: The Entenza Years*, edited by Barbara Goldstein (MIT Press, 1990), anthologized some of the best articles from the magazine, the small reproductions of pages did little to underscore the design. Conversely, the 118 issues of *Art & Architecture*, which he published in ten boxes with text by David F. Travers, editor and publisher of the magazine from 1963 until 1967, resurrects the publication in all its glory. It is the supreme act of preservation.

Facsimiles are obviously not the poor man's design artifacts—far from it. Like re-strikes of Rembrandt or Goya etchings, the best design facsimiles are so faithful to the original that they have their own artistic integrity.

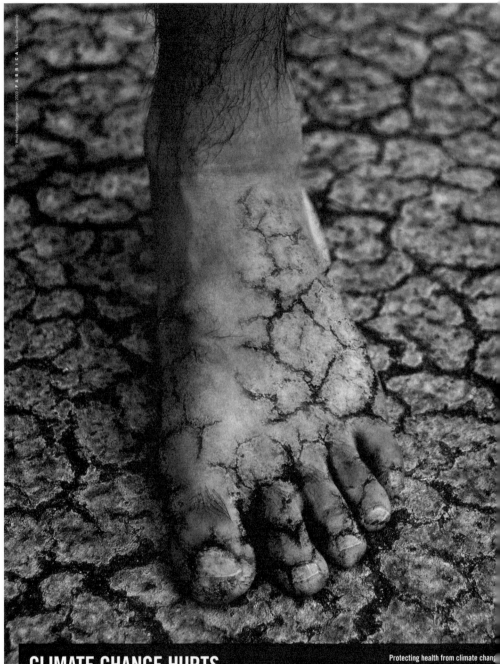

CLIMATE CHANGE HURTS

Besides environmental and economic damage,
the ultimate impact of climate change represents a toll
on our most precious resource - human lives and health.

Protecting health from climate chang

World Healt
Organizatio

www.who.int/phe   www.who.int/globalchange

Illusionism, Meet Dimensionalism

Three dimensions have long been a frontier for the two-dimension designer. Being literate in spatial forms is a great aid in creating memorable and monumental design.

Who could possibly be immune to the sensual wiles of Meret Oppenheim's 1936 Object, featuring a fur-covered cup, saucer, and spoon? Although it was not the first three-dimensional art or design object conceived in the twentieth century, it has doubtless influenced many artists and designers who currently "toil" creating dimensional illusions. It is the gold standard of turning real into surreal—of making something seem entirely plausible when, in fact, it is the total opposite. The fur cup is, let's say, the godfather, godmother, and godhead of what I like to call illusionism.

What is illusionism, you ask? If you do a Google search, this is one of the top tier definitions: "Illusionism in art, a kind of visual trickery in which painted forms seem to be real." It appears as though a lot of mid- to late-twentieth-century art was all about visual trickery and tomfoolery—surrealism, expressionism, and dadaism, to name the major ones. But there is another kind of illusionism—let's call it design illusionism, and it has to do with fooling the savvy among us into thinking that two dimensions are really three, and not just painted forms. In fact, creating the illusion of three dimensions in two-dimensional space has long been one of the graphic designer's foremost—and probably most enjoyable—challenges. In the mid-nineteenth century, when type and typography were first employed as tools to promote industry and business, designers created letterforms and images that were intended to rise beyond their flat surfaces for greater visibility. Types with large, colorful shadows and other faux sculptural elements were commonplace on store signs or windows to suggest dimensionality and draw the eye to the focal point of attention. On paper these stylized typefaces gave the impression of volume, depth, and breadth to the printed page. By the late nineteenth century, what might be called the graphic design tromp l' œil, dimensional illustrative boarders and frames with architectural flourishes, gave everyday advertisements a classical aura—illusionism being something of a classical as well as modern art form.

With the widespread use of photography as a prominent design tool starting in the late teens—what László Moholy-Nagy called a "mechanical art for a mechanical age"—the once limited and difficult means of creating dimensional illusion multiplied. Photographed objects that were combined with typography was called "typofoto," and many progressive early-twentieth-century designers employed this method to, at once, achieve a modern aesthetic and evoke a sense of monumentality. The cover for the designer Norman Bel Geddes' *Magic Motorways*, a 1936 tract about the future of transportation systems in the United States, did not show overt images of cars or highways, but rather presented the title of the book in three-dimensional letters casting a dramatic shadow that clearly spelled out the words. Rather than literally illustrate something specifically future, these dimensional letterforms offered a mysterious futuristic sensation, which could not have been achieved using more traditional image-making methods.

Bel Geddes' book was an exploration into the not too distant, pragmatic future, while Moholy-Nagy's famous Bauhaus Books were experiments with the future of media. When he conceived his three-dimensional cover for *14 Bauhausbücher,* for which he composed type on a piece of plastic and photographed it and its shadow falling on the surface behind it, his goal was to literally add another dimension to how graphic design was used and perceived. It was like a very primitive Photoshop composition whereby Moholy sought to liberate type and typography, images and imagery from the strictures of two dimensions, even if in reality the result was still stuck on the printed page. In so doing, other modernists, including Ladislav Sutnar, Herbert Bayer, Piet Zwart, among them, turned to the camera instead of the pen and brush for illusionary purposes.

By the late 1930s model-making had also become a major element in the designers' tool kit. Building structures—large and small—that were photographed and often collaged or montaged to create new realities was so common it was called "three-dimensional illustration." The camera, of course, enabled designers to freely produce any kind object and wed it to any kind of graphic material. Dimensionality was the next big thing just waiting to become a bigger thing.

While dimensional design was pretty commonly practiced from the 1940s through the 1960s, every so often there were milestones that changed the standards and altered the rules. Peter Blake's cover for The Beatles' *Sgt. Pepper's Lonely Hearts Club Band* was such an icon. In fact, it was a theatrical production of the kind usually seen in stage or film design but not graphic design. It required fashioning dozens of life-sized characters out of cardboard and as mannequins and placing them in an environment that was photographed. Of course, when it was printed on the 12 x 12 LP surface it lost its real-life monumentality but retained the ambitious graphic quality that, for anyone who saw it for the first time, blew the mind and other senses.

In a much less monumental way, but no less acutely conceptual Robert Brownjohn's cover for The Rolling Stones' *Let it Bleed* helped launch the '60s dimensional design trend. After this cover was released many so-called "concept albums" came off the assembly line. Among the most branded were the three-dimensional covers by Nick Fasciano for Chicago's albums. Each was some object—made from wood, plastic, even chocolate—on which was etched, engraved, or carved the groups swash logo.

Dimensionalism (a spin-off of illusionism) is in the blood of many designers. Many of Gunter Rambow's posters combine real objects, photomontage, and flat typography for dramatic effect and conceptual monumentality (his world globe covered in cow hide forming the continents is a masterpiece of wit and irony). Similarly Günther Kieser's record covers use surreal transformations of instruments as foils for real content. On an equally surreal note, the design/photo poster collaborations between Nancy Skolos and Tom Wedell set a standard of visual complexity to dimensional art. While these are elaborate visual concoctions, they don't compare with Gert Dumbar's elaborations whereby intricate symbolic visual narratives are assembled from various representational and abstract 3D components and then photographed in a studio, on a table or floor, to insure an ambiguous dimensional effect that is at once static and kinetic. The compositions could have been done to look 3D by using flat illustrations, but making the 3D elements was a lot more playful and artful.

Now that the computer has made dimensional design, and therefore dimensionalism, so easy, the method still evokes a sense of wonder. Making objects appear to have volume, weight, and mass when they are void of such attributes has the power to titillate the eye and mind. For designers who make these illusions (regularly), they are certainly challenging the perceptions of their audiences, but they are also accomplishing what Meret Oppenheim may have had in mind when she first conceived her fur cup: She made us look! Illusionism or dimensionalism is the art forcing a second look, and that's what every designer wants to achieve, isn't it?

The Adtritus of Viral and Guerilla Advertising

The new advertising is designed to make us look in the most unusual places. Learning the names of the new advertising techniques is just one step in understanding the new media environment.

Viral, suggesting antibiotic-resistant disease, and guerilla, implying [terrorist] warfare, became positive buzzwords during the late 1990s when American advertising appropriated them as labels for attitudinally edgy urban campaigns, also known as "never been done before" (or NBDB) ads. This method (originally co-opted from alternative culture DIY and wild postings) involves the semi-subversive planting of messages in venues and on objects ordinarily free of advertising, like banana peels, body tattoos, and urinal disinfectant pucks (presumably it is difficult to forget a brand name after you've peed on it for a while). Viral and guerilla strategies also depend on unconventional employ of sidewalks, taxi roofs, and vacant storefronts, to engender shock and awe, or at least surprise, in unsuspecting consumers.

Here are some examples: A few years ago, Kirshenbaum Bond Senecal + Partners, in a burst of guerilla-inspired pique, spray-painted some New York sidewalks with the line: "From here it looks like you could use some new underwear," for an intimate clothing company. Last Christmas, an equally audacious "Good Samaritan" holiday campaign for Starbucks, created by Creature in Seattle, Washington, involved affixing precarious red paper cups on roofs of dozens of cabs. If a "Samaritan" warned the taxi's passenger about the errant cup before driving off, a free Starbuck gift card would be given as a reward. During last year's Major League baseball season, Ogilvy mounted a guerilla action promoting

the New York Mets where thin plastic sheets made to look like cracked windshields, as if a baseball had crashed through the glass, were placed on cars, which came with an apology note from Mets management. It was doubtless a heart stopping surprise for victims who hopefully got a good laugh after realizing the joke.

These unorthodox ploys, also known as "ambient" advertising, have so successfully triggered buzz that some ad agencies and marketing companies obsessively comb metropolitan areas in order to commandeer public spaces—legal and otherwise. As a result, new advertising detritus—or adtritus—is visible wherever the eye can see and has earned fervent proponents and angry detractors. Predictably, most advertising experts hold that the ersatz-grassroots approach is simply a new and viable means to put the word out, just another tool in their advertising media toolkit. But critics counter that it is just another desperate scramble to compete in an already over-saturated consumer marketplace, and litter both the physical and mental environment in the bargain.

Whatever one's views, viral and guerilla methods have been adopted for a very practical reason. "Advertising, for all its immensity and importance, is in trouble," writes NYU historian Stephen Duncombe in his new book *Dream: Re-Imagining Progressive Politics in an Age of Fantasy*. With the advent of such anti-ad filters as TiVo, which allows TV viewers to eliminate advertising altogether, coupled with the downsizing of traditional advertising media—TV networks, newspapers, and magazines—due to competition from cable TV and the Internet, mainstream advertisers are finding it difficult to efficiently target audiences. Duncombe notes that ad spending started declining in 2001 for the first time in four decades, and by the largest percentage since the Depression. "Traditional spaces for advertising are drying up and consumers are harder to reach," he says. So if advertisers cannot identify new platforms from which to inveigle their way into hearts and minds, they will perish.

Of course, exploiting new media is not new. As far back as the 1930s, for instance, advertisers conquered the heavens through skywriting and blimps. Whenever advanced technology is introduced, advertisers are among the first to adopt it. The colonization of virgin public space in many large cities is the latest frontier, and digital display technologies have made it infinitely easier to post, plaster, and affix scrims, vinyls, or decals in all sizes and shapes, as well as project laser image messages on almost any surface. It appears that despite certain ordinances every nook, cranny, and scaffold is fair game. But how much "never been done before" advertising can or will the public tolerate before they feel their space has been violated like never before?

"No matter where it is, [NBDB advertising is] filled with equal amounts of shamelessness as well as ingenuity," insists Brian Collins, director of the Brand Innovation Group at Ogilvy in New York. On the shameless side he says there is a "plague of very suspicious 'restoration' scaffolding that covers ancient buildings entirely wrapped and smothered by ads for BMW and Mercedes Benz and Hollywood movies." On the clever side, he insists "this [guerilla] thinking redefines what an 'ad' is." Meaning, it's not enough to simply insinuate a brand into the public's subconscious through mainstream TV, print, or LED screens. Inexpensive viral and guerilla techniques are increasingly essential either alone or in supplementing broader campaigns. Yet to avoid alienating the public NBDB ads must provide something more tangible than a basic sales pitch.

The public will be annoyed by a guerilla campaign that invades their space unless it "rewards them by giving some benefit," argues Rick Boyko, managing director of Virginia Commonwealth University's Adcenter. He says a superb example was Charmin's New York toilet pavilion during the 2006 holiday season. Rather than rent a typical Times Square bells-and-whistles spectacular billboard, on Charmin's behalf the Gigunda Group, experiential marketing consultants from Manchester, New Hampshire, took over an empty space for twenty well-designed, fully stocked, and meticulously maintained public restrooms. Since everyone appreciates clean public bathrooms, users were indebted to Charmin. But more importantly, Charmin garnered considerable press above and beyond the good will of a few hundred thousand people, like me, who used the facilities. Boyko says, although he doesn't use the term, it was NBDB at its best.

Yet most ambient, viral, guerilla, or NBDB ads are not implicitly engaged in public service. I recently stumbled upon the stairway leading up from Pennsylvania Station to 7th Avenue in New York City, which has become a prime place to post huge ads for commuter-targeted products. Just days before New Year's eve 2007 the stairs were taken over by Kellogg's announcing Strawberry Special K; and while it may seem that having pedestrians walk on a large bowl of strawberries and cereal flakes might adversely impact the brand's integrity by linking food to grimy shoes, the display's sheer spectacle of incongruous scale apparently overcomes most negative perceptions. And speaking of scale, sometimes giganticism is its own reward. Case in point: The hybrid billboard in Times Square last summer promoting Cingular cell phone company's claim of fewer dropped calls made a veritable splash (or crash) with a billboard precariously perched on the actual sidewalk to look as though it had literally "dropped" (get the metaphor?) from the scaffolding above (all that was missing was a pair of legs—like the Wicked Witch of the North—sticking out from underneath). Never mind that it actually impeded foot traffic by causing a small bottleneck because it blocked pedestrian space—the conceptual audacity and execution was enough to insure a positive experience (it was also removed before it became too much of an annoyance).

Guerillas cannot afford to make enemies, but sometimes they do take calculated risks. For example, in 2006 MFK New York was commissioned to re-brand Rheingold, a legendary New York working-class beer that had gone out of business, to appeal to a hip "downtown" clientele. Neil Powell, MFK's chief creative officer, decided to use graffiti, still a controversial art form. "With a very limited budget the decision was to get street traction," he explains. So when he scoped out the Lower East Side, Manhattan, and Williamsburg, Brooklyn, where the targeted consumers frequented bars and restaurants, he learned that local storeowners were responsible for keeping their "night shades," those protective pull-down gates, from being vandalized and actually paid fines when defaced. This triggered the idea to enlist local street artists to paint "whatever they wanted" on the gates as long as somewhere they wrote in the word Rheingold—large or small. Ultimately three blocks of Rivington Street were filled with the paintings. Both the artists, most of whom worked at night and were paid in cash or beer, and the storeowners were happy. Even the community declared it a beautification program. As a byproduct Powell learned "since street artists respect other street artists, the screens were unlikely to be vandalized."

Most viral or guerilla ads don't bring such satisfactory results. To truly succeed, the idea must be product specific. Powell has refused to copy the Rheingold campaign for others because "it only works when it is appropriate." He has, however, found other NBDB venues: For Perry Ellis, MFK recently introduced graphic novels to dry cleaning shirt boxes, which tell an independent story while triggering a unique buzz for Perry. In guerilla campaigning Brian Collins believes "ads can go anywhere as long as they add some delight, enhance, or improve the experience." But what happens when even this unconventional method becomes more and more predictable and commonplace? Well, says Collins, "It's just more ugly, meaningless noise."

Beware!

For two years during the mid-2000s I did a regular feature on the WNYC radio show Studio 360 called "Design For The Real World," which focused on everyday designs that impacted popular culture, yet were often ignored—deemed invisible by historians and critics. Called "vernacular" by those who sought to establish a hierarchical or noble status for them, these commonplace things were designed by someone at sometime but have been in our lives for so long—like the air we breathe—that they simply exist. The first "Real World" segment I did was on the common stop sign. Honestly, I never thought about where it came from, why it was an octagon, or even why it was red. I never actually found the ultimate designer either. My musing on the matter was inconclusive, but it opened doors to how graphic design is used to caution us or at least force us to stop and reflect. This section is called "Beware!" because in 2009, when the threat of H1N1 virus was so prevalent, I wrote a few essays on the cautionary graphics published by international public health centers and hospitals. This led me to ponder how other human health concerns were addressed by popular art and design. I was fascinated by how Japanese protective facemasks are packaged and how French medicines were advertised. But health wasn't the only theme for caution. I also looked with jaundiced eyes at how the sidewalks are defaced with gum and, though it may seem like a non sequitur, how the end of the world scenarios have been played out in visual terms.

Got Flu? The Art of H1N1 Posters

The H1N1 swine flu pandemic has aroused poster artists the world over, making flu posters the latest harbinger of popular culture. Many designers have unfairly but predictably smeared the common pig as an object of enmity. Despite a concerted attempt by the pork industry to minimize the negative PR focused on their prized pigs, the term "Swine Flu" is easier to remember and better to visualize than H1N1. Presumably, not even the legendary Wilbur, Porky, or Babe can stem the tide of bad publicity. As cute as they can be, pigs are the virus' original carriers and have been demonized through beastly caricatures and cartoons.

But how effective are these graphic indictments? Public health awareness poster campaigns have been a time-honored means of urging citizens to be vigilant when faced with health crises. Flu is an all too frequent theme, but more effective were the barrages during the early to mid-twentieth century of cautionary venereal disease posters, in which artists show women of ill repute (or skeletons dressed in women's clothes) luring men into dens of iniquity filled with syphilis and gonorrhea. The most fearsome of these had a marked impact on limiting the carnal urges of some. Similarly, but with less of the melodrama and more humor, pictures of sickly pigs with wet dripping snouts, tearing eyes, and ice bag covered heads, lying helplessly in bed are suggesting the obvious while offering no real solutions. The difference between VD and flu posters is context. The former could be controlled through abstinence or protection, the latter is a potent virus, and prevention is not entirely in everyone's control. Even the cute poster showing a pig wearing a surgical facemask doesn't really help prevent the flu, does it?

So what good do the pig posters do, other than make pigs

alternatively appear to be victimizers and victims of the virus. Well, most are amusing, which provides certain intangible benefits. One poster, for instance, a send-up of the famous "Got Milk?" campaign, featuring a drawing of a pig with ice bag on head and thermometer in mouth over the headline "Got Flu?" might take the perceptual edge off the virus by suggesting it's not as deadly as the pandemic of 1917. Yet the "Swine Flu, Beware the Pandemic" poster by Luvatacious Skull, available through the online poster and t-shirt store, zazzle.com, with a more menacing drawing of a pig's head atop that eerie toxic waste symbol, suggests the film *28 Days*, where owing to a virus the world's population is turned into zombies. Zazzle.com is also marketing a tongue-in-cheek version of the Shepard Fairey Obama "Hope" poster titled "Aporkalypse," by Patrioticdissent, which is a double-edged satire conflating the flu scare with the current administration.

Using the pig as mascot for H1N1 has decided limits in the ability to rally the public to action. The majority of people in urban areas who are susceptible to the virus are not in contact with pigs—their bacon, chops, and roasts are so disembodied there is no visual relationship. So the pig simply becomes the logo of a virus that doesn't need a logo. Still, that should not imply that health awareness posters are unnecessary or ineffective.

As a designer I am more drawn to the wit of "Aporkalypse," but as someone who wants to avoid catching the flu, I am not only grateful for the sudden outcropping of liquid hand sanitizers in offices and restaurants, but also for the staid, workmanlike posters and notices emanating from healthcare facilities, the United Nations World Health Organization, and the Centers for Disease Control, that outline prevention steps that can be easily followed. Some of these are bland instruction guides on how to "wash your hands properly," others are more seriously comical, with cartoons of symptoms (fever, fatigue, headache, etc.) and "Prevention" (healthy diet, exercise, etc.). The WHO's poster promotes "How to Protect Yourself and Others" using a genderless, doughy character in proscribed right and wrong scenarios. The CDC's minimalist comics are designed to "stop the spread of germs that make you and others sick," showing how to cover a cough and clean hands.

These are not stunningly designed, but they effectively serve the didactic mission, reminding us of the simple health steps within our control. Now that flu season is here, it's time to retire the pig as object of derision (or caution), and just give the facts and nothing but the facts and the ways to use them.

Japanese Face Masks

Here's a surefire way to prevent germs. You may recall seeing in Ridley Scott's *Blade Runner* scores of surgical-face-mask-wearing passersby navigating their ways through the dense futuristic metropolis that was a cross between Tokyo and LA. It always struck me odd yet somewhat comforting that in the future average people would protect themselves and others from the ravages of germs and inevitability of disease in such a way. But living in New York City, where people have a tendency to sneeze without even covering their mouths, I figured the mass employ of surgical face masks in the streets and on public transportation was simply a utopian fantasy. So I was totally surprised to find on my first trip to Tokyo that not only is it the custom to wear such masks everywhere, it's big business too, with a nod to graphic design.

I have the proclivity for obsession, and I quickly became obsessed with finding where and how Tokyo natives obtained their masks and why they wore them at the expense, I thought, of looking quite eerie. I soon learned that what's eerie to some is decidedly natural for others. According to my calculations, one out of every five people from all social strata, age groups, and genders wore them in virtually every public circumstance. I found a logical preponderance on the streets, especially in the crowded Shibuya and Ginza districts, and on the over-stuffed mass transit trains and buses, but also in fine hotels and restaurants (of course while eating they were placed awkwardly under the chin and looked like drool cups). I even saw one gentleman comically albeit seriously smoking a cigarette through one.

Although some people wore the masks because they had colds or were afraid of catching them (and contagion from bird flu was a real fear), the majority of wearers are actually allergic to the cedar pollen that had become so annoyingly common since the end of World War II. Massive deforestation during and after the war was compensated for by thousands of cedar plantings, which unbeknownst to the agrarians at the time, gave off potent pollen on a par with ragweed in the United States. Apparently, the surgical masks, which cover nose and mouth, considerably reduce the intake of the allergens. What's more, because blowing one's nose in public is considered bad form (as I learned from experience), any reduction of sneezing is as much a question of manners as hygiene. (Interestingly, though, tissue packages with advertising for everything from girly shows to currency exchange are one of the most common advertising give-a-ways on the street.)

But back to obsessions: For the few days I was working in Tokyo I made it my mission to buy as many face mask packages as I could find. I found them in the numerous 7-Eleven and Lawsons convenience stores on virtually every street corner, hanging next to the white business shirts and near the white umbrellas (everything is so uniform). The masks routinely came in silvery mylar packages, usually with a sky blue tinge overall, but also in pink (for the ladies). One was labeled "High Tech Breath Moistener" and was recommended for flying (not a bad idea); another one was promoted as being usable for seven days (though that would give me pause). A few were designed especially for sleeping children, and some, with various layers and ruffles, were more technically complex than others. On the backs of the packages were detailed diagrams on how to use the masks, and also how germs—usually presented as little balls of florescent color—were blocked from entering the breathing passages. The typography is rather clunky in the commercial Japanese style, but entirely appropriate for the mass nature of the product. What I liked most, however, was how soft and comforting the packages felt. Despite or because of the smooth foil/mylar wrapping you could sense the soothing essence of the product inside. What was also intriguing was the number of different brands. In my brief shopping spree I found ten, each with different hygienic attributes, and I'm sure there are more.

When I returned to New York, I visited my local surgical supply store to see whether anything comparable was sold here. The counter person did show me the surgical masks, but they were in drab medicinal packages (near the rubber gloves) designed not for the general public but for healthcare professionals. I doubt, of course, that face masks will ever be as big here as that other Japanese import, transistor radios. Americans may like protective gear, but covering one's face with a mask has gloomy and sinister connotations (what's more Homeland Security would probably ban it). But if there were ever an opportunity, I'd be interested to see how differently we'd design the packages and the masks, too. And I wonder what we'd call them—"Face Off," "GermMasque," "CoffProof?"

かぜ・花粉・黄砂に
ハウスダストが気に
なるときに

ふつう
（大人向け）約9cm×13cm

保管に便利なチャック付き!

フィッティ®

7DAYSマスク
立体ドーム型

高性能
高機能

のどの保湿・保温に有効な密着空間形状

使いきりタイプ 1週間分

細菌・ウイルスを含む飛沫（3μm以上）
花粉（30μm以上）
99%カット

幅広やわらかゴム
耳が痛くなく、何度付け直してもずれにくい!

7枚入

Névrivitamine, Sérifer, Hémoluol, and Pancriol

If face masks don't work, how about medicine that relieves "troubles nerveux de l'enfance" or provides "régénération globulaire" or cures "la grippe" or eliminates "constipation," "crampes," vomissements," and "spasmes"? During the late nineteenth and early twentieth centuries promotion for remedies of various real and imagined physical and psychological maladies were routinely hawked using miracle claims. So-called patent medicine men bolstered by hyperbole and armed with catchy slogans and clever bromides filled handbill and newspaper ads with bogus fears and unsubstantiated promises. The public was gullible or desperate enough to believe anything they read and so ingested the most repugnant (if intoxicating) concoctions. Those were the days before food and drug oversight was written into law and any huckster who mixed pure grain alcohol with sweet syrupy goop was able to call his potion medicinal.

By the early 1920s, however, medicines were coming under greater governmental scrutiny. Legitimate drug companies were waging war with the phonies in the court of popular opinion. Advertising was in the vanguard of this quest for legitimacy and by the 1940s and 1950s pharmaceutical companies developed distinct verbal and visual vocabularies that at once built credibility for their products while eliminating much of the pseudo-scientific mumbo-jumbo. Over time pharmaceutical advertising evolved into a distinct art form. By the 1960s and 1970s, for instance, the Swiss corporation Ciba-Geigy was celebrated for its imaginatively progressive imagery that was built upon Modernist visual idioms. Yet even before this accepted "golden age" other European drug labs introduced surrealism as a visual means of making difficult medical concepts into avant garde art. But this style of advertising was not all eerie barren landscapes, doleful endless horizons, and

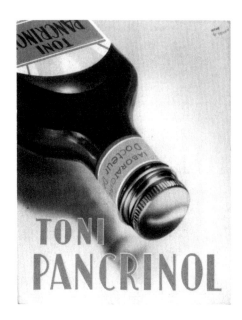

discordant Dali-esque juxtapositions.

In the pre-war 1930s, French companies, like Laboratoires D'Actino-Biologie, Laboratoires Lumiere, Laboratoires Caducia, and Laboratoires du Dr Debat (little known today) employed stylized realistic representation to take the onus off of turgid medical hype. With the exception of a few advertisements featuring heavily airbrushed photographs of happy bathing-suited women (like the one for Curatine for headaches and other pains) or conceptual graphics highlighting the cause of a particular discomfort (like the fire in the mouth for Maxicaïne-Tyrothricine pastilles), the majority of highly colorful ads, targeted at les docteurs, played up the simple beauty (and authority) of a distinct package or bottle. Most package and label designs were typographically bold yet graphically sedate (see Septicarbone for intestinal disorders and Toni Pancrinol for nervous condition). Yet the simple dramatic airbrush rendering of each item provided an allure that no photograph could achieve. The idea, of course, was to help physicians memorize the names of non-generic drugs, which in turn they would prescribe to their patients.

In the early twentieth century, poster artist Leonetto Cappiello created one of his most well known images for a congestion medication called Le Thermogene, which featured a whimsical rendering of an elfish dancer clenching a cloud-like wad to his chest (symbolizing massive congestion in the lungs). While this idea established a conceptual

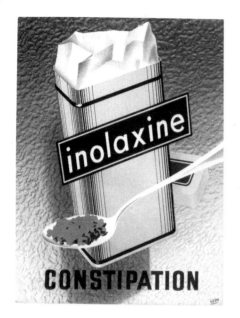

standard for drug advertising, by the late 1930s and 1940s less metaphorical pictorial approaches seemed to be preferred. Despite France's exemplary poster tradition, most of the artists employed for pharmaceutical promotions were among the lesser known. The artists Lupa and Rene Le Terier were quite skilled at establishing a soothing graphic environment but were conceptually restrained.

When graphic concepts were applied they vividly, and also at times sensationally, illustrated what life would be like without these respective medications. The image for Hémoluol shows the legs of a stylish woman, with one covered by a stocking hiding her unsightly varicose veins (a stone gargoyle looks menacingly on). Quel dommage!! Yet even more deliberately disturbing is the ad for Névrovitamine 4 with a night-terror-stricken young child trapped in her crib—who wouldn't take the remedy after seeing that face? But just as effective was the converse: the relaxed man in the Sérifer ad, covered in his blanket peacefully looking out his big picture window at snow-covered mountains—the message being take the medication and life can be a better place (prefiguring the various tranquilizers to come later).

Although some of the ads provided a fair amount of technical explanation on the verso sides, the need for fine print warnings about complications and side-effects were not required. And while physicians needed to know the details, for these advertisements the pharmaceutical firms were less interested in protecting patients' lives than selling their products.

It happens to the nicest of Guys

ORDINARILY he was No. 1 on the hit parade as far as girls were concerned. But tonight he was getting the polite but cold shoulder over and over again. Something was wrong and he knew it...but he didn't know *what*.* It can happen to the nicest of guys.

The insidious thing about halitosis (unpleasant breath)* is that you, yourself, seldom realize when you have it. Moreover, it may be absent one day and present the next. And when it *is* present it stamps you as an objectionable person to be avoided.

Don't Take Chances

Why run this risk? Why offend others when Listerine Antiseptic is a delightful, *extra-careful* precaution against unpleasant breath when not of systemic origin?

You simply rinse the mouth with Listerine Antiseptic and, lo!...your breath becomes fresher, cleaner, sweeter, less likely to offend...stays that way, too, for hours in most cases.

When you want to be at your best, never, never omit this *extra-careful* precaution against offending.

LAMBERT PHARMACAL CO., *St. Louis, Mo*

Before any date
LISTERINE ANTISEPTIC
the extra-careful precaution

P.S. IT'S NEW! Have you tried Listerine TOOTH PASTE, the MINTY 3-way prescription for your teeth?

Hey Stinky, You're Too Fat, and Your Skin's Bad Too!

Medicines—real and phony—are just one way to fleece the public. Sundries and cosmetics have also been made indispensable throughout popular culture. American advertising did not invent body odor, foot rot, bad breath, dandruff, psoriasis, or even acne. These normal, yet annoying, biological occurrences were around since humans emerged from the primordial ooze. Yet it was primordial ad men during the early twentieth century who made them into plagues of such biblical proportions only medicated pads, soothing creams, and scented sprays applied daily could possibly purge the demons from body and soul. B.O., halitosis, zits, and flaking and peeling skin are nothing to sneeze at, but owing to persuasive ad barrages average Americans came to accept that possessing one or all was un-American, or at least unchristian (cleanliness is next to godliness, after all). Madison Avenue's scourges were curable, but if they went untreated, heartbreak (i.e. "The Heartbreak of Psoriasis") was the ultimate punishment for all transgressions.

"Advertising helps to keep the masses dissatisfied with their mode of life, discontented with ugly things around them," reported an advertising trade journal in the late 1940s. "Satisfied customers are not as profitable as discontented ones." And it was this dubious, though effective, incentive practiced during the post-World War II era (when the booming American economy was stimulated by the incredible surges of wartime production) that demanded increased consumption of sundries and medicines to help prop up prosperity. There was no better way to herd consumers into stores than to elevate the importance of ersatz-hygienic values by instilling widespread insecurity through cautionary ads that attacked odor and smeared blemishes.

However, even this strategic paradigm, so endemic to postwar economics and aesthetics, was not entirely new to post-war consumption. In 1919 an ad campaign for Odo-Ro-No, a deodorant for women, first invoked the initials "B.O," which stood for body odor. Previously, ads for perfumed powders and salves merely claimed to be sweet smelling, but once the manufacturers of Odo-Ro-No launched their aggressive assault on perspiration and its odiferous gases, offering customers their patented "Armhole Odor Test," and warning that B.O. would hinder social acceptability, the floodgates opened on insecurity-marketing. And it worked, especially with impressionable female consumers who were the primary advertising targets, but males, too, wanted to be attractive to impressionable females. As a 1950 ad for Lifebuoy soap featuring one such insecure gent attested, "I'd always thought B.O. was something that happened to other people. Then I realized that B.O. was the reason I wasn't popular with others."

B.O. was one of the most damning scolds in American vernacular, and ridding the body of bacterially induced rancid vapors became a national pastime—nay patriotic duty—opening the market for other brand name curatives. Listerine mouthwash, for instance, originally produced as a general antiseptic, was transformed by an advertising campaign that elevated basic bad breath from merely an unpleasant occurrence to major blight. After World War I, when Listerine ads began referring to bad breath as the pseudo-scientific-sounding halitosis, promising "germ-killing action," the brand immediately captured a niche (that continues today) as the leading cure-all. The most memorable of their ads in the late 1940s featured the pathetic case of "Edna," who was "often a bridesmaid but never a bride," approaching her "tragic" thirtieth birthday unmarried because she suffered from halitosis—that "you, yourself, rarely know when you have it. And even your closest friends won't tell you."

These "quick-tempo socio-dramas in which readers were invited to identify with temporary victims in tragedies of social shame," wrote the late historian Roland Marchand in *Advertising the American Dream*, led to a new "school of advertising practice." Copy-heavy, poorly designed cautionary advertisements (that resembled political manifestos) encouraged consumers to revile everything rotten smelling, from head to crotch to toe. A 1950 ad with a silly line drawing of a non-descript fellow underscored the damning point with the line, "Let's be frank... Is your breath on the agreeable side? Don't run risks. Before every date use Listerine Antiseptic. It sweetens breath instantly."

Body odor and bad breath were, however, only two of the biological social pariahs. "Personal hygiene became a crucial piece in the puzzle that upwardly mobile strivers were constantly trying to assemble," wrote Jackson Lears in *Fables of Abundance, A Cultural History of Advertising in America*. "Physical processes that had previously been taken for granted began to acquire ominous qualities, as one can see (or smell) in the changing attitude toward odor." Combining odor and dirt in ads soon tipped the consumer scales towards an obsession with germ infestation. Lears cites an early ad for Kleenex (the first sanitary disposable tissues) showing a nauseated housewife complaining that washing dirty handkerchiefs was the worst job on earth.

Yet even this aspect of the holy crusade for biological purity had its beginnings one hundred years before the post-war consumer boom; as early as the 1850s clean hands joined white skin, white bread, and white sugar as emblems of refinement and were cogs in the wheel of body management, a social construct that Lears refers to as "The Perfectionist Project." This enforced marriage of personal hygiene to regularity, and to efficiency on all strata of the social system underpinned most national consumer advertising.

Laxatives, for example, were promoted in the early 1900s to bring Americans in sync with the complex rhythms of modern life. As work hours conformed to Frederick Winslow Taylor's time/motion performance systems, daily bodily functions were increasingly scrutinized with regard to the average workday. From this the mantra of "regularity," another element of consumption, emerged. Laxative advertisements assailed constipation as a greater menace to society than alcohol, so colonics and enemas were marketed to purge the innards of "intestinal toxicity." Kellogg's Corn Flakes was one such product born of the early individual health obsession. Invented by Dr. John Harvey Kellogg, whose Battle Creek hospital and health spa (fictionalized in T. C. Boyle's *Road to Wellville*) was dedicated to purifying the inner temple of all toxins, and his toasted flakes were advertised with the same fervency as any modern medical miracle. While that particular approach was no longer effective by the post-war era, the "tastes good and is good for you" ethos remained fairly constant in advertising designed to project such a fundamentally unessential foodstuff as key to notions of health and well being that underscored American commercialism. Incidentally this commercial ethos was rooted in so-called democratic freedoms, which consisted of "ignoring politics and worrying, instead, about the threat of scaly scalp, hairy legs, sluggish bowels, saggy breasts, receding gums, excess weight, and tired blood," wrote Marshall McLuhan.

Even after the Federal Trade Commission issued regulations related to "truth in advertising," advertising men sought ways to formulate new, harsher truths about real, but decidedly exaggerated maladies. "There's a womanly offense—greater than body odor or bad breath!" whispered the subhead in an ad for the feminine hygiene product called Zonite. Under the headline "How can he explain to his sensitive young wife?" a photo of a somewhat disgusted young man with a comic thought balloon over his head read, "There are some things a husband just can't mention to his wife!" Meanwhile Zonite was being promoted as the "modern miracle" because no other "douche is so powerful yet safe to tissues."

In addition to ailments such as these, outward appearances loomed large in the minds of ad men. As early as the turn-of-the-century, human fat was deemed a formidable enemy yet oddly enough, although medical books warned against the dangers of obesity, many doctors claimed fat was an energy reserve. But when the advertising industry embraced the notion that being svelte was a marketable hook for them—"thinning down" became an American mission, and dieting a new religion which, in turn, raised the specter of an entirely new and continually replenishing market: American youth.

This consumerist ideal became the cornerstone of post-war consumption strategies influencing advertising for decades to follow. Even when ads were not aimed at physical restoratives and sundries designed to make "Lovelier Skin in 14 Days," pretty girls and handsome men in ads routinely had the same, white, clean, perky looks. The demographic between ages 14 to 18, known as the teenager, did not become a codified market until the post-war era (when both fashion and sundry marketers sold directly to them through magazines like *Seventeen*), but the cult of youth (25 and under) was celebrated by the advertising industry since the teens.

By the late 1940s young women had emerged as the quintessential American consumer for such products as toothpastes, deodorants, shampoos, facial lotions, soaps, and feminine products, as well as major appliances (cars were still the province of men, until the mid-1950s, when it was clear that women had a stake in the looks and performance of automobiles). Young women, particularly those who had sacrificed during the war on the home front, were ripe for seduction by even the ugliest advertisements (which were published in abundance). They also believed they deserved the new bounty, to be free from maladies, and look beautiful in the bargain. Advertising wholeheartedly asserted that civilization would abruptly end if women did not actively contribute to the consumer boom that would make America a better place to live, love, and pursue happiness.

Topanga, We Hardly Knew Ya

True happiness is being skinny, but it comes at a price. Being a design snob, I've always wondered why anyone with taste would pay thousands of dollars to publish one of those text-heavy, type-awful, full-page magazine advertisements void of any semblance of graphic design nuance or sophistication. In other words, an ad so terribly designed the word "design" is irrelevant. Then again, who would take the time to read a 2,000 word promotional screed set in monotonous body type, full of hyped-up assertions couched in moldy clichés? Well, now I know at least part of the answer. I am that reader. And those advertisers must bank on the fact that design is indeed irrelevant when the sales message is its own virtue. Maybe they are right.

I came across such a full-page specimen in a recent issue of the *New York Times Magazine*, opposite a page on which were the final run-over paragraphs of a fascinating article on Todd Haynes' biopic inspired but not about Bob Dylan, titled *I'm Not There*. Having reached the end of the article, and ready to close my eyes for a short catnap, I saw the following headline: "The pressure to be thin in Hollywood is huge! And boy, did I feel it." Such announcements are usually typographic white noise, but when my eyes focused on the typical "before" and "after" pictures, I was hooked.

There was a small but incredibly sexy studio photograph of a woman wearing a bikini overlapping a bleached-out snapshot of her enormous previous incarnation. Although ordinarily not worth an additional iota of attention, this girl, it turned out, was 26-year-old actress Danielle Fishel , who from 1993 to 2000 played Topanga Lawrence on the amusing sit-com *Boy Meets World*. Over the years she grew increasingly more sensual evolving from tween to teen. It was one of my then young son's favorite shows, which I dutifully sat through to monitor his intake of mass media. Now I (gladly) admit that watching her develop over the course of many seasons was not a burden. Once *Boy Meets World* was off the air, however, Topanga left my consciousness, until the Sunday I stumbled upon the advertisement for NutriSystem's Glycemic Advantage. By any standards it was a poorly designed ad, but nonetheless very effective. Design snobbery has its place, yet good design I have learned is often irrelevant in the pursuit of an audience.

I wasn't even in the market for a dietary program, but I was intrigued enough by the come-on to read every last sentence presumably written in Ms. Fishel's own words. "I have been an actress most of my life," she states in the first paragraph. "I love doing it. So when *Boy Meets World* went off the air, I really was looking forward to continuing my career. But my weight got in the way." Poorly letter-spaced and forced-justification of default typefaces notwithstanding, I was hooked.

"Look," she continues as though in a direct conversation with me. "I knew that it was my job as an actress to look my best. And I kind of let that go. I'm just glad that NutriSystem was there to rescue me." And so was I, once her admission turned into a confession. "I first started to have issues with my weight when I was 18... I really didn't pay attention to what I was eating. Plus my body really started to change then. I just couldn't eat whatever I wanted to anymore."

The prose was not Proustian or even Judy Blumeian, nonetheless it seemed pretty honest for an ad. So I found myself drawn from reading one short paragraph to another, until by the time the sales pitch kicked in I was invested enough to continue reading the entire tract down to the coupon. Moreover, as I read, never once did I think of the type or layout; I just wanted to be convinced Topanga was on her path to nirvana, self-fulfillment, or at least another TV gig (you'll have to read the ad to find out).

Of course, I know this advertisement is deliberately "designed" to capture the attention of those who relate to celebrities who after years in the glamour limelight became fat (like that perky Valerie Bertinelli on those Jenny Craig commercials). "Dolling-up" the ads with elegant typefaces is therefore unnecessary since those before and after shots and lengthy personal testimonials do the job so well, regardless of layout. What's more, from a strategic branding point of view, running a text-heavy, sloppily composed full-page ad in an otherwise handsomely designed magazine, replete with beautiful fashion and product advertisements, makes it stand out more. I also presume that if a company is investing this much money in a "direct response" ad, it must know what it is doing. The audience is going to be engaged because the celebrities are sincere about their road back from perdition. Right?

In this blinkered era of design sophistication the lines between good and bad are actually not so clearly drawn. As we see on a daily basis, not all consumers care about good, great, or exceptional design when what they really want is to believe in the message. And the message NutriSystem may be telegraphing is this: Lose your excess weight NOW and worry about design later. Still, call me an old design snob: We deserve better, and so does Topanga.

THE LONG-AWAITED DRAMATIC STORY OF THE ATOMIC BOMB

THE BEGINNING OR THE END

M-G-M presents the picture of pictures...the story of the most HUSH-HUSH secret of all time!

M-G-M's "THE BEGINNING OR THE END"

Starring

BRIAN DONLEVY · ROBERT WALKER

with

TOM DRAKE · BEVERLY TYLER
AUDREY TOTTER · HUME CRONYN

Screen Play by FRANK WEAD · Original Story by ROBERT CONSIDINE
Directed by NORMAN TAUROG · Produced by SAMUEL MARX
A METRO-GOLDWYN-MAYER PICTURE

Look into the forbidden city!
Meet the girl who lost
her identity—the only girl
who knew the world's
most terrifying secret!

The Sky Is Falling

Pop culture has long been obsessed with doomsday and its graphic representation. Remember the scene in Woody Allen's *Annie Hall* in Dr. Flicker's examining room where Alvy Singer's angst-ridden mother tells the doctor her son is depressed? As the doctor furiously puffs on a cigarette, Alvy says the universe is expanding and since "the universe is everything, and if it's expanding, someday it will break apart and that would be the end of everything!"

"What is that your business? What has the universe got to do with it?" screams Alvy's mother. "You're here in Brooklyn! Brooklyn is not expanding!" To which Dr. Flicker adds, "It won't be expanding for billions of years yet, Alvy. And we've gotta try to enjoy ourselves while we're here. Uh?"

Existential gloom and doom scenarios have not plagued just the sackcloth and ash crowd. Many of the most rational among us have been consumed by the specter of endgame. Of course, the world's great religions have built their respective brand stories on one or another version of Armageddon. But even for those without religious underpinnings the apocalypse is nothing to be sniffed at. If it is not a shower of killer asteroids falling from the heavens then it is a barrage of atomic warhead missiles shot from submarines. H.G. Wells' prescient *The Time Machine,* first published in 1895, accurately predicted two twentieth-century world wars, and prophesized a third that promised to send planet earth back to the Stone Age; and he had absolutely no inkling of nuclear weaponry at the time.

He was not the first (or the last). The seer Nostradamus (1503-1566) was famously known for his book *Les Propheties,* which to this day triggers considerable trepidation among those who read too much into his metaphors.

Conjecture about earth-shattering calamities—manmade or not—is a recurring trope of artists and writers. Predicting the unthinkable is a kind of sport for the practitioners of what's called "counterfactual history." Fans of the genre seem to savor the sublime morbidity in the same way we relish extremely spicy food; it takes a little getting used to but the ultimate kick—in this case the pleasure of fear—is worth the discomfort.

I've often considered starting a cable channel exclusively devoted to fiction and faction about the world's end—Endgame TV. While it would not be for the faint of heart, it would have a real voyeuristic following. Maybe, like the old joke about the guy not minding being hit over the head with a hammer because it felt so good when it stopped, once we awake from these "nightmares" we feel so much better, or do we?

In the early 1960s, during the zenith of the atomic scare, Rod Serling's *Twilight Zone* was demise central. Scores of episodes focused on how humans sent the planet earth on a one-way ticket to Palookaville. You may remember the episode "The Midnight Sun" (1961) in which the Earth suddenly changed its elliptical orbit and in doing so began to follow a path that gradually took it closer to the sun. The place was New York City and it was the eve of the end, because even at midnight it was high noon, the hottest day in history. Towards the end of the episode Lois Nettleton, who played the terrified protagonist, awakened from what had been a nightmare. In her *Twilight Zone* reawakening the world is dark, cold and snowing. Whew! However, rather than being saved from extinction, the audience learns that a new orbit is really leading the earth father and farther away from the sun into frozen oblivion. Our protagonist had gone from one nightmare state into another.

Through films and books hundreds, maybe thousands of endgame scenarios have been played out. Movies like the early 1960s classic *The Day the Earth Caught Fire* was but one of the many Cold War cautionary tales that portrayed the planet as a powder keg set to explode. The Bomb (as it was quaintly known) had become the greatest portend of doom and the mushroom cloud was the most horrifyingly dreadful symbol imaginable. In the 1960s fallout shelter kits were being advertised and yellow and black shelter signs were ubiquitous. After seeing the *Twilight Zone* episode, "The Shelter," I begged my parents to build one—now that's successful product placement.

I kind of miss those halcyon days of Cold War fear, when, to borrow FDR's famous phrase, all we had to fear was fear itself—and atomic annihilation. As harrowing as the movies and books on the subject were, there was often a level of absurdity that took the edge off reality. The shocking story of nuclear uncertainty in the film *The*

Beginning of the End, was given such a Hollywood aura of unreality that the A-bomb was transformed into our friend. While films like *Fail Safe* (1964) and *On the Beach* (1959) were tragic tales, we knew once the film was over our lives would return to normal. The unthinkable just wouldn't or couldn't happen. Then, of course, there was the ludicrousness of *Dr. Strangelove* (1964) (years before we heard of Henry Kissinger), which although savagely sardonic made it clear our leaders weren't THAT crazy. By the time *Mad Max* (1979) came along, the endgame had turned into fashion that looked suspiciously like the clothes Vivienne Westwood was making for the Punk scene.

Recently, the world has become a more dangerous place in movies and literature. The bomb is not the only thing to fear: Global warming, killer viruses, and natural and unnatural plagues of every description are only a few of the uglies now feeding apocalypse paranoia. Films like *Waterworld* (1995), *The Day After Tomorrow* (2004), and most recently *I Am Legend* (2007) address the real concerns of our altering planetary conditions and continue to titillate our prurient interest in doom. But now they seem much more likely than ever before. Where once "the sky is falling" scenarios would not, as Dr. Flicker said, "happen for billions of years yet," the doomsday clock is steadily ticking away. Wouldn't it be nice if we could go back to the days when fiction was not fact?

Art for Art's Sake

Design is a process that starts with a problem that calls for a solution. Few designers actually design with only design in mind—and if they do, it seems likely that the result will be more like fine art than applied art. Yet on occasion designers and illustrators turn to art as, perhaps, a respite from the rigors of problem solving. Similarly, artists have turned to design as a means to extend their creative reach. The early-twentieth-century modernists were known for *gesamtkunstwerk* (or the total work of art), the notion that all art—fine and applied—was indeed integrated and both muse-driven and functional. The futurists, dadaists, constructivists, and the Bauhaus were proponents of this idea, and it continues to the present. This section, however, returns to Théophile Gautier's slogan "l'art pour l'art," the notion that true art is divorced from any utilitarian purpose. Although each of the artists and works discussed in these essays were known for functional art, they devoted themselves to art on its own terms. John Baeder turned from advertising to recording roadside America. Ladislav Sutnar created what he called "posters without words." William Copley, a painter, brought others together in an art box called SMS. And Arthur Szyk, an illustrator and caricaturist, well, he did art for the sake of freedom (so indeed there was a real purpose).

SMS—Shit Must Stop: Art to Go, Sixties Style

Imagine opening a box and finding a vinyl glove, renderings of cloud formations arranged as a musical score, six panels of hauntingly beautiful abstract landscapes, two volumes of concrete and sound poetry by a Russian underground poet, a classic portrait of da Vinci with a real cigar stub sticking out of his mouth, a pinwheel for creating chance poetry, and half a dozen other startling and confounding bits of effluvia, esoteria, and artifactoria by the likes of Enrico Baj, Dick Higgins, Roland Penrose, Man Ray, and H.C. Westermann. This was the contents of just one out of six such cardboard boxes—an exceptional anti-art-art-magazine-in-a-box to be precise—the brainchild of American surrealist painter William Nelson (1919-1996), who in 1968 founded the Letter Edged in Black Press to publish the series SMS, a.k.a. Shit Must Stop (based on the punch line of a secret dirty joke that Copley loved to tell), which referred to dissatisfaction of other featured artists—like John Cage, Christo, Roy Lichtenstein, Claes Oldenburg, Yoko Ono, Meret Oppenheim, Diter Rot, and Lawrence Weiner—who were gnawingly irritated with what they perceived to be a corrupt art market.

SMS was the manifestation of protest. It was also a freewheeling mail-order repository of eccentric artistic expression that for a brief moment in art history brought art and design, as well as private and public expression, together in an incomparably democratic sight and sound experience busting, albeit for the moment, the conventions of both contemporary art and magazine publishing. Like Fluxus before it, Copley—better known by the contraction CPLY, which was scrawled onto his comical, brutish paintings and drawings—conceived of SMS as a populist utopian art platform that, in the words of art historian Carter Ratcliff, "bypassed the hierarchical labyrinth of museums and established galleries." The portfolios were mailed directly to subscribers "on the faith that an audience put in immediate contact with art would have a direct and therefore powerful response."

SMS was also a tacit manifesto against art corruption that brought numerous arts from poetry to performance to traditional printmaking onto a level stage, making it available for everyone (at least everyone who subscribed). "This principle of equality carried over to money matters," wrote Ratcliff in a catalogue produced in 1988 by the Rhinehold-Brown Gallery. "Every contributor, no matter how illustrious, received a flat $100 for his or her work." The fee may have been miniscule (even by 1960s standards) but Copley guaranteed he would not scrimp on the production. "It was possible to replicate a fragment of an artist's oeuvre with astonishing accuracy," added Ratcliff. One such was painter and assemblagist Domenico Rotella's 6 Prison Poems (SMS #4) written clandestinely on cigarette packages while the artist was jailed in Rome for possession of marijuana, and reproduced with exacting verisimilitude. Another is Italian painter and founder of the Nuclear Art Movement Enrico Baj's Glove, a real folded vinyl glove over a bright pink tissue covered in heavy clear plastic. Why a glove? Why not?

The serially anarchic SMS, which originally was scheduled to come out every two months but ultimately fell short of the goal, lasting only six issues before the money ran out, was not, however, the first of its kind. Marcel Duchamp's Box in a Valise (only twenty copies of which were produced in 1941) was a portable gallery of reproductions, not unlike a salesman's carrying case, on foldout panels and individual folders. Copley, who counted Duchamp as a pal, admitted he was influenced by this work but enslaved by it. Two decades later, ten issues of ASPEN (from 1965 to 1971) further explored the boxed magazine format and prefigured the SMS nexus between art and design with its third issue edited by Andy Warhol, featuring his now famous cover parodying a FAB detergent package. Copley was interested in similarly bringing art to a larger audience, and with his SMS partner, the lesser-known surrealist painter Dmitri Petroff, who had spent time on Madison Avenue and knew advertising techniques, the mag-box format bridged the gap between a solely esoteric art assemblage and a more viable publishing venture. Petroff also introduced Copley to commercial printers, notably Sherwood Press in New York, who were equipped to economically reproduce many of the simpler artifacts. Yet Copley noted in an interview shortly before his death that they also would shop around their printing "'til we could find somebody who would do the impossible. We were always looking for the impossible at that point." While designed for the box, many of the artworks transcended its confines.

During the late 1960s, when SMS was conceived, Americans were not allowing themselves to be boxed in; they aggressively protested for peace, civil rights, sexual liberation, and against the Vietnam War. Music, theater, and plastic art merged into a critical mass of explosive sociopolitical power. These were tumultuous times when the 47-year-old Copley leased a third floor loft on the Upper East Side of New York on 80th Street and Broadway (near Zabar's, the legendary gourmet delicatessen) for artists of all stripes to freely mingle and spontaneously create.

Between marriages and being psychologically unable to paint, Copley was looking for something to do and found joy in the pure unadulterated joy of doing SMS, especially publishing young artists: "If you see the issues, there's a lot of ... very young artists [who just walked in and showed me their material]. And it was invariably of interest to me."

The majority of the New York avant garde was found on the Lower East Side—or in the East Village—where, among the many provocateurs, Claes Oldenburg had his storefront Mouse Museum, Lil Picard fomented art happenings, and three radical underground papers, the *East Village Other*, *Rat*, and *Other Scenes*, published political and sexual contraband and promoted cultural extravaganzas in, among other venues, grungy Tompkins Square Park. Only a few avenues west, but still downtown, Andy Warhol was making his band of artistic gypsies famous (if only for 15 minutes) in the legendary Factory. But Copley, a prince of contrarians, decided that uptown—actually not far from where playwright and Brecht scholar Eric Bentley opened his radical DMZ cabaret and another underground paper the *New York Free Press* published anti-establishment journalism—was just as culturally fertile as anything below 14th Street. He was right.

The SMS loft was a place where "it was impossible to anticipate what would happen next," recalled Lew Syken, SMS's chief designer, in the Rhinehold-Brown catalog. The venue was a nest of surrealist, dada, pop, and all manner of unaffiliated artists, including frequent visitors Richard Artschwager (whose cover design featuring visible coffee rings graced SMS #6), Roy Lichtenstein (who contributed a vinyl sheet silkscreened in red, yellow, blue, and white, hand folded like one of those classic newspaper-made peaked commodore hats in SMS #4), and fabled hermit, the correspondence artist Ray Johnson (whose three duotones on a sheet of glossy paper, titled "A Two-Year-Old Girl Choked Today on an Easter Egg," was in SMS #2). Art students hired to help stuff the boxes and construct the more difficult pieces (including burning 2,000 bowties, one-by-one, for Lil Picard's untitled piece in SMS #4) also called the loft home.

Copley was the ringmaster of this arts circus, but SMS developed into a unique publishing organism that brought artists out of the seclusion of their studios and the ghetto of the gallery scene. It was also intentionally edited in an unedited manner, keeping the work individual. "We didn't want to editorialize at all," Copley once said. "We didn't want any critical comment. I wanted something that would just open up and be full of what was going on."

While only 2,000 copies were produced of each of the six portfolios, rumor has it almost 1,500 were mailed. In 1981 Copley made a gift of the remaining 500 or so sets to The New Museum of Contemporary Art, which sat, presumably forgotten, for a number of years in basement storage until a flood destroyed many of them. Had it not been for the flood, however, SMS might have become a veritable Dead Sea Scrolls of 1960s art. On the twentieth anniversary of SMS in 1988, Robert Brown and Susan Reinhold of Reinhold Brown Gallery in New York resurrected them in an exhibition where they offered them for sale. Presumably various museums have preserved a fair number.

When SMS ceased publishing after six issues in 1969 the potpourri notion of amassing art seemed to die as well, although the magazine-in-a-box was not totally rejected. Every so often someone decides to box a collection of something. The more fashionista Visionaire continued the tradition with its rather expensive boxes, and currently a new box idea, "A Very Short List," is offering subscribers monthly boxes of different media—culled from DVDs to CDs, from comedy to news. It may not be as artistically pure as SMS, but the spirit and pleasure of surprise is nonetheless there.

Another Side of Ladislav Sutnar

Ladislav Sutnar is known as the father of information design, but he was also a pop artist—though he loathed the term. When Sutnar emigrated from Czechoslovakia to the United States in 1940, the avant garde designer, who brought constructivism to American corporations, lived on 52nd Street between Fifth and Sixth Avenues. He rented a one-room apartment on the third floor of a converted townhouse, in an oak paneled former library with a large French window overlooking the street. On his first night, after going to bed at eleven, he was suddenly awakened "to the realities of where my ignorance of native custom had led me," Sutnar recalled in a brief essay titled "The Strip Street," which he wrote to accompany a portfolio of racy images that have been more or less ignored since his death in 1976.

What was ordinarily a quiet midtown street during the day, was transformed every night after eleven into "the famous strip street known far and wide as the sexiest place in town," he wrote. "It was never charming or neat, but the embodiment of the shrewd business of pushing the sale of liquor with attractions of the flesh under bright colored lights. In the grab for the fast buck, tawdry physical vulgarity, obscene language, and a close low view of human behavior unmasked in a quest for a variety of temptations, were the predominant attributes of the street's world of dubious entertainment. Intangible, perhaps, yet the phenomena expressed itself distinctly by its own strong and indescribable mood."

During the hot summer, a shimmering, purple-red neon glow projected from the street high into the dark skies, and it was against this Sutnar was introduced to what he called an "exotic shadow-play, moving to the swinging beat from the clubs." During the 1960s the street was transformed by the city's building boom. The steamy and tawdry urban lifestyle was bulldozed under and would have been forgotten, had Sutnar not decided to celebrate his early New York experience in paintings and prints that he alternately called "posters without words," "Venuses," and "Joy Art." These flat, brightly-colored canvases, somewhat resembling Saul Bass' expressionist movie graphics wed to elements of pop art "offer my personal comments on the old times and the shapely disrobing ladies who were so essential a part of the strip street scenery," he added. Tomas Vicek, who has written about this relatively forgotten aspect of Sutnar's work, suggested the influence of pop, but he also noted that Sutnar hated pop and op art.

He began making the paintings and prints in 1960, the year he left his fruitful and influential consultancy with Sweets Catalog Service, where for around a decade he altered first the look of industrial catalogues through modern typography and second raised the bar on information design through precise pictorial systems. What was a totally alien style for Sutnar, and in retrospect a look doggedly derivative of contemporary art trends, was a means of combining his design and narrative concerns into seamless imagery. What's more he viewed these works as representations of the strippers' "unpredictable, mischievous, and sometime hilarious exhibitions ... as they were often seen through the open doors of the clubs, to dazzle passer-by."

The Venus series (which were shown in a few New York galleries between 1966 and '69 and at the NY Art Directors Club in 1975) in the private edition of twelve silk-screened prints (January 1963) interprets the impact of the swift, "passing glimpse in the dim, murky, aphrodisiac atmosphere of female bodies in movement, shaking, swinging, quivering, twisting, rolling, and jerking. Or, maybe just an arm loosening the hair reflects the vivid, live, and lasting echo of the experience of living on the street." The accented silhouette with its emphasis on the simplified form of the figure in action together with the contrast of the flat, unshaded colors laid out one next to another were the visual techniques he borrowed from his graphic design and used to make dramatic impressions. His visual shorthand resulted in bold, simple patterns. The term "posters without words" refers to Sutnar's distinct poster-like design that characterizes the individual prints of this series.

After 1960 Sutnar's commercial work was fading fast. These paintings and a series of retrospective design exhibits were an attempt to revivify his business. Not surprisingly, as the graphic design dried up, he more prodigiously devoted himself to these lesser-known paintings and prints. His career nonetheless languished. He died a year after his Art Directors Club exhibit, believing he had been forgotten by the field.

The Arthur Szyk Renaissance

Popular art sometimes comes hidden as religious iconography, and
Arthur Szyk (pronounced schick) (1894–1951) produced his fair share.
Szyk was a Polish émigré who lived in New York, and who, given a
career that began in 1914, illustrated over thirty books, created scores
of caricatures and portraits as covers for *Collier's* and *Time* magazines,
numerous cartoons for *PM* (the ad-free liberal/left daily), the *New York
Post*, and *Esquire*, as well as posters, medallions, stained glass, and a large
body of images on various Judaic themes. He was one of the most prolific
visual satirists of his day and his World War II anti-fascist imagery was
comparable to Goya's *Disasters of War*. But his mission went beyond mere
topical satire; he employed art as an engine of spiritual transcendence
and human liberation. A victim of anti-Semitism in his native country,
forced to move to Paris, England, and later the United States., he still
fervently fought for a free Polish state as both soldier and artist, and later
devoted his energies to freeing Palestine from British rule and building
a Jewish state. Indeed almost all his art, even the numerous books of
fairy tales and fables he illustrated, were somehow imbued with appeals
for universal social justice. "To call Szyk a 'cartoonist' is tantamount to
calling Rembrandt a dauber or Chippendale a carpenter," declared an
editorial in a 1942 issue of *Esquire*, one of the many accolades he received
during his lifetime. In fact, with articles about him published in the *New
Yorker* and the *New York Herald Tribune*, among others, his artistic renown
was undisputable.

Yet by the late 1970s even this incredibly impressive body of
work (for instance, he was the most illustrious of the *Rubaiyat* of Omar
Khayyam illustrators), which painstakingly wedded the exquisitely
crafted detailing of Persian-style miniatures to the symbolic acuity of
Renaissance iconic masterpieces, was all but forgotten by contemporary

critics, as well as young illustrators and caricaturists who really should have known and admired the work.

So for me, thirty years ago it was a revelation to see Szyk's art for the first time at the Martin Sumers Gallery, which during the late '70s was the only New York (perhaps American) venue exhibiting his originals. I was totally seduced by Szyk's searing cartoons, which, as his biographer Joesph P. Ansell wrote in *Arthur Szyk: Artist, Jew, Pole* (The Littman Library of Jewish Civilization, 2004), were "often ironic, but never comical." Yet they were so highly charged with conceptual intensity that even his most topical (and ephemeral) themes were made to seem timelessly monumental. Unfortunately, however, Szyk's impeccable draftsmanship had been made unfashionable during the '70s and '80s by the art brut, and neo-expressionistic, raw-edged mannerisms were exerting a hold on illustration. Nonetheless, having discovered his legacy, I truly believed the time for a Szyk renaissance was imminent, just waiting for someone with a passion for his work to revive him.

Enter Irvin Ungar, a practicing "pulpit rabbi," who in 1975 was innocently enough introduced to Szyk when he was looking for gifts to bestow on members of his own wedding party. He recently recalled walking into the now defunct Bloch's Book Shop in New York and where he saw a pile of Szyk's *Haggadot* on a table. "The colors jumped out at me, the price was right, and I think I must have purchased 10 copies at $18 each!" The craftsmanship also appealed to him, but more importantly he was enthralled by their spiritual richness and innate humanity of the work. A decade later, after leaving the Rabbinate, he became a rare book bookseller, specializing in historic Judaica, which is when the Szyk renaissance began to pick up steam.

In the early 1990s Ungar uncovered another dusty cache of prints comprising Szyk's Jewish holiday series. Once again the signature fluorescent colors jumped out. At the time all Ungar knew was that religion seemed to be the sole theme of Szyk's work, but as his interest piqued, he launched an investigation that allowed him to find the 1941 anti-Nazi book *The New Order* (G.P. Putnam's Sons) with an introduction by the late Roger W. Straus, Jr. (of Farrar, Straus, and Giroux), filled with blood curdling caricatures of Axis leaders—Hitler, Mussolini, Hirohito, et al.—composed with plausibly monstrous features. These were arguably the most caustic propaganda artworks of the entire World War II era. Although this book now surfaces at antiquarian book fairs, then *The New Order* and the limited edition *Ink and Blood* (The Heritage Press, 1946) were virtually impossible to obtain, if only because they were not highly valued. Ungar saw their value.

Although he was only three when Szyk died, Ungar made it his personal calling to restore the artist to prominence. He eventually acquired the Szyk Family Archives, became close to his daughter Alexandra Szyk Bracie (now in her 80s), and took over the major responsibility for the nonprofit Arthur Szyk Society, which enables him to curate international museum exhibitions of Szyk's art, including *Justice Illuminated: The Art of Arthur Szyk* at the Spertus Museum in Chicago (1999) and *The Art and Politics of Arthur Szyk* at the United States Holocaust Museum in Washington, D.C. He also edits the Society's series of Art History Publications; each contains an illustrated essay that further builds a library of scholarly documentation.

What accounts for Ungar's devotion to Szyk has a lot to do with how the artist speaks to his value system. Szyk once said, "Art is not my aim, it is my means." And Ungar noted, "So much of his art has a message: fighting against oppression, tyranny, and for freedom and justice. In essence, he translated his Jewish values into democratic ideals, being an advocate for mankind at large. [And] what Szyk says to me is this: care about your own people and use the best of that value system to contribute and make the world a better place for all people." In this spirit Szyk developed exhibitions of his work during the war years that raised funds for the Chinese, Czech, Polish, Greek, and British refugees.

Although Szyk was not alone in this philanthropy, he was unique among most mainstream American illustrators. Harry Katz, a former curator of Prints and Graphics at the Library of Congress in his paper for The Arthur Szyk Society, entitled "Democracy's Weapon: Arthur Szyk in America," draws comparisons to other American illustrators of his period—both Norman Rockwell and Szyk illustrated the Four Freedoms (Freedom to Worship, Freedom from Want, Freedom from Fear, Freedom of Speech) based on precepts put forth in President Franklin Roosevelt's 1941 State of the Union Address. Each has a remarkably different interpretation. "While Rockwell's *Pictures for the American People* during WWII depicted people who were almost exclusively middle class and white, Jews were rarely seen and black virtually non-existent," wrote Katz. "Szyk's rendering on the other hand includes the Virgin Mary, a black man, and a Jew together with Lincoln's Gettysburg Address, as a Renaissance pieta type unified work. Rockwell and most of his contemporaries in America lagged behind Arthur Szyk in their awareness of and concern for social justice and civil liberties."

For Ungar there is no more lasting a testament to Szyk's humanist legacy than his interpretation of the *Haggadah* (the text read during the Passover seder recounting the story of the Exodus). Ungar explained that from Szyk's earliest years the concept of freedom and how to achieve it were at the forefront of his creativity and commitment, so it was only natural "that he would be drawn to the Exodus story and the need to confront adversity, and oppression, and to fight for freedom. The *Haggadah* which tells that story and how God led the Israelites out of Egypt was not mythology for Szyk—and it was not only a historical event of its time, but an event once again happening in his own day—for this time Hitler was Pharaoh and the Nazis were the 'new' Egyptians." Szyk recognized that in every generation there would be those who would rise up to destroy the Jews, and he felt it was his job to be a spokesman for his people. So the *Haggadah* was one of Szyk's most powerfully chosen ways to present to his "people and the people of the world the unfolding saga, drama, and challenges facing Jews in the world in which they live."

In 1940 when the initial vellum edition first appeared, the *Times of London* reviewer wrote that this book "is worthy of being considered one of the most beautiful of books ever produced by the hand of man." But to appreciate the *Haggadah* in its fullness, insisted Ungar, one has to see the brilliance of the original art Szyk created in Poland between 1934 and 1936. "No other printing of Szyk's *Haggadah* has ever been able to capture the luminosity and detail of Szyk's originals, that is, until now."

Ungar's mission to raise consciousness about Szyk is currently focused on impeccably and flawlessly reproducing the original *Haggadah* art in an exacting edition. "I officially began one year ago, but have dreamed of it for more than a decade," he said about the project.

The edition of 310 copies, planned for January 2008, and costing $15,000 (for a premier edition) and $8,500 (for the deluxe edition), is being produced entirely by the digital process. "It is the first time, to our knowledge that anyone has embarked on this venture on this scale. We hope to do for the 21st century what Szyk's 1940 printing did for the 20th century, that is, to create a bibliographic landmark that achieves a level of excellence that will be sustained in each generation," explained Ungar.

To achieve the accuracy required he has employed one of the world's leading digital photographers, Ardon Bar Hama who photographed the Dead Sea Scrolls for the Israel Museum and the Codex Vaticanus for the Vatican. He also commissioned production of the finest digital paper for the project, which is made in Germany. But the project has had it share of challenges—from the selection and testing of paper and the proper profile to fit the Epson printer, to creating the most perfect typographical text design to complement Szyk's art on the facing page, to presenting the *Haggadah* with the very "right" binding which has elegance and class, and invites the viewer to anticipate what is held within its pages.

Struggles have also plagued the *Haggadah*. The original designer/ typographer, Scott-Martin Kosofsky, who produced *A Survivors' Haggadah* in 1998 as a limited edition for the American Jewish Historical Society, is no longer involved in the project, which is regrettable as he brought a decidedly objective eye to Szyk's work as a whole. "Though I am always impressed, as one must be, by Szyk's virtuoso technique, his aesthetic sometimes seems to me a bit too heavy-handed for its own good," said Kosofsky. "In his political cartoons, the combination often hits a home run, but in the book illustrations, including the *Haggadah*, the result can be less satisfying; more concerned with the quantity of imagery and decoration than with the emotional power of the topic he is representing." Kosofsky argued, for example, that the tableau showing the princess of Egypt taking the infant Moses "borders on the insipid, whereas the justly famous plate of the father and son reading the Four Questions makes a powerful illuminated page."

While Kosofsky admitted Szyk was a brilliant illustrator, he was far less imaginative as a book designer. Some pages contain few words, while others are crammed with excruciatingly small text in long, tight lines. Szyk's basic plan was for a page-for-page presentation of Hebrew (right) and English (left), and in Kosofsky's original design scheme he tried to preserve that, "but do it better." The English pages of the original edition of 1940, executed in England, attempted to mimic the geometry of Szyk's pages: Where Szyk had Hebrew text, the English text was placed in parallel; where Szyk had pictures, an English commentary was squeezed into an equal space; and where there was less English text than Hebrew, the space was filled out with type ornaments (always the Giolito arabesque). This was all done in (metal) Monotype Plantin, that heavy old dog that the British loved so much, much in the same way that Americans of the period loved Goudy Old Style. "The English pages of the 1940 edition looked like bad William Morris," added Kosofsky, "and they created tremendously noisy spreads," so his design aimed to create pages that were clear and readable, complementary but not competitive—and certainly not noisy. "Since I was the author of both the new translations and the commentary, as well as the designer and typesetter, I had an unusual amount of control, but still there were great challenges dealing with the most crowded pages."

Kosofsky also selected the production team (the binder Claudia Cohen and printer Stephen Stinehour), as well as the authors who would write the companion volume essays, which he was to design and edit. He enlisted Pavel Repisky, of Atlantic Papers, to persuade Hahnemühle, in Germany, to make a sheet especially for the book. Kosofsky's own Montaigne type, a French Renaissance letter influenced by the work of Jan Tschichold, was applied to texts that are meant to be read out loud, while the commentaries are set in Lucas de Groot's The Sans, and the titles are set in Penumbra, designed by Lance Hidy. Some of the original design components have been retained by the current designer Irene Morris who, the current prospectus says "offers a new interpretation of Szyk's intricate page layouts." About Kosofsky's contribution, Ungar acknowledged, "He provided guidance, and helped lay the groundwork for the first phase of the project, and for that I am grateful." Still with so much passion concentrated on this project egos clashed and controversy persists.

Nonetheless Ungar insisted his biggest trial is more fundamental: "What would Szyk have approved of? How does what I create provide the perfect match to what Szyk created. This, I believe has become the essence of the project, providing the greatest challenge, yet the greatest joy and excitement." But ultimately, after the *Haggadah* reaches its audience, Ungar has an even larger goal in mind. "I believe Szyk is a mine so deep and so rich that the art world has yet come to grasp with how rich and diverse it is—but when they do, they will realize it is a gold mine."

Why Does John Baeder Paint Diners?

John Baeder paints diners, and what could be more pop than that? His goal for the past three decades has been to record on canvas and paper just about every diner, roadside eatery, and virtually every possible monument of American consumer culture. His work has been shown in scores of galleries, collected by dozens of collectors, and reproduced in numerous books, magazines, and, appropriately, on postcards. He is a master of photorealism, but his work is more than mere technique and process. Yet each of his detailed images is a document of a disappearing design epoch. They are not nostalgic reprises of bygone days, but paeans to the guileless moments when common consumption was couched in vernaculars unique to the regions in which they were fostered.

But Baeder was not always an artist-documenter. He began his life in the service of clients as an art director at McCann-Erickson. Unlike many who failed to escape advertising's pull, Baeder found the intestinal fortitude to move elsewhere and onward, with his intestines intact.

I've long admired Baeder's work since before Harry N. Abrams published *Diners* by John Baeder over twenty-five years ago. But I never knew why he was able to break from the art directorial rat race to the calmer pace of soulful painter. I recently asked him to explain why. He responded frankly, albeit poetically.

For the Atlanta native, art direction wasn't creatively satisfying. "Spending millions of dollars of clients' money became demoralizing," he told me. The agency system became stifling. And yet working in a gregarious atmosphere was a high, as was working with very gifted photographers, illustrators, TV production houses, and musicians. "It was fun, but shallow," he admitted. Agency life was a "boot camp" for the art world. And like the pop artists Warhol and Rosenquist who were toilers in the commercial art world, Baeder found the six degrees of separation between advertising and art. He left the business out of "self-respect, to see if I could do what I loved most and paint full time." Fortunately, an exhibition at a prestigious gallery was scheduled; his art dealer was Ivan Karp, who was a pioneer of the pop art movement, and was then advocating the photorealism movement. "It was the completion of a fantasy I had since a teenager," said Baeder. "I was observing George Beattie, a well-known southern artist, remove paintings from his station wagon for a show at the High Museum of Art in Atlanta. I said to myself, 'I'm going to do that someday...' [and] I did. It was September, 1972, on West Broadway, with my station wagon, an extension of myself, that took me to magical journeys, and images I'm still painting." He paid homage to the car in the canvas titled *John's Diner with John's Chavelle*.

But what was it about diners that appealed to his passions? Did Baeder choose diners, or did they choose him? For the answer, a little retrospection is required.

Growing up in Atlanta there were no diners, per se. Diners are New England bred, born in Providence, Rhode Island. Most manufacturers were in New York and New Jersey. "Around six years of age, I had the opportunity of going to a 'restaurant' that had an exposed grill and low counter, like a real live diner, with short stools where I could sit in amazement becoming mesmerized by the cacophony of the grill men going about their duty," recalled Baeder. "My eyeballs astonished at their dancing and juggling." Yet even more inspiring was riding in railroad train dining cars, ordering his meal with a pencil on a light green newsprint stock pad, while gleaming silverware welcomed his sensitive nature to all "the surrounds, sounds, smells, and waiters who were in dressed in their crisp white coats, contrasting their dark skin with the same purity as the table setting."

As the train chugged on, Baeder imagined the backsides of small towns were little paintings, framed by the large expanse of window. "I was on a rolling museum, complete with chicken à la king, and aspic salad."

He visualized diners as temples from lost civilizations and this intrigue triggered a photographic quest. At that time there was no indication of any future as a painter, much less using diners as subject material. He documented them with no particular agenda other than the solace he felt as a little boy in the dining car. Diners were stationary dining cars.

Baeder turned into manic collector of diner postcards, especially a genre of simulated linen cards. "I had always negated the linen era postcard because of their gross retouching, losing so much reality for the sake of 'romancing' an image. I always felt cheated [because it] wasn't real looking. I discounted them." But when he met his first postcard dealer at an antique show he fell head over heels for linens. "The retouched image surfaced into a very surreal visual excitement," he said. "I saw them as small paintings, and wondered what they would look like enlarged and transformed to canvas. The linen stock was used to trick the consumer's eye. It was faux canvas." Baeder said he forgave the retouching, and filled in the blanks. Once the postcard bug bit, he started to go to shows with more dealers from local and regional areas and was introduced to the photo postcard. "Now, a new reality was upon me; traveling with a keener focus, more detail, and realizing these small 3.5" x 5.5" images were becoming important for me to pay deeper attention. Getting to these parts of the American landscape, one had to get gas, eat, and sleep." These places had more visual impact as architectural and roadside artifacts. Baeder got more serious and placed classified ads in antique tabloid newspapers to locate gas stations, diners, motels, and tourist camp postcards. Postcard lingo calls them "approvals." You pick what you want, write a check, return the rest. "Voila! Joy! My mailbox began to overflow daily," he joyfully recalled.

As an advertising art director, Baeder worked with most of the best still life photographers in New York. One day a rep came to see him with a photographer named Dick Steinberg. "I intuitively knew he was a painter from looking at his images. There was a spirit that the other photographers, as great as they were, didn't have." The two were instantly drawn to each other on an aesthetic and intellectual basis. Steinberg had been a painter, but needed to provide for two families; the advertising business kept him busy. One of their connections was the love of Marcel DuChamp. "Dick projected his desires to paint again onto me and urged me to leave the business. I still remained cautious. As I was beginning a collection of more postcards, images that appealed to me were starting to come into focus: diners, gas stations, motels, tourist camps—the mainstays of roadside culture. Photorealism was just beginning to be noticed in the art world. I had gone to an exhibition that had a few paintings I related to. I knew none of the artists, it didn't matter what they were doing or who they were. I recalled saying to my wife at the time, 'I can do that, and better....'"

Baeder's shift to painting occurred when he saw an Ed Ruscha installation at the Iolas Gallery in New York. He had purchased Ruscha's small booklets of gas stations, swimming pools, and the Sunset Strip. He related to his unpretentious point of view. "The paintings on view were the beginnings of the word series. I was smitten," he recalled. He had always identified with the social realists. But he also had a compulsion to enlarge postcard images, and once he made the linen image appear retouched, it would take on a surreal nature—that's when his "calling started to happen."

Baeder recalls stretching a 42" x 66" canvas, the exact scale of a 3.5" x 5.5" postcard. It sat blank for a long time. He couldn't decide what image to paint first. "Excitement and fear mixed together are like oil and water," he confessed. "A particular diner stood out—its retouched areas shouting be re-applied, its presence in need for more attention. It felt good to paint flat areas representing the dull printed halftone. Using acrylic paints added to the flatness. I did it." He completed his first painting.

After that he came home from what were increasingly tedious days producing ads and TV commercials. All the new campaigns and new accounts seemed decidedly senseless. Every night he feverishly painted. His next painting was a gas station, then a motel, and then a tourist camp. He painted the Copperplate Gothic font so many cards of that era used for their descriptions on the upper or lower corners of the white borders.

Baeder was introduced to Ivan Karp of OK Harris Gallery in New York. He came to Baeder's small apartment on a Sunday morning on one of his usual forays to visit new artists. No other art dealer had such passion and zeal for finding new artists. He saw the four raw paintings, as Baeder called them, and immediately offered him a show to open the new season in September. It was the middle of February 1972. "I quit my job at McCann-Erickson, the first of April," Baeder told me, "and entered a new world—my new world—a vital rebirth."

l

Intel-
ligent
Design

During the 1990s religious fundamentalists challenged Darwin's theory of evolution. They replaced it with a ludicrous notion called "Intelligent Design." The definition of this seemingly secular term was that, as the bible says, a superior being created the world in seven days (or thereabouts). This cosmic designer created man, woman, animals, insects, and what all, not through eons of evolutionary trial and error, but in a snap of his fingers. Annoyed that a relatively benign term was usurped and transformed into such a dubious anti-scientific concept. I wrote an essay, which is included in this section, questioning the provenance of the term "Intelligent Design." For a while, groups have attempted to curtail the teaching of evolution in certain schools, but the term in question has not been resurrected. So given the less inflammatory meaning, most of the essays in this section do not address the evolution debate at all. Rather, included here are essays that question intelligence and how designers acquire it. For instance, "How to be Motivated" questions the language of design motivators and what's now called "design thinking." "A Designer by Any Other Name" looks at the new role designers play in an intelligent world. What we designers call ourselves and how not to motivate designers through jargon and motivational-speak are subjects that require more intelligent inquiry than did the world begin with the flick of a biblical switch.

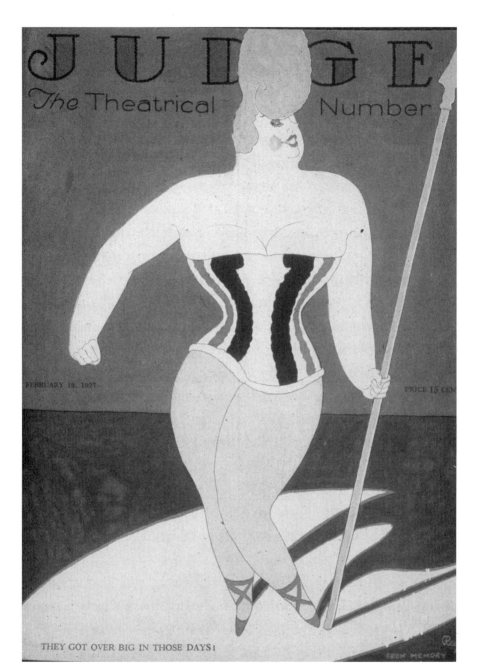

Who Owns Intelligent Design?

While recently reviewing a designer's portfolio, I was struck by the brilliance of a certain campaign and enthusiastically exclaimed, "Now, that's intelligent design!" The designer looked at me with a knowing smile. Of course, I said what I meant and meant what I said, but given contemporary argot, that simple phrase triggered a moment of introspection, and a second later I self-consciously added, "It's also smart and sophisticated." But after uttering this caveat, I asked myself why I was compelled to do so. Is the phrase "intelligent design" so totally co-opted that it no longer means what it means?

As Bill Clinton made absurdly clear, even a word like "is" is subject to various interpretations. Words and phrases are routinely repurposed to evoke ideas that may alter their original meanings and provide new ones. Advertising copywriters and designers routinely manipulate common usages then graft them onto products or ideas to define or identify brands. Verbal puns and ironic twists are advertising's raw meat; in fact, I remember how clever *Fortune* magazine was in the '80s when it turned the Communist derisive "capitalist tool" into its own PR mantra. Calling the foremost American business magazine a capitalist tool neutralized the Marxist-Leninist criticism that workers are dupes of evil money-grubbers. And it became a positive identifier for the magazine in the bargain. I also recall when in the '70s Wells, Rich and Green took a common vernacularism, "the city never sleeps," and recast it as "The Citi never sleeps," creating an indelible tag for Citibank. For the generation exposed to the slogan, the city never closing down will always be associated with the bank that is always open for its customers. Now, that was intelligent wordplay.

Like commerce, politics is terra firma for verbal and visual language manipulation. During World War II, Winston Churchill made the word "victory" and letter "V" (formed by his two cigar-gripping fingers) into the ineradicable symbol of British resolve against Nazi blitzkrieg. The V was also adopted in occupied countries as a sign of resistance. So by claiming ownership of "V for Victory," the Allies effectively kept it out of the Nazi's otherwise rich propaganda lexicon. In *V for Vendetta*, Natalie Portman rhetorically (and polemically) asks when innocuous words like "rendition" and "collateral" started taking on such nefarious meanings as they do in American foreign policy today. The answer is simple: It happened when the government realized it must make bad things palatable to good people, and made terminology such as "torture" and "civilian casualties" sound more sterile. But surely co-option of words and phrases is as old as visual and verbal language. After all, turning the crucifix (the sign of the cross), a Roman method of execution, into a symbol of martyrdom and redemption was truly intelligent design.

During the twentieth century, obfuscating meaning through transformed common words and phrases, or what George Orwell termed "newspeak," became de rigueur in politics and media. And the trend continues. The Nazis were, of course, masters of turning venal acts into benign phrases: deportation to concentration camps was "resettlement"; gas chambers were "showers." But they were not alone; the American military command in Vietnam referred to the torching of villages as "pacification." During the Cultural Revolution the Communist Chinese used the term "rehabilitation" to describe the official humiliation (and at times murder) of its internal enemies. Today's term for mass murder, "ethnic cleansing," is not as obscene as genocide (even though at times they are used in the same breath). "Regime change" is a polite way to indicate an overthrown government. "Surgical strike," a devastating bombing raid or missile attack, suggests a clean medical procedure. Then there is "shock and awe," which really means destruction on a grand scale designed to produce death and induce capitulation. Oh, by the way, not all wordplay is tied to war; tax cuts for the rich are now called "revenue enhancements."

"Instead of language we have jargon," wrote Eric Bentley, the playwright and translator of Bertolt Brecht. "Instead of principles, slogans; and instead of genuine ideas, bright suggestions." Maybe it's all just semantics. Maybe institutions, organizations, businesses, and individuals are free to nuance language and images all they want.

Maybe one of our responsibilities as citizens is to learn how to discern, translate and interpret the multiple meanings. Maybe it is our job to be savvy enough about verbal and visual vocabulary so we are not fooled or flummoxed. Maybe.

Nonetheless, I am bothered that common words and phrases (some, such as "intelligent design," I had taken for granted) have been turned into trademarks for certain agendas, and therefore owned by those people or groups. "Patriotism" connotes everyone's loyalty to nation—America for instance—but through a few clever slogans and jingles and ceaseless rhetoric, it is often used to signify those in power against those in opposition. In my mind, the true patriot is not simply a conformist but a nonconformist, but when the word is spun to mean a patriot is one who supports administration policies, it also must imply one who disagrees is unpatriotic. Whoever claims a word or phrase first—or uses it more persuasively—seems to own it. Using patriotism in this way establishes dichotomies, so in this particular scuffle the opposition has relinquished the word—and has not found a better one.

Intelligent design is a vivid description but a debatable concept. Regardless of whether one accepts evolutionism or creationism—two decidedly clear ways of labeling distinct views of how life developed on earth—the theory called "Intelligent Design" throws a monkey wrench into the linguistic works because it co-opts a phrase that should belong to all of us. When William A. Dembski, author of *No Free Lunch: Why Specified Complexity Cannot Be Purchased Without Intelligence,* and Philip Johnson, the pioneers of the Intelligent Design movement, coined this label, they truly muddied the waters for all who would use the term in a benign but clear manner. "Intelligent Design, if separated from any right-wing agenda," said branding expert Brian Collins, "could be a straightforward term for anyone who seeks proof that the unifying patterns of existence may be connected to a broader intelligence at work in the universe. Fair enough." But in its current state the baggage weighs heavy.

Intelligent design is based on an alternative scientific theory to Darwinism, arguing that life developed from deliberate natural design (perhaps from a higher being) rather than from random natural selection. It could have been called "natural design" or "natural forethought" but intelligent design has a better ring and is a brilliant branding method to drive creationism (with its more biblical overlay) back into public classrooms. "It is not coincidental that its use appeared shortly after the United States Supreme Court rejected Creationism from American public schools," Collins added.

This is not an argument for or against either of these hot-button issues, but rather a rationale for retaking ownership of the term. A linguist once said, when you change your language you change your thoughts, so it is necessary that certain terms and phrases be freestanding. Words are empty vessels. But once a memorable word or phrase has entered a public dialog filled with a powerful emotional charge, its takes on that meaning until a stronger one replaces or dilutes it.

No one should own intelligent design. "For those who wish to reframe the debate," continued Collins, "one way would be to make the term more emotionally charged as the search for scientific truth rather than a term for the assertion of religious faith." Another use would be to celebrate what is truly extraordinary about what graphic, industrial, product, new media, and all other designers do. Intelligent design is design that understands and serves the public, and that's the best use of the term.

A Designer by Any Other Name. . .

Speaking of popular terminology, since graphic design is not a licensed profession, we can call ourselves anything we want, with the exception of maybe doctor or monsignor (although Monsignor Dr. Heller has a nice ring). Likewise, anyone else can claim the graphic designer mantle (or "graphics designer," which is the dead-give-away that you're not a graphic designer), without an iota of schooling, simply because they made a letterhead, newsletter, or Web site on their home computer. So, if our nomenclature is this fungible then it stands to reason our bona fides are in question too, at least in the eyes of the outsider looking in and even the insider looking out. A designer by any other name may still be a designer, yet make no mistake, what we call ourselves is key to our professional health and well-being. As professionals we are hired to be clarifiers, organizers, and even namers for our clients. So, if we don't know what to call us, who does?

Nonetheless, given the current growing intersection of graphic design with time-based media, information design, and other associated disciplines, including writing and producing, as well as boundary blurring between fine art and design, who and what we are (and ultimately want to be) is becoming more complicated to define and, therefore, to name. Yet it wasn't always this confounding.

Before W.A. Dwiggins famously coined the term "graphic design" in a 1922 Boston newspaper article as a means to describe the wide range of jobs he personally tackled, "commercial artist" was the accepted label for the interrelated acts of drawing, specing, comping, and laying out. Dwiggins, however, was a jack-of-many-graphic-trades, including, but not exclusively, illustrating books, composing pages, designing typefaces (including Metro and Caledonia), producing calligraphic hand lettering,

DEC. 1923

No. 99   PRICE 25c

ART MAGAZINE

Cartooning
Designing
Illustrating
Lettering

G.H. LOCKWOOD EDITOR
Kalamazoo, Mich.

stencil ornament, book covers and jackets, book interiors and title pages, advertising and journal formats, along with handbills, stationery, labels, signs, not to mention writing his own critical essays, fiction stories, and marionette plays. Being an iconoclast he wanted to distinguish his activities from more humdrum, less prolific commercial artists and coined a term that was uniquely his own. Graphic design, which was derived from, but much broader than, "graphic arts" (signifying drawing and engraving) defined such a personally esoteric pursuit Dwiggins could not have predicted that decades later graphic design would become the standard professional description. Although he never actually called himself a "graphic designer," his coinage was cast like bread upon the sea and eventually washed up on professional shores.

I recently asked for a show of hands at an AIGA/New York student conference (I moderated) on the nexus of commerce and passion to the question, "Does anyone here call themselves commercial artists?" Predictably, not one among these college juniors and seniors raised their hands. But surprisingly, only two-thirds of them embraced the term graphic designer, and a few of them were rather tentative. Over a decade ago, when schools and design firms started affixing loftier monikers to academic degrees and business cards, the most common newbie was "communications design," which, along with "graphic communications" and "visual communications" (or the marshal-sounding Viz-Com), seemed to address the transition from old to new media. A little while later, thanks to Richard Saul Wurman, in a milestone talk before the first AIGA Conference in Boston, the field was given his quixotic appellation "information architects." In the mid to late 1990s, when the Web became a dominant presence in design practice, this tag became much more commonly applied along with "user interface designers," "human-centered interface designers," and "experiential interface designers." All of a sudden, the name game turned into something of an Olympic sport to outdo the next guy, with designers adding all sorts of in-your-face or interface verbiage to their credentials.

Currently there is something of a schism between the newly coined and the curiously pejorative affixation, "conventional designers," which indicates solely print-orientation, and other art/techno/science sounding job descriptions. The first time I ever heard the term "conventional design" it was uttered by a guru in the "Web standards" movement, who was obviously trying to drive a wedge by making a huge distinction between Web designers and print designers, who, incidentally, were designosaurs (try that on your business card—or Web site).

If graphic design is synonymous with print, and print is "conventional" then a priori anything in the non-print realm is "unconventional." While this makes linguistic sense, the last time I looked print was still a vital medium in which many progressive designers continued to experiment with type and image in brilliant ways. In theory, the Web and other digital platforms are the proverbial new frontier, but in practice too much "standardized" Web design (i.e. the major news and commercial sites from Amazon to the BBC) is replete with—and at times drowning in—brand spanking new conventions. Achieving comparably great design on the Web has yet to happen. Additionally, whether on the page or screen, designers are still making graphic things. Still, the term graphic design is on its way to becoming obsolete. (Full disclosure: even the School of Visual Arts' MFA Designer as Author program, which I co-chair, dropped the "graphic" when it began almost ten years ago to indicate more than just print studies.) What's more, some "conventional" designers even buy into the designosaur concept: Recently, I heard a highly reputed print designer announce the end of printed books is near, to be replaced by the "tablet" or digital reader, a technological advancement that will allow pages be read like print but in pixel form, and end the need for book or book cover/jacket designers, perhaps in favor of a new job description, "tablet-interface designers." With the evolutionary onslaught of new tech already upon us, the day may come when designers will be called "-ologists," as in designologists, typologists, or interfaceologists.

It's not so farfetched that in a few years' time the academies and profession will totally sweep out all the old nomenclature—as it did commercial art—for labels that completely alter and elevate the outside and inside perceptions of what we do and who we are. For instance, a number of the students attending the AIGA conference told me they "do branding," which incorporates graphic, Web, and experiential design in one total, integrated package. So I asked them, what in their classes do they call this field? The answer was Brand Specialists—not too far from my anticipated answer, brandologists—which eliminated both the words "graphic" and "design" entirely.

Citing a "dysfunctional name" out of touch with the times and technologies, back in 1993 the AIGA—originally founded in 1913 as the American Institute of Graphic Arts—considered calling itself the American Institute of Graphic Design. Massimo Vignelli said about the venerable moniker, "So the name AIGA has been around for 80 years. Even if it had been around for a thousand years, it would still be wrong." Yet despite a wellspring of lobbying to change, the naming committees soon rejected

COMMERCIAL DESIGN

DIVISION

ON

ADVERTISING LAYOUT

ART INSTRUCTION, INC.
MINNEAPOLIS, MINNESOTA

graphic, fearing it would be out-of-date by the time the letterhead was redesigned. AIGA is no longer initials but a melody, with the qualifying subtitle "The Professional Organization for Design" suggesting there are many sub-professions under (or perhaps replacing) the broad rubric of what was once graphic design—which makes sense in this radically integrated new media world, although, truth be known, I still like the word graphic, if only for the comfort it provides.

Funnily, not all the students attending the AIGA/New York conference knew exactly what the initials AIGA stood for, nor did they much care. Knowing it is the "Professional Organization for Design" was enough for their immediate needs. But like the organization itself, which is in the process of looking towards the future, these students face a naming (or rather branding) conundrum. How, through their names and labels, do they telegraph what they do? With such a growing menu of terms to choose from maybe graphic designer is, at least, not so nebulous, though clearly for many it's incredibly confining.

Which leads to another profound shift: These very new media causing an identity crisis are also enabling designers to do more independent, authorial, or entrepreneurial work. For previous generations independence was daunting. But now, all that prevents a designer from inventing, fabricating, and selling unique wares is talent, ingenuity, and drive. I know some undergrads, and many of my own grad students, who have made products for the marketplace. So what do we call ourselves when the practice shifts from service-provider to producer? Maybe my own story will have some resonance.

When I first started out, forty years ago, I called myself a cartoonist. When that went sour because my talents were limited, I became a graphic designer, but really I was an art director, which is how I labeled myself for over 35 years. An art director, by the way, is one of those jobs that even a non-graphic (or graphics) designer can do, as long as she knows how to collaborate with designers, photographers, and illustrators. A few months ago, I quit being art director. The worst part of the decision was not leaving a job I loved to broaden my horizons, but coming up with a new title to identify me. Since I've been writing articles and books, I thought I might call myself "graphic writer" but that sounds almost as archaic as commercial artist. So I thought ex-art director sounded appropriate until I realized it was like "ex-husband" and was too negative. Para-designer has a nice cadence, but lacks meaning. Since I work with students, design educator had the right ring, but is also too limiting for what I do. Design impresario is too pretentious and design consultant sounds like a non-job. Interface engineer doesn't quite sync with my purpose in life. And I think Design Slut is taken. So as of this writing I no longer have a title. Though I still think of myself as a graphic designer, I worry that without a tag that defines me in relation to my peers and betters I will simply be a former professional. A designer by any other name is still a designer, but it's important to have a viable name, whatever it may be.

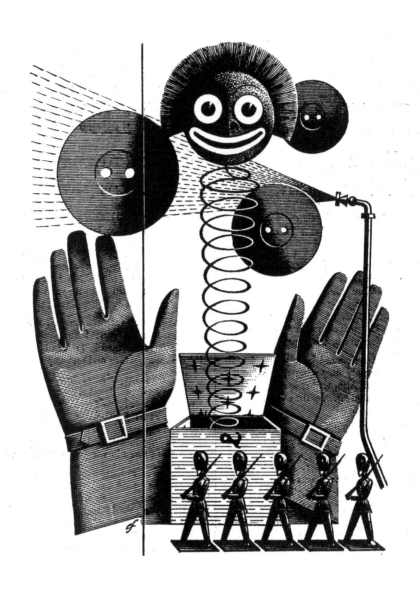

How Not to Be Motivated

Motivation demands inspiration, which requires insight. I often wonder how insightful some of design's motivational speakers really are. Although they may put forth the occasional pearl of wisdom, I cannot tolerate them. Their imperious, self-bloated stagecraft is, for me, like listening to chalk screeching on a blackboard. Nonetheless, I know people who draw real inspiration from this twaddle. In fact, at a few conferences I've seen audiences become rapt in devotional attention as motivational gurus toss out bromides about how to achieve design nirvana.

Maybe I'm just being a little too cynical. Maybe that nagging voice inside my head is correct when it says, "If you gave these folk half a chance, you'd learn what you need to become a better designer/business wonk and actually find true fulfillment in your chosen field—which, incidentally, might help you rise above the pitiful pettiness of your current existence." Well, faced with such a persuasively articulated argument, perhaps it is time to drop my resistance and open my ears and heart.

My problem, however, is this: while you can remove the cynic from the skeptic, you can't lead a horse to the waters of motivational salvation when prejudices are deeply ingrained. And mine are definitely deep. Listening to motivational speech cadences—tough-love vibrato alternating with earnest, sing-song rhythms—is about as annoying as listening to the TV pitchman who slices and dices or sells male enhancements on infomercials. I hate the patronizing timbre that others seem to find hypnotic. Despite the fact that, to me, they offer little more than robotically formulaic liturgies, I finally gave in to the inner voice urging me to give motivation a try. Understanding that the key to acclimating myself to such rhetoric would best be done, at least initially, in a more palatable way than attending another design conference, I curled up with a book.

As luck (or fate) would have it, I stumbled onto Tom Peters' *Essentials: Design*—published several years ago and adapted from *Re-Imagine!: Business Excellence in a Disruptive Age*—a decidedly evangelical, motivational tome that promises to empower its readers to "innovate, differentiate, and communicate" through the marvel of DESIGN. It is written by "the most influential business thinker of our age," or so says the flap copy. Tom Peters and his persuasive powers are indeed legendary: the coauthor of the celebrated *In Search of Excellence*, he is a pioneer image consultant for Rolls-Royce, Starbucks, Virgin, and Intel, among others. Thanks to the *Essentials* pocket-sized edition, I could dip a toe in the waters of his knowledge and experience, and, if his lessons sunk in, maybe I'd become a more enlightened design person (and just maybe those nasty headaches and that annoying twitch would go away, too). I might even graduate to his others on leadership, talent, and trends.

But first, an admission: in case my snarkiness sends the wrong message, this essay is not a rag on Mr. Peters. He is an acute business thinker and, more importantly, a tremendous design advocate. His motivational rhetoric is sincerely intended to prevent designers from being "odd ducks who should be confined to their desks." Actually, Peters' laudable mission is to release us fowl from stereotypical bondage—and from the fiction that we are inarticulate passive-aggressive artistes who routinely push our own aesthetic agendas at the expense of our clients' need. Rather, he insists we should "sit at the CEO's immediate right at the boardroom table," which I presume means not as servile concubines but as meaningful strategic contributors. And it takes an "über-guru"—one of the many honorifics applied to Peters on the book's back cover—to help the rest of us get our acts together.

Peters' goal is to both bolster designers' confidence while proselytizing the value of design to business. For instance, there is nothing more rousing to this designer's ears than Peters' forceful directive to execs to "have a formal design board," "routinely invite top designers to address the company as a whole," and make certain "the chief designer is a member of the board of directors or, at the very least, a member of the executive committee." Having read these words (twice), I felt he was that proverbial big brother—the one who protects and defends against the bullies—we all wish would be at our sides at all client meetings. (By the way, he further urges those execs to "have great art on the walls" to improve their visual literacy. Who could argue with that?)

Peters' sprightly tome is packed with visual aids, including typographically explosive manifestos, insider tips, bullet points, lists of to-dos and not-to-dos, homilies, slogans (e.g., "Design = Soul"; "Believe It"), screeds, rants and raves, asides, declarations, and "words of wisdom on design's large (and potentially enormous) place in the universe...." The book looks like an ambitious PowerPoint or (better yet) Keynote presentation, with each sentence—and almost every word—meant to jolt and stimulate. Among Peters' many quotable truisms, for example, is this message to corporate executives that can't help but feed a designer's optimism: "You don't become 'design-minded' by opening a checkbook, spending a few hundred thousand dollars on a 'great designer'—and then telling him/her to please 'do the design thing.'"

Peters' collected aphorisms are like "Home Sweet Home" samplers for us designers, and his rationales for how and why design is essential to all facets of corporate culture is so solidly absolute it is difficult for even this cynic to find ways to puncture his logic. Even his frequent hyperbole is indisputable. He clearly loves design and hates those who misunderstand it. He wields prose like a battle-ax against the hordes that encourage mediocrity or worse.

Peters believes design makes dreams (or at least "dream products") come true. As a contraction of the term "marketing of dreams" he uses the coinage dreamketing. On one of his many bullet-pointed pages peppered throughout the book he explains that dreamketing is: "touching the client's dreams," "the art of telling stories and entreating," "building the brand around the 'main dream,'" and "building 'buzz,' 'hype,' a 'cult.'" Another of his many motivational mantras—"Enthusiasm begets enthusiasm. Technicolor words beget Technicolor responses"—seems to define his entire philosophy. So, after reading the 160 pages in but a few short hours, I was convinced that if he were Secretary of Design for the United States, designers would definitely enjoy an elevated status heretofore unknown in this or perhaps any country. In fact, I was so sincerely motivated that while reading I even punched the air with my fist: "Right on, Peters!"

Yet despite that unbridled surge of excitement, I find something troubling about his motivational method.

You see, Peters' *Design* is as much a reservoir of motivational tropes as it is a bible for the motivationally needy. It is a stunning example of what he himself calls buzz, hype, and cult, and I have this nagging feeling that his motivational rhetoric, which reads so convincingly, is powered by hubris, fueled by generalization, and depends entirely on packaging to succeed. If I succumbed to this allure, just think about the more malleable reader.

Are design motivators really just hucksters? Must design-speak really be hyped-up marketing speak? Peters basically says yes. To truly persuade clients that design is worth something, designers must exhibit what Tibor Kalman called "the bullshit factor"—the gift of doubletalk—which is the point at which all this motivational hooey gets depressing. While I understand the realities of business—and I realize that Peters and other motivational gurus simply want us to do better (or as he says, "dramatically alter perspective"), must we build our credibility on a foundation of hype? Why must the rhetoric be so calculated that it sounds disingenuous, even if it is not?

Intense repetition of a single idea, phrase, or doctrine is called brainwashing, and that is exactly what motivational speaking (and writing) is all about. Motivational speaking, like advertising and propaganda, is part psychology, part philosophy, and part ideology (religious at times), couched in any mannerism that sells the big idea. Frankly, I was taught that brainwashing (a torturous practice first administered to American prisoners by the Chinese Communists during the Korean War and best illustrated in *The Manchurian Candidate*) is wrong. Of course, all successful motivational self-help authors or lecturers are at least tacitly brainwashing their audiences, and exude hubristic self-confidence to command their listeners or readers long enough to impart their wisdom. The über-guru must satisfy the need of his audience to be bettered, if not transformed, through sage advice, convincing promises, and corrective admonishments.

Sure, people wrote inspirational books—Dale Carnegie was the pioneer with *How to Win Friends and Influence People* in 1937—but the practice was not as cliché as it is now. Turn on any channel in the early hours, and someone is at the pulpit motivating. The design field is a fairly recent recipient of this gift, but now has more than its fair share. Today, anyone with a good stage presence, convincing oratory, and catchy slogan can be a motivationalist. Some certainly hit the right nerves and stimulate strong responses. But it is just too easy to get sucked in for all the wrong reasons.

After reading *Design*, I feel a bit shucked and jived. And believe me, I tried to be tolerant—really, I did! So maybe it is just me. Maybe I find it hard to believe that being formulaically told what to do will make my work, my life, better. Still, I believe that we all must find our own answers—our own blissful motivation—for ourselves. Or maybe you should take two bromides and call me in the morning.

Art for the Masses

Arguably this book could be titled Art for the Masses, since design (even the most expensively produced) is created with an audience in mind. The vast majority of said audience would fall under the rubric of masses. As a rule designers do not work with exclusivity as their ultimate goal but rather develop ideas and objects that have both long-term and wide reaching impact. Some design is focused on the zeitgeist, which may be fleeting, but most design—graphic, product, etc.—is meant to last, or at least anticipate change. This section includes essays about objects and ideas for which mass appeal is more or less a prerequisite. I admit that some of the themes are a bit quirky. The essay on home movie titling in the 1950s (before iMovie) is not simply a nostalgic romp but a serious view of how type entered our lives through the basest of methods. The story of Notgeld, the ersatz currency issued in 1920s Germany during its worst inflationary period, is a study in how art for the masses helped ease economic pain. The critique of awards and trophies addresses the poor design and manufacture of objects that every school child has received and every parent covets. And the profile of a supermarket chalkboard sign writer is as beautifully mass as design can be.

How Much Is That Artifact in the Window?

Many of us have bought mass-produced design objects for pleasure and/or scholarship. We've paid varying amounts—high and low. But what or who determines the value of a design artifact? Is it simply supply and demand, or some curiously abstract idea of worth? I recently found a reference on the Web to something I edited many years ago for sale through a highly respected antiquarian book dealer. A complete set (seven issues) of *Design and Style*, a paper promotion created by Seymour Chwast and me for Mohawk Paper Mills, was sold for $1,200 or $150 per copy. Granted, it was expensive to originally produce back when we began the series in 1986 (ending in 1992), and it was a limited run to begin with, but how was this dollar amount determined?

Monetizing fine art is a fairly logical process. Artists who have reputations command more money than those who do not. Gallery shows usually create the baselines for value, while museum exhibitions exponentially raise that line. Collectors often inflate worth by virtue of buying into and amassing collections of certain artists or movements, and from there value is further determined through sales, auctions, and forms of cultural barter. Posters are among the few graphic design forms that follow this essential model. Since a poster is a displayable object, often marketed to a broader audience than just designers or design scholars, it commands a higher price. Since various poster artists are known as masters of the craft, their respective works also have greater resale value. The most well-known of these "affichistes," despite the fact that the item might be printed in a large print run, are also intrinsically more desirable. Add to that the condition of the poster and the price is established.

But what about those objects produced in medium or large

quantities, by historically less significant designers? What about the more contemporary work produced by significant current designers or those who recently passed away? What determines, for instance, how much a Paul Rand El Producto cigar box (the one with the photogram on the top) is worth (I paid $95 ten years ago) compared to Milton Glaser's Dylan poster (I paid $95 for a first printing). And what about the price of original sketches, comps, or final artwork compared to the reproductions? How are these items prized?

"Real value for ephemeral productions is ostensibly determined by the notoriety of the designer of the piece (be it catalogue, brochure, mailer, point of purchase design), the relative scarcity (if it can be determined—how many were printed based on how often they turn up on the market, etc.), and condition (point of purchase displays, for instance, tend to have been banged up, or thrown away, so one in pristine shape will often command a premium)," explained John McWhinnie a partner of Glenn Horowitz Bookseller in New York. "I bought a number of examples that Sutnar created for Roneo and Vera at auction years ago and paid handsomely for them because they had never been unwrapped."

But sometimes, valuable objects fall between the cracks. Over ten years ago Steven Guarnaccia, chair of the BFA Illustration Department at Parsons, breathlessly called me to say he just found nine mint-condition copies of Sutnar's *Catalog Design Progress*, the Czech designer's seminal book on the subject, for $10 each at the Strand. I had purchased a copy a year before from a rare book dealer for $100 and six months later I saw one for sale at $500. I suggested he keep two, sell one to me, sell one to a friend for $250, and sell the rest to a dealer for $200 each. I learned later the dealer sold them each for between $300 and $450. And I bet the buyers were happy to have them.

Not all Sutnar materials are this expensive, but most have high price tags because they are historically valued (in other words in all the history books). In the '90s libraries were paying high prices for avant-garde materials, so selling them to individual collectors became a high stakes game. "There has been a market for these sorts of ephemeral productions going back into the early eighties," continued McWhinnie. He cited Ex Libris and its proprietors Arthur A. Cohen and Elaine Lustig Cohen as one of the pioneer booksellers that promoted and sold this type of graphic design and helped establish a market. To a certain degree their ambitious pricing set the tone for the '80s and '90s. Other dealers followed suit. European avant-garde movements commanded the highest prices (and monographs about those movements helped push the prices upwards). Then a flood of monographs on American and European émigré designers helped raise their public profile and collectors began paying attention to their work.

There are other considerations besides the most obvious names or initials of designers. James Fraser, former librarian of the Friendship Library at Fairleigh Dickinson University, Madison, New Jersey, follows these principles when appraising graphic design: "1. Skilled die cutting with a design concept that begs for the technique and is perfectly conceived for the product, etc. Not just a die cut for the sake of it 2. Ephemera style that is so much of the period in color, typography, image, and text that it 'dates itself' 3. Ephemera producer's position as 'design leader' in a field in a given period, e.g. Knoll, I. Miller, PKZ, DTV, PTT, etc., 4. Ephemera that is by or carries the mark of influence by a coterie of 'agenda designers,' e.g. Peter Alma, August Tschinkel, Otto Neurath, Gerd Arntz, Seiwert, Hoerle, etc." If you don't recognize these names, that's in large part why they are valuable. Their work represents the roots of modern graphic design but their names are known only by a rarefied few.

Because ephemera is of the moment—and usually destroyed rather than preserved after use—most of these fleeting objects are rare, which has always kept the price relatively high. "eBay, however, has shifted the field a bit as many dealers have sold work in that forum and collectors have discovered that what they thought was rare was often scarce merely because they didn't have an international sales forum they could routinely search," noted McWhinnie. "Now they do, and I've found that American post-war graphic design has flattened in value because eBay has demonstrated that it isn't as scarce as it seemed to be fifteen years ago."

Books are a different story. Some are worth much less than when they were sold retail. Others, owing to scarcity are priced much higher. The book market has clear guidelines and some intangible ones, too. If a book is important and rare the price will be predictably high, but what's important and rare is subjective. Often it takes a mediator—historian, critic, or dealer—to convince others of such value. I once had the opportunity to buy A. Tolmer's *Mise en Page* for $25. Five years later it was $350. In the meantime, it was written up in a few design histories.

What about setting a value on contemporary designs (i.e. the past twenty years)? If I were pricing *Design and Style* would I have given it such a high tag? Probably not, but then again valuing one's own work is incredibly difficult (and I have a few complete sets). Given that many designers control their inventories, they can price according to what the market will accept, and withhold what doesn't bring the price they want. I will expend large sums based on only one key factor: I can't live without the document. Regrettably for my pocketbook, that covers a lot of design artifacts.

GUNNAR PIHL

GERMANY:
the last phase

A Mass for Mass-Market Paperbacks

Some of the most affordable artifacts are paperback books. In the beginning was the hardcover book, comprised of multiple typeset pages containing knowledge and insight—tales small and tall—fiction and non. As the vessel of word and image, it offered pleasure and enlightenment; it bound messages and stories together, illuminated the mind, and darkness became light. And as time passed the literate few did multiply and purchased more books, and the publishers who roamed the earth were blessed. Yet the hardcover was too costly for many people, so in its image, though somewhat more condensed and less smartly typeset and splendidly adorned, publishers begat another, somewhat smaller format that was fertile and appealed to more masses at a cheaper price. Thus it was dubbed the mass-market paperback, and it sold well, bringing low and high literature to those who might never have read a book before. Publishers quickly realized how successful was their offspring and the industry rejoiced.

This homily should not imply the inevitability that mass-market paperbacks would be successful, yet the genre was a calculated risk that certainly paid off over the past century. The consuming public, it was proven, yearned for volumes that they could read anywhere without having to lug around cumbersome tomes. A book that could fit into a coat pocket—hence the trademarked and generic classification "pocket book"—was perfect for train, plane, or beach chair and sold on racks in drugstores, supermarkets, and terminals. They were an economic boon for their producers and economical savings for their consumers. Inexpensive to print, they could be disposed of or passed on to others. This was key to the evolution of modern Western civilization that began with the invention of moveable type and the printing press during the fifteenth century. Mass-market paperbacks may not have been what Johannes Gutenberg or the Church had envisioned when the presses started pumping out ecclesiastical texts, but they were a force that altered what and how the masses consumed and digested everything from pulps to classics, and eventually self-help books too.

Sometime during this evolutionary process, however, conventions were established that forever distinguished the look of mass-market paperbacks from hardcover books from yet another genre called trade paperbacks (which were ostensibly "soft-shell" hardcover books because they looked the same only without the casing). At some key juncture it was decided in the bowels of the publishing industry that mass-market books should be a particular size (based logically on the most cost-effective, standardized printing formats), and look a particular way (doubtless based on the pseudo-scientific assumption by marketing experts about the aesthetic tastes of the masses). Some of those distinctions are as follows: Hardcover books looked more imposing, mass-market paperbacks looked more informal. Hardcover jackets were more artful, paperback covers were more commercial. Hardcover graphics were more nuanced, paperback covers titillated by leaving little to the imagination. Hardcover graphics merely suggested the content, paperbacks pounded the plot and/or the characters home. Many hardcover books relied entirely on type to announce the book while most paperbacks were realistically, romantically, or surrealistically illustrated. Nonetheless, despite the contrasting approaches (distinguished as commercial versus literary) at their very best and most effective, mass-market paperback covers exemplified distinctive artistry. Moreover, the best of those who practiced the art of mass-market paperback design really understood how to capture the readers' attention and imagination.

Although it does not take a cognitive psychologist to know that a scantily clad woman will appeal to a certain segment of the male population or that a well-endowed male, usually embracing said woman, engenders interest among the female audience. It does, however, take talent to render the human form—expression and gesture—and the garments, be they torn or tight, to stimulate a viewer's prurience. Not every illustrator is capable of being evocative. Yet not all mass-market paperbacks are so sensual or sexy. Mysteries must look mysterious, thrillers must look thrilling, horror must be horrible, and science fiction must be other-worldly. All book jackets and covers are ostensibly advertisements, but the mass-market paperback must be the most totally convincing of them all. With only a limited timeframe in which to attract the proverbial fish, the lure must be bright and shiny. Mass-market paperback artists and designers prided themselves on making the best lures and being incredibly alluring.

The most alluring (and at times disturbing) for its noir-like melodrama (albeit in color), Dell's popular Mapback book series serves as the model of the mass-market ethos. Influenced by dime novels of the nineteenth century and pulps of the early twentieth, Dell's Mapbacks were seasoned with a hint of B-movie. The Dell Publishing Company was founded as a pulp house in 1922 by George Delacorte, Jr., a twenty-eight-year-old entrepreneur. The pulp, which takes its name from the cheap newsprint on which it was printed, was, according to *The Pulps* (Chelsea House, 1970) editor Tony Goodstone, "the cradle of sensationalism in American art and literature" and featured some of the best and worst fiction ever written by the likes of Dashiell Hammett, Edgar Rice Burroughs, and Ray Bradbury. Delacorte's biggest sellers were adventure monthlies, such as *Danger Trail*, *Sky Riders*, *Western Romances*, and *War Birds*, all inexpensively printed and distributed through news dealers rather than bookstores. Soon he became successful, and by the late 1920s branched into magazines, including Radio Stars, Modern Screen, and Ballyhoo, one of the most popular American humor magazines of the 1930s.

In 1942 Delacorte started Dell Books, and by 1943 the first editions were released. To limit his liability and insure efficient production he forged a partnership with Western Printing & Lithographing Company of Racine, Illinois, one of America's largest commercial printers, whose staff selected titles, created art, and printed the books while Delacorte distributed them. It was estimated that between 1943 and 1945 between eleven million copies of Dell books were sold at a cover price of 25 cents. By the end of the decade sales soared to twenty-five million (which was still short of the other major mass-market publishers including Pocket Books' fifty million and Bantam's and New American Library's thirty million each). Dell Books were successfully competitive because the cover art that promoted an enticing selection of titles—initially crime solvers by Ellery Queen, Rex Stout, and Brett Halliday, among others—was eye-catching for their raw sexuality. But to suggest that they pandered only to prurient instincts would be an overly simplistic characterization of Dell and the paperback industry in general. Sex was periodically used, then disavowed, and then reprised by an industry that wanted to mirror public tastes rather than alienate its audience. Experimentation was not a concern.

In an attempt to transcend the saucy and hardboiled pulp aesthetic perpetuated in Delacorte's magazine division, Dell Books, under the art direction of Racine-based William Strohmer and his assistant George Frederiksen (who also painted a number of the covers) turned to expressionistic covers that used surrealism and dramatic symbolism to suggest the plot. Dell's leading staff artist, Gerald Gregg, had adopted Dali-esque tropes which he rendered primarily in airbrush. Gregg had a distinctive, simplified, symbolic style that was enhanced by the airbrush's continuous tones and his preference for bright colors. Gregg referred to his covers as "stylized realism," and cited Norman Rockwell, Winslow Homer, and Andrew Wyeth as his influences. Despite these influences, Dell covers from this period also borrowed graphic devices to elicit fragmentation and isolation as practiced by French posterists A.M. Cassandre and Jean Carlu. Many of their tropes such as the disembodied hand and eye were adopted for Dell Book covers.

Mass-market paperbacks in the '40s were also known for hand-lettered titles that were similar to the splash panels of comic books. Dell's lettering, however, almost exclusively drawn by Bernie Salbreiter, was more reminiscent of movie titles. American paperbacks had a very close relationship with the Hollywood psychological thriller (the plots of which were often torn from paperback pages). Most paperback covers, and particularly Dell's, had a crude aesthetic, largely owing to the fast pace at which they were produced, often between five and ten titles a month and as many as 150 a year. In Dell's case, though it is reasonable to assume this applied to the industry as a whole, such simplicity may have had something to do with the fact that most of the artists rarely, if ever, read the manuscripts but instead were given titles and a verbal statement about the contents, a process that was bound to result in a reliance on clichés.

The covers were based on brief summaries, while the Dell Maps on the back covers required intense reading to determine what part of the plot would be depicted and then rendered (almost exclusively) by Dell's in house map-maker, Ruth Belew. Her unmistakable linear style was as endemic to Dell Books as its unmistakable eye and keyhole logo. Dell used maps as a standard feature from 1943 to 1951. They were based on the often-photographic "scene of the crime" diagrams used in sensationalist newspapers.

The realistic period of Dell Books cover art ended around 1951 when it was decided that the art department should move from Racine to New York. The style that distinguished Dell Books for less than a decade was also becoming passé across the industry. Romantic realism was increasingly becoming a prevailing trend in illustration, especially in magazines. Dell's New York art director, Walter Brooks, not only preferred the sexy realism of Robert Stanley, one of Dell's leading artists, but one might say he modernized the overall look by adopting sans serif lettering, and replacing maps with blurbs. These changes did not hinder sales (in fact, in 1957 Dell made millions from the sales of eight million copies of Grace Metalious' *Peyton Place*, the highest selling paperback at that time), but a special era in poster-like paperback art had definitely come to end.

Mass-market paperbacks evolved other conventions. While the basic size has remained the same over the decades, the tricks and tropes have been pushed along with advances in technology. Multiple covers produced in different colors are de rigueur. Die-cuts, embossing and debossing, metallic inks, and fold-outs and gatefolds are used to distinguish and attract. The design is still not as sophisticated or nuanced as the hardcover, but many kinds of hardcover bestsellers have liberally borrowed from the paperback. In the beginning there was the hardcover book, and there is no indication that it is going away (despite the Kindle), but the mass-market paperback remains the most economical and portable of all the books on the market—may it stay that way.

Confessions of a Book Catalogue Reader

I read publishers' seasonal catalogues the way some people go to the movies, in part to watch the trailers for coming attractions. You get the gist—if not the best parts—but don't necessarily have to see the film. Likewise, from catalogues I glean what's up and coming, but I don't necessarily have to buy the book—or conversely, after seeing what's not yet in the stores, I have something special to look forward to, another reason to live.

Book catalogues are considerably more elaborate lately—full-color object photographs of books are alluring (and the covers and jackets look better in miniature anyway, especially with drop shadows). A few, like the Taschen bi-annual magazine/catalogue, even include excerpts and other exclusive editorial content; so as not to be simply sales pitches but proxy cultural experiences, like receiving the *New York Review of Books* without the pressure of having to read the long essays or the guilt of not doing so.

Most publishers issue catalogues twice a year (some three times), so it is around early to mid-summer that fall and winter offerings come through the mail. When I was art director of the *New York Times Book Review* I looked forward to the en masse arrival, and while I'm not at that job any longer, I'm still on a few choice mailing lists.

Yesterday the Thames and Hudson U.K. catalogue arrived, and after ripping off the plastic, I found myself on the couch perusing the glossy pages. I'm not just singling out T&H because (full disclosure) I have a new book in this catalogue, but because I truly enjoy scanning the coming attractions and reading the florid promotion copy—and florid it often is, even to the point of making me wince, but that's a large part of the experience.

In fact, the only problem with book catalogues these days is that some tend to read like computer software mail order circulars. The book business is just so competitive, and so few books actually make big bucks, that hard sell has become de rigueur. Decades ago, promotion for books was itself a literary art—much of it written either by wannabe novelists or interns from Smith and Sarah Lawrence.

Nonetheless, what I particularly like about the T&H catalogue is that it is laid out in a small journal format, featuring twenty-one categories, from "Art" to "Children" (obviously not in alphabetical order, but rather based on what the T&H sales force sells the most). It also includes sections on "Product Design," "Visual Communication" (i.e. graphic design), and "Popular Culture" (the catchall for all manner of weird and wonderful things).

I'm always anxious to see what other authors have done in my field, although it can be depressing when I find that a book I'd been working on, or dreaming about doing, is already on the list before mine is finished or even started. It has happened more than once, but this season I'm free and clear—at least with T&H. Still, in this catalogue I admit to being rather green-eyed over quite a few books I would have wanted to do.

The first in this category is *Creation: Artists, Gods and Origins* by Peter Conrad, about all the major and minor art ever produced featuring deities—or as the catalogue copy intones: "A book of breathtaking scope in which the mystery of how the world began unfolds in an epic narrative that sets the Gods against the world's great artists, their rivals in creative energy." How can you not be inspired? A few pages later I was struck by *The Society Portrait: Painting, Prestige and the Pursuit of Elegance* by Gabriel Badea-Păun, which surveys "a dazzling array of works of art" from David to Warhol, "a lesson in elegance, grace, and style." Yummy.

Jumping to "Textiles" there is a global survey of trends and traditions, and a world guide of quilting, patchwork, and appliqué (you might knot know it but I live for appliqué). In the "Decorative Arts" is a history of the shell as decoration and ornament (a long time in coming, I'd say) and *The Majesty of Mughal Decoration*, ("an essential reference work for art historians, designers, and anyone interested in the arts and life of India"). In "Architecture" is offered a "vibrant, quirky survey of the finest examples of parking garages," called *The Architecture of Parking* (and at under $40 it costs less than my monthly garage payments).

Jumping to "History" I'm simply yearning for *The Story of Measurement* by Andrew Robinson (who would have thought that "the first fully-illustrated guide to the human passion for measurement—of ourselves, our experiences, and our surroundings" would be so fully illustrated?). And in the "Food" section I can't wait for *Food: The History of Taste* ("The perfect foodie's gift for Christmas 2007"). In "Travel & Transport," an area I've never been too keen on because I hate to travel and am not found of transport, I was nonetheless smitten by *How to Fly a Plane* by Nick Barnard ("Get airborne with the aid of this lavishly illustrated guide to flying")—sign me up.

Then there's "Visual Communication" with entries on the following tantalizing themes: "the ultimate book on signage in all its different forms, packed with real-life examples from around the world," "AGI's who's who of the world of international graphic design," and "the bible of street culture, in the same format as Graffiti World." But the two I most envy are *Vietnam Zippos* by Sherry Buchanan, which showcases for the first time the "personalized Zippo [lighter] engravings by American soldiers during the Vietnam War (1964-1973)" and *War Posters: Weapons of Mass Communication* by James Aulich, "a mesmerizing collection of hard-hitting propaganda and groundbreaking graphic design."

Other than browsing bookstore shelves, there's probably nothing better for this bibliophile than browsing publishers' catalogues. If only the books themselves took up as little space.

Music Design:
Think Small

The era of large LP art is long over. Those elaborate typographical and conceptual extravaganzas typical of The Beatles' *Sgt. Pepper's Lonely Hearts Club Band* (1967), Cream's Disraeli Gears (1967), the Grateful Dead's *Aoxomoxoa* (1969), and The Mothers of Invention's *Weasels Ripped My Flesh* (1970), have been eclipsed by more sedate, less ornate, minimalist compositions. For early CD packages, LP art was simply reduced to fit the smaller spaces without regard for overall design integrity. But in the mid-1990s, when it was clear that CDs had become the industry standard, designers finally began to seriously design for the smaller space. Then came the MP3 and online (iTunes and iPod) platforms that demand even smaller images—tableau turned into icons. Yet surprisingly a significant amount of visual information can be communicated even in a thumbnail size, so from a design perspective all is not entirely lost to progress.

LP designers took for granted the luxurious scale of their 12 x 12 inch canvas. With the CD and later the MP3 they learned that excessive typographic detail and visual nuance was unreadable. Yet according to many designers, the mandate to downscale album designs did not come directly from the record companies. "To be honest, we've never had a record company ask us, specifically, to make a CD design more minimal than an LP design," said Jon Forss and Kjell Ekhorn, of Non-Format, the music-centered design firm based in London and Minneapolis.

"People in the music business don't really use words, or logic for that matter," said Stephen Doyle of Doyle Partners, the designer of a number of elegant CD packages for the likes of Roseanne Cash and others. "If anything, they might've said that the images have to be bolder, or have more impact. But we knew that already, being designers and all."

The industry invariably sets its own standards, yet it starts with

designers who, as Doyle duly noted, understand pragmatics better than anyone. The MP3 is clearly the next (if not the final) stage in music packaging and the form demands simplicity, bold color, stark image, and unadorned type, which in routine doses can become monotonous. According to Forss and Ekhorn, there is indeed a profound a sense of unrest amongst designers, similar to that which accompanied the transition from the LP to the CD format. "If the best a designer can hope for is a 240 pixel square cover image, then it'll be a depressing time for the music packaging industry." But, there is a ray of optimism if designers can embrace new technology and produce packaging like Big Active's special visual material for The Enemy's album *We'll Live And Die In These Towns*; the future is not altogether bleak. The design for The Enemy's album is based on digital railway departure boards. Each time a new track begins, the track details change on the listener's iPod screen, just as a railway departure would be displayed. "It's this kind of innovation that will keep music 'packaging' thriving, well into the future," said Forss and Ekhorn.

Sweeping innovations not withstanding, often the best results come from just plain old common design sense. When it comes to thumbnail representation knowing where, when, and how to modulate visual noise is the designer's best asset. The sneering smiley face, for instance, on Bon Jovi's *Have a Nice Day* (2005) is an aptly minimalist rendering, while the abstract pixels for Coldplay's *X & Y* (2005) is somewhat questionable at a small scale because it appears like a smudge. The typographic overlay of the P and 3 for Portishead's *Third* (2008) invokes a mid-century modernist aesthetic while signaling a contemporary graphic sensibility. Of course, nothing works better in any size than a sensual photograph, and Rihanna's *Good Girl Gone Bad* (2007) fits neatly into that category, with a stark, elegant, and legible cover headline. But it does not push the boundaries like Nouns' *No Age* (2008), which is possibly the most effective miniature application, at once simple and complex, readable and abstract. The dimensional letterforms are made to jump off the screen, and the sculptural shapes serve as a logo for the music if not the band.

Music will never again be packaged with the same triumphant fanfares of the LP, but that does not mean graphic representation will cease to exist. In a world of branding, a logo or icon is an invaluable mnemonic for any product. Graphic design continues to complement and enhance listening. "Music is a big experience, so cover design should be big in aspiration even if consigned regrettably to a small physical space like the infernal CD," said Storm Thorgerson of the British design group Hipgnosis, which created album covers for Pink Floyd, Genesis, and Led Zeppelin. In other words, designers must embrace the small-scale challenges as opportunities to develop new visual languages. "So long as visual material is welcomed alongside music," insisted Forss and Ekhorn, "there'll always be opportunities for designers to produce music packaging, no matter the format, and no matter the size."

Sorry, We're

SORRY

Yes, We're

BROKE

Blue Q: Novelty Typecasting

Blue Q has been manufacturing "Life improving, joy bringing, mind altering, universally praised products since 1988," according to the company's Web site. Although I cannot vouch for the aforementioned life improvement, the so-called "joy bringing" and "mind altering" is not far from an existential parsing of the truth. This is particularly true for an ever-expanding coterie of artists, designers, and typographers who have conceived, designed, and fabricated Blue Q's joyful brands of eclectic novelty products—from body fragrances to soaps, from chewing gums to candies, from bumper stickers to magnets, from vinyl tote bags to coasters, from car air fresheners to breath sprays, most featuring quirky (often taste challenged) brand names like "Cat Butt," "Dirty Girl," "Total Bitch," "Get Real," "Hot & Flashy," "Miso Pretty," "Mullet," "Gnome," "Virgin/Slut," as well as the spiritually sublime "Wash Away your Sins," and, my personal favorite, "Steve's House of Charm."

Under the creative direction of co-founder and pop culture maven Mitch Nash, who was never trained as a graphic designer but has the zealous obsessions and keen eyes of one, Blue Q has cornered the boutique specialty gift market in the United States with products that appeal to a visual culture comfort zone. This perhaps sounds speciously high tone since in this article I am referencing, among other things, breath sprays with titles like "Ass Kisser," "If Marijuana Were Legal," "Understand Modern Art," and "Instant Swedish Accent Spray," and boxed sweets called "Candy from Strangers," "Instant Irish Accent," "I'm Not a Republican," and "I'm Not a Bigot," to name a few, but given his sly blend of high-performance crass design and highly sophisticated infantile wit, Nash has astutely tapped a flowing consumerist vein in the body politic.

Despite some of its decidedly goofy, strip-mall-looking designs, Blue Q is a well-oiled strategic machine with a clear understanding of its audience—youthful (but not always young) fans of irony—and how the delicate balance of design and wit telegraphs moods and messages that, in turn, tickle funny bones. As the brain behind Blue Q's corporate brash brawn, Nash inspires unique ways of using design, and encourages designers to twist their innate senses of humor to make visual products that are at once serious and self-mocking. He would have done quite well as the captain of a more mainstream branding ship—Cap'n Nash—but always felt happiest as the prodigal outsider, breaking those stilted rules that pound creativity into mediocrity.

Nash does not follow conventional wisdom. He works in a two-story, turn-of-the century former piano factory located in a once vital, though long depressed, old New England industrial city, Pittsfield, Massachusetts. Blue Q's historic headquarters—reminiscent of Pee-Wee's Playhouse—is brimming with products as well as drawers overflowing with toys, gizmos, gadgets, curios, and other stuff that inspire Nash and his staff.

During a recent daylong visit to his lair I wanted to learn how Blue Q's peculiar design mojo is conceived and developed. So for starters I asked Nash how he selected typefaces appropriate for his products. "I never look for fonts," he responded. "It would be like picking paint chips to paint the kitchen! So I only reject submitted fonts [submitted by designers] that look cluttered. A brand name can be stylized and be over the top, but the type must protect the idea."

Type that protects (as well as serves) is a novel concept. Yet Nash has his visceral preferences, which include shadow and outline fonts he said "feel heavy and dramatic." So I asked him, even with these "over the top" products, shouldn't the type echo or support the content of the product rather than merely have a heavy and dramatic presence? "Type wants to help the reader see the point as fast as possible," he sagely replied, which led, by way of example, to a brief discussion about the typographic scheme for the best-selling product "Miso Pretty," a line of body washes, soaps, mists, and more, with a pun for a name and designed with an ironic, loving eye towards hybrid Hong Kong commercial vernacular. With this product, the illustration and lettering must be in perfect sync for the graphic concept to succeed, otherwise it could come off as just plain silly, or worse, dumb. But because the illustrator/designer Fiona Hewitt, who was born in Scotland but lived in China, has been given a relatively free hand to evolve the image—"we actually wrote the brand around her," explained Nash—the product is always fresh in many ways. "She's always using new serif fonts and likes to stack a script font on top of them which looks really handsome," added Nash. "And it's cool to have two fonts in the span of two or three words, because the change acts like a comma." It may not be the type purist's dream solution, but "Miso Pretty" is not about typographic purity.

Still, I wanted to know whether Nash ever considers more neutral type treatments for his conceptual products. "Anytime we try to be too neutral we end up in the close-out bin at TJ Maxx [the American discount department store, and franchise of a British chain]. Overall people look to Blue Q for cheeky humor. It's harder to be humorous than handsome. So when we can do it well, as in the case of [Seattle based design firm] Modern Dog, for example, which has done some of our most hilarious stuff [including 'Less Kill More Bill' and 'Get Lucky'], you get a lot more bang for it."

Modern, post-modern, and cheeky typography—is this the next new wave? The fact is much of Blue Q's aesthetic falls somewhere between retro and grunge typographic styles. But I was curious whether Nash saw qualitative distinctions even within his own wares. Did he think of them as high-end or low-end cheekiness? "It is all quick concepts with a quality execution," he explained. "The retailers who buy our stuff wont put up with bad gum or a bar of soap with cheap fragrance. So we have to over-deliver a bit," he said, "It ain't Estée Lauder but we aren't the local drugstore gift shop either." But since Blue Q is a company that must sell wares to survive, does he test the products in any way—like the mainstream branding firms do, ad nauseam? "No," said Nash, without hesitation. "If my brother's into it, it sells. He's an engineer, very out of the box but still very logical, really smart seeing instantly what will work. Or not."

So by now, I was wondering what has been the most successful of the Blue Q products both in terms of numbers and buzz and what success means to a small company. The answer: "Dirty Girl" has been the biggest with almost $20 million sold of that brand over the past seven years. And is this attributable to the sketchy brush portrait of a girl composed over hand-scrawled lettering? "The brand name's pretty snappy! Not the design," said Nash. But at the time the product was launched, "it was very spot-on. Retro-Parisian, very simple to suss up, flirty, and the copywriting is not too linear. It's got an artsy mood. The illustrations of the character show the designer/illustrator's understanding of the human body. The limbs work well; she gesticulates like Vanna White [the American TV hostess for "Wheel of Fortune"].

While some of Blue Q's design concepts are dictated by Nash, he allows for various design methodologies: Seattle's Modern Dog is really "fast and furious" and goes for a quick gag. Then there are the "finesseers," like Haley Johnson, who has done "Sins," "Bitch," Dirty Girl," "Get Real," and "Hot & Flashy." Recently, the London and New York ad agency Mother has been brought on to treat products like ads, including "Joint" candy in a box that has a joint on it. Other contributors include, Michel Casarramona ("Joy Stick"), Roy Fox ("Bird Shopper"), Methane Studios ("Cubical"), Buttery Smooth ("Most Tattoos"), and Louise Fili ("World" candies). "It's that combined mish mash that makes Blue Q strong," said Nash proudly.

The real trick behind the design of Blue Q products, however, is knowing how to write and work with writers. "Alex Isley, who used to work with Tibor Kalman, taught me a lot about how design is really writing," said Nash. "Blue Q is really a writing exercise." Nash further noted that illustration and writing together is the ultimate. "I love a designer who can illustrate because it triples the chances of what you can do. Though it is also fun teaming an illustrator and a designer. Also I like the designers who let me be a baker in the cake. I am happy to receive art that is ready to go to the printer; hey I can go home earlier! But I still feel that I am in charge of editing a certain curious voice. I like being cute and clever in a certain way, and more often than not I am talking to the creator about tweaks to make it tighter."

Yet after all is said (and done), Blue Q creates novelty and novelty—even the cleverest—is not essential. So I asked Nash how he feels about adding more clutter to the world. "There is the saying that 'the most beautiful things are always the most useless,' like peacocks and lilies for instance, and our customers have no use for merely good, beautiful stuff. I would love to make things that are more pure art but that is not our core retail customer." So what would he like to make that he has not? "Something with giant eels. Just kidding. I am working with independent artists more. Rather than building a package, being more organic." Now Nash is taking Blue Q into the literary realm with a series tiny books, sold in countertop displays, on a broad range of weird and wonderful themes—like *The Holy Bibel*, an exploration into what the bible would be like if not for a good copyeditor, and *Sleep,* a collection of photographs of people, yes, sleeping. Maybe cheeky typography has come and gone, and the age of the post-cheeky book has arrived.

Titling Home Movies, Mitten's Way

Back in the days before desktop technologies like iMovie and Final Cut Pro the easiest way to create titles for 8mm or 16mm home movies was actually not easy. In fact, it was ridiculously messy and cumbersome. Yet it was the only way for the do-it-yourselfer to learn a little something about type and lettering while snazz-ing up the old celluloid. The results weren't always pretty, but making film titles with Mitten's Movie Titles, Struhl Movielux Titling Set, or any of the ersatz letter systems like Judy's Alphabets (originally plastic letters made for children but adapted for films) was how any novice filmmaker could, as the promotion slogan went: "Give your titles that Hollywood touch."

Although most weekend cineastes couldn't be bothered to spend their time composing the individual two- and three-dimensional letters, gluing, filming, and splicing the film, titling was being pushed as a big enough hobbyist's business that guidebooks were written, lettering sets were produced, and hardware was manufactured to encourage "attractive" (which was the mantra) home movie typography.

James W. Moore, the leading expert in the field, wrote in his book, *Titling Your Color Movies*, that the three elements necessary for any "well-prepared" title card were: "The card itself, or background; the lettering or letters which go on it; and the decoration which may or may not be used to enhance these two practical elements." It all seems fairly fundamental but never underestimate the ability of even the most serious amateur to screw things up. I know—in the 1950s, I remember my father trying his best to compose the titles, getting impossibly frustrated, and then fobbing the entire job onto me. It's a wonder, given the trauma I went through, I don't get hot and cold chills whenever I see a Mitten's box. It is even more incredible I love still typography after suffering through the aborted titling tasks I was given to do.

Nonetheless, amateur movie titling is a slice of popular culture, a remnant from the time before computer "automation," and an artifact—the letters themselves—that is reprised in contemporary practice by designers who used the letters to create 3D typographic illusions without resorting to digital tricks—a satisfying anomaly.

There were five fundamental ways of creating titles: "With a typewriter; with moveable letters—either flat or raised; with draftsmen's lettering guides; with press (actual typeset) printing; with hand lettering—either traced or freehand." The masters of titling had certain rules that made "execution more effective." They are worth noting. First, the typewriter: "Typefaces should be freshly cleaned and free of all embedded ink. A studied evenness of touch in hitting the keys

should be practiced. The ribbon should be set in the 'stencil' position to get soft, textured outlines to avoid unattractive magnified projection." Predictably, however, typewriter type is risky, as James W. Moore warned. "Titles set in movable letters are unquestionably more attractive than the typed title; they are therefore more widely used by both experienced and aspiring movie makers." A lesson used is a lesson learned.

The most popular lettering sets were Mitten's white plaster letters, which came in eight different sans-serif styles, including one called Tempar and another that looked suspiciously like Kabel. "Smartly designed and cleanly cast" these tri-dimensional tile letters were meant to have the most graphic impact under harsh cinematic lights. While they lack the grace of printed letterforms, Mitten's "tri-dimensional bulk (which can be cross-lighted for shadows with dramatic effect, their upper and lower case fonts (which are almost mandatory in setting subtitles), and the general clarity and elegance of their design" were a plus. The minus is that they needed to be very carefully mounted on background surfaces, which could cause accidents.

The lighting was critical. "Directionally speaking, there are three ways of lighting titles: from the front, from the side, and from the rear. The last of these three lighting methods, since it requires that letters be in transparency is used primarily in making double-exposed titles." Systems for lighting were surprisingly elaborate to achieve the "hot spot" and capture the best possible shadow to increase dimensionality. For the advanced hobbyist, creating double-exposures was even more complex. A light-box for the transmitted-light system of illuminating title letters required feats of engineering using brains, brawn, and patience.

The experts agreed that for linear sharpness, variety of styles, and general clarity of design, "the press-printed title is hard to beat," wrote Moore. In addition to standard faces, lettering guides, used by architects and engineers, make "workmanlike" title legends. Hand-lettering was generally recommended for use only in main and end "title cards." Typesetting was best for "credits."

Mitten's offered the most versatile size options; and size definitely mattered. "Intelligent care should be given to determining suitable letter size and spacing," stated Moore, adding "letter line up and spacing should be done with a ruler for absolute balance." Since titling rules were aimed at the uninitiated "typographer" the most valuable advice was this: Don't overdo. "In other words, keep it simple, keep it small, and keep it subdued. Remember that title art is an adjunct, not an end in itself." Take that, Saul Bass!

50 HELLER

NOTGELD DER

50 HELLER

GEMEINDE TRAUNKIRCHEN.

Notgeld: The Design of Emergency Money

In some parts of the United States communities are responding to the recession by designing their own money in popular styles. This practice, however, dates back to the deep inflationary period in post-World War I Germany. "How can one describe those incredible times," wrote Stefan Lorant in Sieg Heil, a personal history of pre-World War II Germany. In the morning a newspaper and punitive reparations had virtually depleted Germany's treasury and drained its resources. But even more crippling were the large sums (40 million gold marks) spent daily by the Weimar government to support "passive resistance" in Germany. Never in the history of industrialized nations did an economic crisis have such ruinous short- and long-term effects as the German inflation of 1922-1923. Five years after Germany's ignominious defeat by the allies in the First World War, Germany's immense war debt in the Ruhr, a major industrial area of Germany then occupied by French troops, caused the mark to take such a nosedive that its value in the world market and buying power inside Germany changed virtually minute by minute. At the beginning of 1923 the American dollar was worth 7,424 marks. By August the rate had risen to over a million, In November the rate increased to 600 billion, and by December the figure skyrocketed to 4,210,500,000,000. The 35 Reichsbank printing presses working night and day could not print the new denominations fast enough to satisfy demand or keep up with inflation, so a flood of unofficial "notgeld," or emergency currency, was issued daily by towns and businesses..

Famous are the black and white wire photographs of Germans pushing wheelbarrows piled high with cash to the local bakery to buy bread or carrying trunkloads of bills to the grocery for butter. People could not keep up with the rising cost of living. Individual salaries in the billions could barely pay for the needed staples. Savings were ruined and pensions were worthless. Reichsbank notes became wastepaper since the smaller denominations of these otherwise impressive looking bills had no purchase power. Their only tangible asset was as heating fuel. This untenable state of affairs continued for over a year until the government, lead by the chancellor Gustav Stresemann, issued a proclamation ending passive resistance in the Ruhr, introduced the Rentenmark (a more manageable denomination that literally knocked nine zeros off, bringing the exchange rate from 4.2 billion marks to 4.2 marks per dollar), and thus was a first step in stabilizing the ravaged economy by 1924. Other firm-fisted measures helped slow the downward turn. But as history vividly reports, the economic condition fueled other hatreds and resentments, for the Weimar Republic was doomed by the power of German nationalism.

The only minor bright spot to emerge from this devastatingly critical period—and very minor it was too since even after stabilization unreasonable fear continued to envelop German society leading, of course, to the acceptance of the Nazis less than ten years later—was the exemplary artistic quality of the emergency currency (notgeld and ersetzgeld) issued by cities, states, banks, political groups, and businesses to ease the burden on Reichsbank presses and, more importantly, provide some semblance of economic stability for the individual citizen who was naturally panicked by the state of economic affairs.

Practically speaking, since official Reichsbank notes were virtually worthless, most emergency money issued by municipalities was worthless save for an investment of faith. On the other hand, since they were used as instruments of barter ersetzgeld and notgeld issued by businesses were redeemable for goods or services (and even entertainment such as films). In fact, notgeld began as a kind of redeemable coupon in prisoner of war camps during World War I as an instrument for paying wages to allied prisoners for laboring outside their camps for the local community or private industries. Officially, these vouchers had value only for POWs in the camp kitchens and with ersatz wheeler dealers, but despite government regulations some bills managed to circulate among civilians causing problems leading to strict rules on the official use of notgeld.

The issuance of "civilian" substitute money (which preceded the large-denomination emergency money that came shortly after) began a few years before the inflationary vortex began to spiral. With the permission, or in most instances the silent agreement, of the government ministry of finance, local and private institutions could cheaply print, usually on newspaper presses (or, in the case of coins, at locksmiths or machine plants), bills on rag paper or cardboard. Since these printers were not subject to government standardization the sizes, shapes, and designs were wildly inconsistent. The images reflect the variety of talents and technology ranging from artful to primitive execution. Though many of the bills are beautifully rendered by professional artists and designers, many were simply scrawled by rank amateurs. Since a majority of the printing is inferior compared to the standards of the government printing offices, falsification was easy, as well as difficult to police.

In addition to providing redeemable scrit to workers and citizens, municipalities found that substitute money had inherent value to collectors. German provinces garnered extra needed income by selling directly to dealers and collectors for prices higher than face value. Dealers advertised and sold albums to collectors from all over the world.

Though substitute money was officially illegal tender by 1922, the German government found it difficult to forbid what was referred to in government circles as "the money folly." For many German and Austrian graphic designers and poster artists the designs of the most intricate notes were replete with images of death. Sporting and political groups used their own iconography, such as the steel helmet that appears on the notes issued by the Stahlhelm (a nationalist group that would later merge with the Nazis). Not even forgery of official banknotes was taken too seriously due to the speed at which people had to dispose of large quantities of cash to avoid hourly price increases. Some of the notes included stylistic lettering, while others were rooted in classicism. Many were vibrantly colorful, others somberly monochromatic. Actually, money—real or counterfeit—was essentially worthless at the moment of printing.

By summer of 1923 paper money wasn't even accepted as having value. Only real products (or things) had any value. Leather producing firms gave out their salaries in the form of shoe soles, brickworks in bricks, food processors offered sugar or margarine. The suppliers of electricity, gas, and water issued vouchers, but even these vouchers had to be redeemed on the day of issue—wait a moment and the rates would dramatically increase.

Stresemann's conciliatory stance with the allies and his government's attempt to regain control of the railways and other vital industries relinquished to private owners as conditions of unconditional surrender helped stabilize the German economy, but ignited further acrimony among left and right factions who were tired of paying and suffering for the war. Although certain allied plans were put into effect that reduced the costly reparations, returned some resource centers, allowed the mark to have some parity in the world market, and otherwise improved domestic conditions, civil war between communists and nationalists would trap Germany in a political vortex even more tragic than its economic plight. Of course, in 1933 Adolf Hitler democratically gained dictatorial powers and the rest, until 1945, is tragic history.

The history of notgeld, however, briefly picks up again in 1944 when, certain of Germany's defeat, the allies printed up new currency for occupied Germany—but the denominations were small and ineffective.

Though much of the notgeld issued throughout Germany was destroyed by war, the artistry of these bills inspired some to maintain collections that until quite recently were little known. Thousands of different variations were produced between 1918 and 1924. The genre was even recognized in issues of *Das Plakat*, Germany's most respected advertising arts magazine. Since 1939 the law stated that it was forbidden to produce substitute money, but the same law demanded that the Reichsbank would provide the proper "value signs." By 1945, with the war over and the nation in disarray, the Reichsbank was in no position to forbid anything, nor could it produce enough currency itself. After a short period of crisis the allies quickly stabilized the currency.

The Art and Craft of Grocery Signs

During the recession, grocery signs sometimes take the edge off of spending. Admittedly they are low on the scale of marketing priorities and usually produced without an iota of nuance or style—yet they are essential to knowing when and where the toilet paper is on sale. While these signs generally don't deserve so much as a sentence of design analysis, I'd wager that after this story is posted an earnest cultural studies grad student will write a thesis on the semiotics of vernacular store sign graphics, if it hasn't been done already. Nonetheless, I have found the exception to my assertion.

As a regular patron of Guido's Fresh Marketplace in Great Barrington, Massachusetts, I have long admired the anonymous impressionistic portrayals of apples, cantaloupe, lemons, and cherries exquisitely rendered with Rembrandt and Sennelier pastel chalk on sign boards. I recently learned that for the past five years the signs are created by a pastel artist and landscape gardener named Erin Piester of Hillsdale, New York. Her chalkboard signs, promoting fresh fruit, vegetables, meat, and fish have raised this mundane craft to alluring art. Her tomatoes are so expressionistically ripe you can taste them, the Vidalia onions shine like gems, and the highlights on the red peppers are translucent and transcendent.

Although she is not channeling Cézanne, Piester's drawings are soothingly naturalistic while engagingly abstract in an early-twentieth-century-fauvist-sort-of-way. With just a strategic smear of pastel she handily creates textures and shadows that echo Giorgio Morandi's signature bottles, only colorful. What's more she does not work from tried and true, monotonous templates—not every pear is the same pear, not every grape is perfectly round. Granted, on any given day some of the drawn fruits don't look exactly like what they are supposed to

represent—for instance, the orange-fleshed melon looks more like an apple, but what a robust apple, so why quibble.

Piester, who went to school for nutrition and dietetics, works during the day at a local nursery and does landscaping on the side, and moonlights an average of three or more mornings (starting at 6:30 a.m.) per week drawing new signs and freshening up the old ones. Given their high quality, you'd think she would be kept quite busy sign-writing throughout the Berkshires, but to the contrary, Guido's is her only Medici.

In a geographical area inhabited by many artisans of different kinds, Piester pays close attention to other store signs and sign-makers. She is always looking at what people are doing with color and technique or other mediums. And if you think sign artists are slaves to one particular style, Piester takes risks, especially "when I use different colors that may not work, but then you start to use them and then it pops and looks good," she said. Predictably, green dominates her signs—leaves serve as the frame for most signs—but burnt umber gives her imagery its signature underpinning. Yet to catch the eyes of the customer, she uses bright neon colors, especially in the lettering. Indeed, the handcrafted letterforms involving a layer of linear letters overprinted with shading sets her apart from the bland typeset signs at a nearby supermarket. "I have always had compliments on my handwriting, I love how it changes with your mood." Have you ever thought about mere store signs having moods? The Guido's signs run the gamut from joy to jolly and even the frequently high prices (usually rendered in white chalk) are not off-putting.

The sprightly marriage of letter and image changes with the seasons, but always retains a fresh feeling, even in the dead of winter. Unlike standard store signs, this little touch of humanity subtly adds pleasure to the supermarket experience. Nonetheless some of her signs are better than others. Some fruits just lend themselves to more exciting rendering approaches. Moreover, "some days are very hectic and I am not able to do the best work," she lamented. "I have another job I must get to, which makes it hard if, for example, the list is late or the [managers] do a lot of line changes. It gets me down but other people don't seem to notice." Well, I do, but it really doesn't matter. Hers are still the best grocery signs I've ever seen.

And the Trophy for the Most Generic Trophy Goes to...

In springtime the culture turns to outdoor athletics, and if you're related to a child on any sports team or other organized activity it is the time when millions of trophies are handed out for the best, runner-up, and show-er-up for just about everything from sports and academics to chess and checkers. You don't have to be an over achiever to get one. Some schools are so zealously democratic that no one leaves the award ceremony without some token of esteem—no matter how inconsequential. And while that's a nice thing for students and parents, what does it say about the importance of the trophy as object and artifact?

I was reminded this week just how badly designed—materially and conceptually—trophies have become. While cleaning out my college student son's closet of no less than three-dozen trophies won while in middle and high school, it dawned on me how much the poor design diminishes the honor.

When I was in school awards were not the cheap molded plastic capped with generic little symbolic figurines and poorly detailed laurels and wreaths. They were real metal—sometimes brass, even stainless steel—loving cups custom engraved with the student's name and personal achievement. Most were majestic and had a venerable aura, even if they were recently cast. What's more, possibly since the ones from my generation cost more to produce, they weren't given to just anybody (I know firsthand, since I rarely received them).

Today too many trophies look distressingly similar to "the world's best dad" novelties. Typically, they are cheesy gold plastic on faux marble (sometimes faux wood) bases. Shiny colored foil or mylar with stars, balls, and other lackadaisical decorations wrap the stands on which the figures of contorted soccer players or tackling fullbacks reside. Now there is a new trope called "Spintastics"—solid figures with spinning balls that add a kinetic fluff that is both unnecessary and unappealing. Most contemporary trophies are so shoddily made that if one is not careful they self-destruct before reaching the trophy case. Too often the respective batter or shooter on my son's baseball and basketball trophies lost heads or appendages on the way home. Like a burst birthday balloon, the trauma of such a decapitation was palpable (especially for me, because I could never easily fix it).

While industrial designers (and design students) spend their days thinking up more beautiful and efficient ways of making almost everything, I have yet to meet one who cares about the state of the common trophy (of course there are some uncommon trophies around). So are mass-produced trophies such a lost cause that, like fast food menus and laundry tickets, designers cannot be bothered to improve them?

But why reinvent the wheel or the statue? As much as I love the National Magazine Award's elegant Calder elephant trophy, just retaining the classic trophy style is good enough for me. The gold or silver loving cup simply cannot be improved upon.

Trophies have long been cherished as symbols of exceptional accomplishment. Yet as I carried the cardboard box filled with years of memories and dozens of my son's plastic honors down to the curb for Saturday recycling pickup, I watched as one after another passersby passed them by. Despite the little sign I made admonishing them to "give them a home," indifference reigned. They were rarely given even a second glance (and nobody took one of them). Now that is a design problem that needs solving.

Canned Laughter

Mass produced trophies may stink but recently I caught a whiff of a pungent odor emanating from a local construction site and noticed a thick, green, anaconda-sized hose running from a tank on a truck emblazoned with the words "Call-A-Head" in bold gothic letters on the side. I was immediately reminded how indispensable portable toilets are to many, and how verbal and visual puns are copious throughout this indispensable industry. Manufacturers and suppliers go to great lengths to make the portable toilet experience clean and sanitary, as well as warm and cute. Portable toiletry is only second after hair salons (i.e. Mane Street, Clip Joint, Hair Today, etc.) for warm and cute, albeit excruciating, pun names. This is a dirty job, so why shouldn't those who attend to our bodily hygiene have the opportunity to practice a little wit and double entendre?

With this in mind, I set out to determine how widespread this branding phenomenon really is. Is it localized in comedy-centric locales, like New York, Chicago, Waco, or Walla Walla? Or is it a trend that knows no regional boundaries? For the better part of a day I visited New York City's numerous construction sites, a veritable forest of portable outhouses, copying down names and numbers. Not surprisingly I learned that Porta-Potty was the most common brand, with Call-A-Head a close second. Scattered throughout the city were the variants on John, including Sani-Jon, Porta-John (note the former spelling may be paying homage to Jon Stewart), Johnny on the Spot, Johnny on the Potty, Mr. John, Gotta-Go-Johns, and Little John. There was also Port-o-Let and the regal A Royal Flush. My favorite, however, was Zack's Shacks (which could also be misidentified as a chain of roadside eateries).

I wondered who came up with these puns—was it people who lacked internal monologues (Tourette's sufferers, perhaps) or professional copywriters? After an unsuccessful attempt was made to contact an official at the Porta-Potty company, I admit I did not pursue the quest. I did, however, find that there were other people (an online group of sorts) who had been collecting novel names unique to other regions, which are listed below for your edification in no particular order:

Happy Can Portable Toilets, Atlanta, Ga.
Drop Zone Portable Service Inc., Frankfort, Ill.
Best Seat In The House Inc., Bradley, Ill.
Plop Jon Inc., Port Saint Lucie, Fla.
Port-A-Pots Inc., Hampstead, Md.
Ameri-Can Engineering, Argos, Ind.
Bobby's Pottys, Joppa, Md.
LepreCAN Portable Restrooms, Chicago, Ill.
Loader-Up, Inc., Sarasota, Fla.
Royal Throne, Washington, D.C.
Tanks Alot, Tomball, Tex.
Tee Pee Inc, Roseville, Mich.
Wizards of Ooze Ltd., Anacortes, Wash.
Oui Oui Enterprises Ltd., Chicago
Gotta Go Potties, Tobyhanna, Pa.
UrinBiz.com, Chicago
Willy Make It?, Oregon City, Oreg.
Doodie Calls, New Orleans

With the exception of the last (and most juvenile), they are not all that cringe-inducing. But what does this branding technique say about American popular culture? Perhaps all it needs to say is that a little levity can go a long way in making such an essential product, and therefore everyday life, more pleasant. I agree that two thirds of a pun is PU, but since these toilet names do, in fact, trigger chuckles, they serve a purpose. I don't see any need to can the laughter, do you?

Tracking the Street Measles

During the Beatles' first U.S. tour in 1964 John Lennon marveled at how New York's sidewalks were paved with diamonds. He was referring, of course, to sparkling glassphalt—asphalt mixed with crushed glass routinely used to fortify the concrete. But I wonder whether he also saw the so-called street measles, those ugly black blotches that have long marred urban pavements. Actually, I've been seeing a lot more of them lately, and if you live in a city (and look down to avoid eye contact as I do) you must have seen them, too. But if you don't know what they are you might be surprised to learn that each splotch is a piece of chewed gum brazenly spit from pedestrians' mouths, then ground by hundreds of walking feet into black grout that forms into hardened viscous globs. To me this suggests that gum chewers are possibly filthier than cigarette smokers, whose butts, at least, can be easily swept up. Conversely, caked amebic gum spatter is extremely time consuming and costly to remove using "gum-busting" steam-cleaning machines. My aim in this essay, however, is not to raise mass consciousness about gum pollution, although someone should.

Although discharging wads of goop on public walkways is truly disgusting (would you do this in your own home?) and arguably more dangerous than throwing banana peels on the sidewalk, I cannot support, as some have suggested, a ban on public gum chewing and its dubious disposal. Actually there are already ordinances on some municipal books from the days when chewing tobacco was in vogue that prohibits such wanton spitting, but enforcement is difficult at best. "Gum has been a problem since the beginning of time," proclaimed Joseph Vas, mayor of Perth Amboy, New Jersey, about a splotch outbreak in his city. Now that the major gum producers have introduced upscale gum products—Orbit, Eclipse, Carefree (though I've always been partial to Black Jack) which have increased overall gum sales and advanced chewing over the past couple of years, the amount of splotches have exponentially increased (at least according to my unscientific survey), and in New York City the problem is consequently frequent in a greater number of neighborhoods.

Given these epidemic proportions, last year I decided to take a closer look at gum splat as a kind of social and visual phenomenon—a veritable vernacular street "language"—that speaks to certain behavioral patterns of city life. Over the past year I've been something of a gumshoe when it comes to investigating and documenting these patterns, visiting devastated areas and talking to perpetrators and victims alike. Now I'm ready to share my findings.

Just so you know, chewing gum has existed since the ancient Greeks chewed a substance made from the resin of a mastic tree. Subsequent gums were made from the sap from spruce trees as well as paraffin wax. Modern gum was extracted from Mexican chicle (remember Chiclets brand? I always wondered where the name came from), originally used as a rubber substitute but was found to work better in a chewable form. Most gum companies currently use synthetics, although some still rely on natural glutamates. There are scores of different gum genres—bubble, medicated, breath-freshening, laxative, and more—and gum display shelves in candy stores and delis are filled with well over a score of different high- and low-end brands. Gum chewing is used to relieve stress, freshen the mouth, even clean the teeth; it's great when flying and even has certain cool panache, either macho or sensual. It's done by the likes of artists and musicians, but police, firemen, and plumbers also seem to be frenetic chewers. Kids, of course, are massive chewing machines (although most schools prohibit chewing in class, the bottoms of school desks are testament to how effective such rules really are).

Speaking of kids, my survey (which covered a geographical area between 23rd and Houston Streets in Manhattan) reveals that the largest concentration of gum goop is usually right outside public school entrances. It was in front of New York's School of the Future high school where I found a veritable Jackson Pollock cement canvas of splotches so dense it could easily be compared to an Ad Reinhardt, and so black that the sidewalk is barely visible. The most intense of this particular splattering is located within five feet to the right or left of the entrance, which leads me to believe that the students either dispose of their gum immediately before entering or after leaving (if the latter is true then they've been chewing for hours). I also checked the entrances to nearby Simon Baruch Junior High, P.S. 40, Washington Irving High, and a bit further away at Asher Levy Middle School and the proportion of goop to sidewalk was also much denser than at other locales. Surprisingly, this was not true at private schools located in the same general radius. Friends Seminary, Immaculate Conception, Little Red School House, and Elisabeth Irwin High School all had less gum buildup. To determine why this was true, I loitered outside of a few of these schools for a few hours at a time recording students' habits. Those in the public schools did indeed spit more than private school students. When I asked a few kids for rationales, I was told to mind my own business. I had to find another way. So I decided to focus on "adult" areas.

Lower Fifth Avenue has a uniquely high occurrence of gum stains, not as bad as the school infestation but enough to raise eyebrows. In the five blocks either to the north or south of the AIGA national headquarters on 21st Street and Fifth Avenue the density was much greater than around nearby Madison Square Park. These admittedly random patterns of splotches seem also to be better designed in front of AIGA than elsewhere in the vicinity, but this could just be my imagination. The fundamental reason for this distinct occurrence pattern (a term I apply to formations of goop) is that Fifth Avenue is a highly congested street during weekdays, with many offices housing music, fashion, design, and other creative industries—all full of potentially highly stressed gum chewers—so in addition to stains in front of building entrances, it's possible to trace a gum line from office buildings to various popular lunchtime eateries, with cheap-food delis having the largest concentration of stains outside their doors. Madison Park is where people go to eat lunch or sit calmly watching birds, which reduces the need to nervously chew. In addition, on the weekends Fifth Avenue gets a large tunnel crowd from New Jersey, which for reasons best left vague, have the highest sidewalk gum spitting ratio in the region. After nailing why Fifth was the way it was, I moved east.

Over the past decade Union Square has been strikingly transformed—the park is beautiful and the five-day-a-week farmer's market has raised the energy level of the entire area. In addition to New York's usual park denizens, it is Mecca for many young professional and hip people, and because of this demographic gum goop prevails at least on the perimeter of the park. Inside there is limited coverage because of what appears to be a rapid cleanup force, made up, oddly enough, by gum chewers. Conversely the sidewalks where skateboarders often hang-ten and itinerant musicians place their hats is fairly dense with goop. It also appears that the average customer of the Virgin Mega Store and Circuit

City, which face the park, does a good share of the area's daily chewing (I speculate five sticks of Winterfresh every two hours if my 18-year-old son is an indication).

After time well spent in Union Square I was ready to head uptown to the more swanky New York neighborhoods—Turtle Bay, Murray Hill, and Sutton Place—where splotches were noticeable but in considerably lesser quantities. What was on the ground was put there, apparently, not by residents but interlopers. Since these neighborhoods do not have a lot of retail traffic the volume of interloping is kept to a minimum. In fact, I was looked upon with suspicion. So when I asked a randomly selected Murray Hill pedestrian why he thought there was so little gum goop in the neighborhood, I was told to mind my own business. Maybe I should not have been chewing when I spoke.

In any case, my survey turned up the following results: Gum splatter is disgusting. Students and kids, who have no respect for their environment do it to excess. Adults who work in stressful industries chew too much and potentially spit it on the sidewalk, unless they live on Sutton Place. John Lennon chewed a lot of gum, but to my knowledge he never spit a wad on a New York street.

Nothing Sacred

I am a maven for political commentary and satire. Having worked for 1960s "underground papers" I developed an appreciation for cartoonists and artists who popped the bubble of complacency through images designed to make the viewer uncomfortable through hard-to-swallow truths. It wasn't just the audience who needed to be shaken from their acquiescence. The objects of attack were to be unhinged, first and foremost. While not all political or social satire hit the mark—and very little radically altered public opinion—the act of doing it is more important than whatever success or failure there may be. We all agree that there are sacred cows, but it is the satirist's job to undermine their sanctity. This section begins with an essay about my first (at least as far as I can remember) taste of political satire, the play *MacBird*, a stinging dark comedy about Presidents Kennedy and Johnson. I later became wrapped up in the study of turn-of-the-century satiric journals, here represented by *L'Assiette au Beurre*, the French cartoon magazine. During the 1960s my favorite cartoonist was Ron Cobb. *MAD* magazine would also trigger my anti-establishment feelings. During the 2000s, perhaps the worst political decade of my life, anything that jabbed at George W. Bush was welcome. Herein an essay on ads that targeted W along with other dubious world leaders.

You Mean,
Not All Designers
Are Liberal?

That all graphic designers are liberal or left-wing is a fallacy perpetuated among liberal and left-wing designers that all creative people are somehow politically progressive, even if the majority are not Marxist firebrands. History actually tells a more complex story—just look at F.T. Marinetti, Paolo Garretto, Fortunato Depero, or Ludwig Hohlwein and their respective links to fascism, assuming, of course, we can agree that fascism is not progressive. Nonetheless, each believed that their art and design served a social revolution, and in that sense it was progressing the cause.

Yet if you read design magazines and blogs, classic liberal views dominate, especially in the United States where one would have been hard pressed to know for certain that any conservatives or right-wingers were in attendance at Next, the AIGA National Design Conference in Denver, October 2007. Many main stage speakers liberally railed against President George W. Bush and the Iraq War, and although the war is unpopular, active opposition in the United States is still almost exclusively from the left. When half way into the conference, the master of ceremonies, Kurt Andersen, announced that former Vice President Al Gore had just been awarded the Nobel Peace Prize there was such enthusiastic applause one could assume all attendees were in total accord.

Not so. There are various shades of political gray within the design world—as well as stark black and white—particularly in the United States where for a majority of the Bush years the electorate's loyalties were almost equally split. Nonetheless conservative and right wing designers were largely underrepresented or drowned out entirely in the political design discourse. All the recent books about design and politics in the United States and UK (*Design of Dissent* by Milton Glaser and Mirko Ilic, *Conscientious Objectives: Designing for an Ethical Message* by John Cranmer and Yolanda Zappaterra, and the recent *Street Art and the War on Terror: How the World's Best Graffiti Artists Said No To The Iraq War* edited by Eleanor Mathieson) present unapologetic liberal/left perspectives. The design magazines, *Print*, *CA*, *EYE*, etc., also featured more stories about oppositional graphics and guerilla advertising than on pro-Bush media. Meanwhile, mainstream design associations in the United States, but also in Europe, were not reticent about voicing oppositional views: In 2003 and 2004, respectively, the New York AIGA Chapter sponsored two evenings of talks and panel discussions devoted to political protest called 'Hell No!' and 'Hell Yes!' (the latter so-named because it was an election year in which it was assumed Bush would be voted out of office). Each respective evening addressed preparations for, and the ultimate declaration of war against Iraq. In 2005 the traveling exhibition *Graphic Imperative: Posters for Peace, Social Justice, and the Environment 1965-2005*, supported by AIGA and other design groups, began appearing on numerous college campuses and at design organization events throughout the United States. In 2006 the New York Art Director's Club hosted "Designism," featuring Milton Glaser, Jessica Helfand, George Lois, James Victore, Brian Collins, and Kurt Andersen, which volubly promoted a liberal agenda of social responsibility. A follow-up event in December 2007 attracted a large, supportive crowd. (Full disclosure: I was involved as a speaker or moderator in all these events).

Since Bush assumed office, flash points—from ballot fraud to abrogating civil rights to starting wars against Islam in Europe's backyard—have been addressed with various degrees of vigor and passion at conferences and symposia. Conversely there have been no exhibitions, conferences, seminars, or "small talks" advocating conservative policies sponsored by design organizations. Conservative designers have not managed to garner support for political events of their own; hence those who hold these views doubtlessly feel frustrated.

At the Denver AIGA conference following one of the main stage sessions where President Bush was lambasted, I talked to a few attendees who readily complained that injecting partisan political rhetoric into what they believed was supposed to be a "neutral" organization challenged their faith in AIGA's ability to represent them. Although they wanted to remain members of the sole national professional design organization in the United States, they resented having to put up with what they construed as negative, and at times offensive, propaganda, treated as though their opinions were irrelevant. When I asked whether they would consider starting their own counter initiatives, they lamented that their views would never get any traction, so why bother? Most of the anger about mixing design and politics, therefore, surfaces when partisan politics is debated on blogs and listservs, which create a somewhat more anonymous and safer playing field than the conferences where dissenters may feel uncomfortable. The Web allows unprecedented public access and the capacity to argue without filters. Usually, it is liberal/leftist political posts on Web sites like Design Observer and Speak Up that trigger vociferous disdain for what conservative critics see as politicized design discourse. The majority of complaints, like this one submitted to Design Observer in response to William Drenttel's May 31, 2007, post "Gore for President," argue that this is an inappropriate place for political posturing: "I'm not the least bit pleased to see a place that is usually home to great critical design writing turned into an ad for Al Gore."

This response raised sincere concerns over whether this blog (which, despite the proprietorship of its founders, has become a leading voice of the design field) should take partisan stands. Bitter responses like the following referring to Drenttel's Gore essay, reveal stronger antipathy to designers who impose political punditry on others: "This is probably the worst article I've read on Design Observer. It seems it's based on nothing but personal (political biased) opinion." Objections run the gamut from mildly civil to harshly personal, and while some complaints, such as this by a Speak Up commenter in response to a 2003 review of AIGA's "Hell No!," appear to be non-partisan, they express disdain for the "knee-jerk" nature of liberal/left politics: "I fucking hate being preached to as much as being lied to and misled by propaganda." While politics has been part of the design discourse for decades, only recently has the argument on both sides been so vocal.

Overall, those who oppose politicized design discourse seem to fall into two camps. One faction objects to being ambushed by political messages and also believes design writers have no credibility in the political arena (which is not unlike how some people view movie stars and other celebrities who stand for causes). "Designer writers could do the political processes of the world a great favor by taking... their nonsensical idealism elsewhere and leaving the heavy thinking up to people who actually have clue," wrote a reader of Design Observer. The other faction simply resent being confronted with challenges to their own passionate views. A commenter on Speak Up referring to the discussion over "Hell

Yes!" noted: "No good design critique can come of this because you've created a hostile atmosphere. You've made part of this audience feel unwelcome so that you can make easy jokes about the other side."

Whatever your particular opinion, injecting politics into the design discourse is a recipe for antagonism. But why must this be? Designers are no more divorced from politics than any other aware citizens, so to restrict, as some have proposed, designer discussion on blogs or at conferences to only designer-specific themes, like typography, would misrepresent the design discourse. Even type has political ramifications in how it is used to convey messages. What's more, some practitioners are designers in order to promote the causes in which they believe, while understandably others want to keep their politics to themselves and away from their clients.

Those uncomfortable or unwilling to engage in political discourse can opt out of the Web discussions, although it is increasingly more difficult to do so since so much discourse is taking place on the Web. The temptation for some to rebuke unacceptable views is just too great, particularly when personal values are under attack. Here is a response from 2004 on Speak Up to a discussion of anti-Bush policy buttons designed by Milton Glaser: "Am I the only one who sees this hypocrisy? Where are the posters and buttons and AIGA conventions and designers voicing outrage against abortion?" Interestingly, the anti-abortion graphics rarely make it into design shows. And the accusation that there is a liberal/left conspiracy to deny access of this view in this kind of competitive forum is probably true. Additionally there are other prejudicial concerns that transcend Left versus Right. When an exhibition of pro-Palestinian posters was hung at the AIGA VOICE conference in 2002 in Washington, D.C., vehement outrage against images apparently supporting suicide bombing in Israel triggered a fierce debate among otherwise socially simpatico liberals. (Full disclosure: I led the charge against them, although not against showing them.)

Certain hot buttons are guaranteed to raise blood sugar, but angry responses can also be unpredictable, as this response to a historical essay on AIGA VOICE about the legacy of revolutionary Cuban posters (January 10, 2007) indicated: "This article made me decide to never support or get involved with the AIGA again. I will not be part of an organization that publishes articles promoting Communism and makes lite [sic] of the millions of deaths attributed to this evil movement. Have fun in your utopia. Keep those rose-colored glasses on, you won't see the blood that way." Five days later another reader rebutted: "I've read through this (fine) article three times, and I cannot see what the hell [the respondent] is on about. There is no 'promotion' of communism or any other 'ism', and there certainly isn't any making light of any deaths. May I suggest that [the writer] actually reads the article before jerking his knee."

There is never a paucity of argument when one view clashes with another; but sadly the tenor of such things rarely develops into rational conversation. Rather politics seems to be a wedge.

When once asked about the role of political discourse in the classroom, Paul Rand asserted that design education was not good venue for politics, which did not mean it should be ignored but rather kept at bay. Political content, he suggested, was so charged it could distract from teaching formal issues. It is true that politics often ignores design formality given the mandate to communicate message. However, this should not be a reason to reject politics from design discourse, which is there in any case.

In a letter to *EYE* (#48) British designer Quentin Newark acknowledged that design journalism is rooted in social or political bias: "Isn't all judgment of design about employing values, and aren't these always informed by hidden factors? I find much of the journalism in *EYE* strongly colored by barely disguised 'factors'—a loathing of commerce; fetishisation of the idea of the avant-garde; fantasies about radical politics." Ultimately he rhetorically questioned the proverbial elephant in the room: "Do these 'factors' behind a good many of the pieces in *EYE* make it inadequate?"

The design field is not as homogenously political as some may assume, yet politics is certainly one aspect of what designers are called upon to communicate. Expressing political views, no matter how difficult to swallow (on either side) must be embraced, not shunned (a liberal view for sure). I became engaged in design largely because design was so integral to the political process. This is why I was encouraged after reading this note on Design Observer: "Reading Design Observer and saying 'hold the polemic' is sort of like going to Hooters [a U.S. restaurant chain known for its buxom waitresses] for the food. Thank goodness the art of Pamphleteering lives on. Designers, where do you draw the line?"

Yes, the lines have changed because new technologies—blogs, digital video, podcasts, and a wealth of community sites—have made soapboxes out of our desktops. Designers increasingly take advantage of these opportunities—in fact, are drawn—to express political opinion (and fact). As the traffic grows, doubtless more dissenters will challenge liberal/left assumptions, and that's a liberal thing.

When Satire Was More than Funny

At the turn of the century the French Republic was threatened by a military-church-aristocracy coalition and a huge bureaucratic machine dominated by "l'assiette au beurre" or the butter dish—the entrenched job-holders who dispensed favors for a price. They were despised but curiously tolerated. Until ...

During this period Paris was emerging as the art capital of the world. The Belle Epoch was in full swing. Artists were streaming in from Europe, joining ad hoc Salons des Indépendents. Many socially conscious artists turned to anarchism as a way to transcend the insularity of bohemianism and openly vent their political frustrations. They often created cartoons as a weapon in their struggle and, therefore, required outlets that projected their images beyond the hermetic salons and ateliers. It was propitious that in 1901 Samuel Schwarz founded a satiric visual weekly, aptly titled *L'Assiette au Beurre*, expressly poised to attack the functionaries who made their fortunes off the sweat of the citizenry. One of many graphic periodicals at the time, it not only critiqued the ruling classes but altered social mores in the process. Would that the same could be done today.

The acerbic art of *L'Assiette au Beurre* was produced by an assortment of international artists who contributed radical points-of-view. The journal provided a matchless opportunity to exhibit biting satires within a virulent, highly innovative artistic environment whose professed mission as the overseer of social foible and immoral excess was successfully carried out for the next twelve years.

L'Assiette au Beurre was loosely patterned on the German satiric magazine, *Simplicissimus*, with full page drawings as the main content. The text was minimal if used at all. Art nouveau was the predominant graphic style although the more decorative aspects were subservient to the caustic polemical ideas. The mastery of line—expert use of lights and darks—and subtle composition were all components of the socio-political message. Since virtually all of *L'Assiette*'s content was visual, it offered artists room to breathe while experimenting with various rendering media, including woodcut, pen-and-ink, and lithographic crayon. Art nouveau was dominant but not the sole style. The representational approach, void of stylistic flourish, was also effectively employed as polemical method. Toulouse Lautrec, whose poster style inspired considerable mimicry among many of the artists, was refused admittance into *L'Assiette*'s ranks because his art was deemed too superficial.

L'Assiette published weekly; its issues were based on single themes that scrutinized specific events or international personalities, such as Franz Kupka's satiric trilogy devoted to "Money," "Peace," and "Religion." Usually a single artist was responsible for all the artwork in an entire issue—approximately sixteen large-scale drawings (some reproduced in two or three colors). At various times groups of contributors were invited to tackle a particular bête noire, including the faulty judicial system, the hypocritical Catholic church hierarchy, or the inept medical profession. The most memorable single issues of *L'Assiette* are those executed by artists with fervent biases, such as Vadasz on homosexuality, Veber on reconcentration camps in the Transvaal, Gris on suicide, and Hermann-Paul on Lourdes, the religious retreat that he believed exploited atavistic superstitions.

Some graphic commentaries nibbled rather than took deep bites, such as those aimed at snobs, cafes, sports, high fashion, automobiles, and technology. A curiously provocative issue entitled "Le Lit" (the bed) was devoted to the sleeping habits of various social groups—from rich to poor, as well as married couples, prostitutes, and prisoners. "Predications" was a futuristic view of the human condition by Roubille. Another special issue was devoted to the second coming of Jesus Christ, this time resurrected into the "modern" fin de siècle world. It speculated on how the Son of God was repulsed by many deeds (i.e. those of organized religion) done in his name. Juan Gris' pre-cubist contributions revealed his fascination with geometric formulations predating his later experimental canvases. And in Nabis artist Félix Vallotton's special issue of original lithographs, titled "Crime and Punishments" and exquisitely printed on heavy paper stock, each original stone lithograph was given an unprecedented single side of the page. They are masterpieces of brutish expressionism aptly representing the cruelty of France's criminal system as well as punishments meted out by clergy and parents on children and adults alike.

All officials could be pilloried. Leal da Câmara's issue titled "Les Souverains" was complete with caricatures of the world's leading monarchs. And no friendly or belligerent nation was beyond the range of satiric ordinance: England, France's historic enemy, was periodically attacked through caricatures of its leaders and farcical tableaux for what L'Assiette's editors described as heinous foreign polices, notably the establishment of the first twentieth-century "concentration camps" for use during the Boer War to imprison Dutch South African civilians and combatants. L'Assiette's few central European artists kept a watchful eye on the machinations of the Austro-Hungarian emperor and condemned his thirst for European dominance. But closer to home, the abusive treatment of black Africans in French colonies was also abhorred.

Particular rancor was reserved for la Belle France herself: For one special issue a group of L'Assiette's contributors marshaled their journalistic fervor and critical zeal to reflect on a tragic "accidental" gun powder factory explosion at Issy-les-Moulineaux where hundreds of workers were killed owing to inadequate safety measures. Another exposé targeted a scandal involving a dairy company that knowingly distributed spoiled milk throughout Paris, resulting in fatalities among young children. In addition L'Assiette's sharpest barbs and venomous graphic commentaries were reserved for French Papists.

L'Assiette was often banned by French authorities. On one occasion, one issue titled "Les Cafes Concerts" was coerced into being previewed by an ethics committee that stamped each acceptable drawing with "Vise par Le Censor" (passed by the censor). A frequent L'Assiette contributor, Aristide Delannoy, was arrested, sentenced to one year in jail, and fined 3,000 francs for depicting General d'Amade, the military occupier of Morocco, as a butcher with a blood-stained apron. Later the same artist was threatened with imprisonment when he visually attacked the French leaders Briand and Clemenceau. Minor witch-hunts were practiced with L'Assiette as the target and yet efforts to restrain often backfired, resulting in greater publicity and sales.

L'Assiette au Beurre made an impact on a generation, and continued to do so even after it ceased publication in 1911. Its spirit continued in satiric journals such as Le Mot, edited by Jean Cocteau, and Le Temoin edited by Paul Iribe. But L'Assiette was a wellspring of critical and oppositional graphic journalism in France and the model for many satiric journals to follow. Today this kind of print media has been replaced by film, video, and TV, which, in blander ways, carry out the stinging comedies and stark satires of the past.

"The Play's The Thing
Wherein I'll Catch The Conscience of the King"

BARBARA GARSON

My First Taste of Political Satire

It's funny how events spark memories that have been forgotten. On the sad day that Ted Kennedy died I came across a tattered copy of *MacBird*, the 1966 play by Barbara Garson that accuses President Lyndon B. Johnson of being culpable in the John F. Kennedy assassination. At the time this ludicrous accusation seemed curiously plausible given the tenor of the times. Popular opinion had turned against LBJ owing to the unpopular Vietnam War triggering many weird conspiracy theories. But *MacBird* was not the run-of-the-mill lunatic fringe fantasy. It was the first post-Kennedy satire to receive serious public attention. Pulitzer Prize winning poet Robert Lowell wrote: "I have nothing to say about the political truth of this play, but I am sure a kind of genius has gone into the writing." And Dwight MacDonald in the *New York Review of Books* said it was, "The funniest, toughest-minded, and most ingenious political satire I've read in years."

I was sixteen years old when I first saw it at the Village Gate Theater on Bleecker Street in New York. I went with my parents and I can remember virtually every detail, as this was my first exposure to really biting (adult) anti-establishment political satire. It was also the first time I saw the then young actors Stacy Keach (MacBird), William Devane (Robert [Kennedy]), Rue McClanahan (Lady MacBird), John Pleshette (Ted [Kennedy]), and Cleavon Little (as the Muslim Witch). In this case a black Muslim witch, the idea of which was scaring the bejesus out of white America. Some of you may remember the late Mr. Little was the African-American marshal in Mel Brooks' comic western *Blazing Saddles*. If only for the cast, many who went on to stellar careers, this was a historic theatrical experience, but the theme was heatedly controversial, too.

MacBird, a send-up of *Macbeth*, was published three years after the Kennedy assassination, an event so psychically devastating that it was hard to believe back then that humor was not forever dead, in the same way it was said that irony died after 9/11. LBJ had less than two years remaining in his term and there was no indication that he would ultimately not seek re-election. It was a critical, tumultuous, and angry time.

MacBird was a full-dress Shakespearean costume "drama," with Texan and Bostonian accents replacing the Bard's English. The first act began at the 1960 Democratic National Convention, where in reality the powerful Senate Democrat leader LBJ sought to wrest the presidential nomination from the upstart JFK. In the scene, MacBird and Lady MacBird scheme to manipulate the selection of King. MacBird, however, looses to John Ken O'Dunc and as a consolation is named Viceroy (VP)— much to the consternation of Ken O'Dunc's formidable clan.

ROBERT: Hail MacBird, Vice-president thou art—
            That is, if you'll accept the second place.
            My brother Jack has picked you for the job
            And hopes that you'll agree to grace the slate.

MacBird happens upon three witches (sound similar to the sirens of Homer's *Odyssey* or *Oh Brother Where Art Thou?*) who speak to him in riddles, urging him to become King by whatever means are necessary.

WITCHES: (chanting together)
            The bosses shall be booted in the bin,
            The kings unkinged. We have a world to win!
MACBIRD: Vice-president—and President to be!

To make his fantasy reality MacBird, adroitly played by Keach who even looked identical to LBJ, invites Ken O'Dunc and kin to his ranch following the coronation. As this fateful event unfolds, Lady MacBird, who insistently complains of the dirty work she must endure as a Viceroy's wife, finds an opportunity for MacBird to seize the throne and becomes the brains behind the coup.

Following the real Dallas scenario, a procession is planned headed by Ken O'Dunc, followed by his brothers and lesser nobles of the court (i.e. its chief, the Earl of Warren). Unexpectedly, shots are fired—and I can still viscerally recall violently flinching in my seat.

ONE VOICE: He's gone!

(Right after the shot is heard, a projector throws an X in a sixth
floor window of the building, trajectory lines extend from the building to
the sidewalk, and lettering appears, reading "Grassy Knoll," "Railroad
Overpass," etc. In this way the backdrop becomes a newspaper diagram of the
assassination.)

3rd VOICE: They've shot the President!
5th VOICE: Oh, piteous sight!

The King is dead. And although the right of succession insures that
Robert will be crowned, complications arise. The not so subtle implication
leaves no doubt that MacBird was responsible for the deed. MacBird takes
power but things go wrong and wronger with the war, race riots, and
more. The witches return:

WITCHES (all): Bubble and bubble, toil and trouble,
                      Burn baby burn, and cauldron bubble.

In the end MacBird realizes his greatest enemy is Robert (who in
1968 would run for president in the primaries against LBJ).

ROBERT: Your charm is curse. Prepare to hear the worst.
              At each male birth my father in his wisdom
              Prepared his sons for their envisaged greatness.
              Our first gasped cries as moist, inverted infants
              Confirmed for him our place as lords and leaders.
              To free his sons from paralyzing scruples
              And temper us for roles of world authority
              Our pulpy human hearts were cut away.
              And in their place, precision apparatus
              Of steel and plastic tubing was inserted.
              The sticky, humid blood was drained and then
              A tepid antiseptic brine injected.
              Although poor Teddy suffered complications,
              The operations worked on all the others,
              Thus steeling us to rule as more than men.
              And so, MacBird, that very man you fear,
              Your heartless, bloodless foe now lifts his spear.

(ROBERT slowly raises and aims his spear, but before he can hurl it, MACBIRD clutches his heart)

MACBIRD: My heart, my heart! (staggers)
                          Thus cracks a noble heart!

There are so many things that I now vividly recall from the viewing and reading of MacBird, not the least being the illustrated logo and the drawings that ran through the book (which incidentally sold over 200,000 copies in 1967). The hand-lettered title "MacBird!" with a caricature of LBJ running with spear and shield in hand, wearing a veritable mini-skirt and cowboy boots with spurs, symbolized what many believed was his recklessness in Vietnam. Also, until that time most satire (other than Lenny Bruce) was held to certain standard of decorum. This play stripped off that civil façade.

As Macbeth and MacBird were tragic figures, so, in truth, was LBJ whose legacy was not his progressive civil rights legislation but his unreasonable escalation of the war. Of course, Robert Kennedy was assassinated only two years after the play was published, although he lived long enough to fulfill Barbara Garson's prescience with his run in the Democratic primaries against LBJ. And Teddy had myriad problems that prevented him from the ultimate envisaged greatness—the presidency—although his life as senator was extraordinary and significant.

It's odd that I would find this book after four decades on the very day that Ted Kennedy died. But there is usually a reason for everything. This made me realize that it is important to take heed of hope and build upon it. There are just too many forces conspiring against it. Let's "lift aloft the banner of MacBird."

Once Upon a Time, There Was a Big Bad President

On Lil' Bush, the Comedy Central animated cable show, George W. and his cronies are reduced to pint-size caricatures who, like unruly children, wreak havoc on the nation. In one episode, noting that "American Awesomeness" has plummeted and "we are now the most hated nation in the world," lil' Condi Rice introduces a plan to re-brand the entire country. America will be called "The Land of the Funsies" and the "scary old bald eagle" will be replaced with funny wisecracking unicorn named "Larry the Fun American." Sound silly? You bet, but it also derives from a venerable tradition of satire dating back to the nineteenth century when kings, queens, prelates, and presidents were transposed onto characters from children's literature for the sole purpose of ridicule.

Classic children's tales with characters that reflect the comédie humaine are perfectly suited for parody. The Brothers Grimm, Mother Goose, and even Dick and Jane, provide ready-made vehicles to, with just a twist of wit and irony, attack the foibles and follies of any leader or political entity. One of the most "beloved" (if that's the right term) of this genre is Struwwelhitler a 1941 British parody of the German fable Struwwelpeter (Shaggy Peter), originally about a nasty little unkempt boy who demonstrates that his misbehavior can have disastrous consequences. In the parody written and illustrated by Robert and Philip Spence, Hilter and his henchmen are thwarted at every turn or punished for carrying out their evil deeds. And when not being thwarted or punished, they are ridiculed, as this rhyme vividly illustrates:

GOODNIGHT BUSH

by Erich Origen & Gan Golan

Just look at him! There he stands
With his nasty hair and hands.
See! The horrid blood drops drip
From each dirty finger tip:
And the sloven, I declare,
Never once has combed his hair;
Piecrust never could be brittler
Than the word of Adolf Hitler.

As with *Lil' Bush*, sometimes infantilizing those in power does not require parodying specific characters, but simply placing the target of ridicule in a children's context. In the Italian *Mi Chiamo Adolf*, written and illustrated by Pef (Giannino Stoppani Edizioni), Hilter is portrayed as an eerie child (replete with mustache) who oddly enough carries out nightmarish acts of cruelty and pays the price. While not the most effective satire, it is nonetheless an unsettling portrayal.

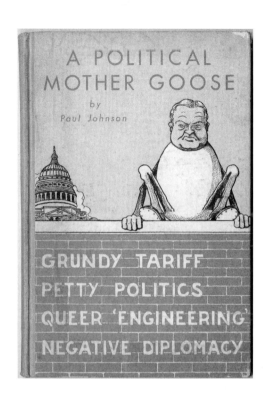

In the United States one of the most well-received send-ups was published in 1931, just after the start of the Great Depression, titled *A Political Mother Goose* by Paul Johnson (published by The Non-Partisan Press). Here, like in *Struwwelhitler*, rhyme is expertly crafted to bring out the venal in politicians of both Republican and Democratic parties, like this one that accompanies an illustration of future president Franklin Delano Roosevelt walking with his arm around a corrupt Tammany Tiger (Tammany was the powerful New York City Democratic political machine):

> I like little pussy, her voite is so warm,
> > And if I don't hurt her she'll do me no harm,
> So I'll not twist her tail in the way that I should
> > For I fear if I do, Puss will fix me for good.

Many caricaturists have used children's characters to great effect but few in recent memory have done it with more rapier wit than Robert Grossman. In his comic strip version of *Snow White* (published in *New York Magazine*, 1973) President Richard Nixon, under the scrutiny in Watergate Committee hearings, dreams happily of being Snow White with congressional elves at her beck and call. But then dream turns to nightmare when the elves turn against and disrobe her. Nixon awakes in a panic, exclaiming, "Oh my!"

While more recently the perennially popular *Where's Waldo* was transformed by cartoonists into variations of *Where's Osama*, a jab at the Bush Administration's inability to find the elusive Al Qaeda leader, the most pitch perfect of current parodies is *Goodnight Bush* by Erich Origen and Gan Golan based on the Margaret Wise Brown classic *Goodnight Moon*. For any parody to live up to its promise, every nuance of the original must be precisely copied, and this is done here from the flat color drawings of George W. in his room in bed—with the red phone by one bed stand and lines of cocaine on another—to the black and white pull-outs of all the details in the room, which was a key conceit of the original. The text superbly follows the sing-song cadence of Wise's version, as in:

> Goodnight toy world
> And the flight costume
> Goodnight ballot box
> Goodnight FOX
> Goodnight towers
> And goodnight balance of powers.

Fun with Dick and Jane, with its staccato "See Dick run" sentences, has also been repurposed, but when targeting the *Bushies in Yiddish with George and Laura*, by Ellis Weiner and Barbara Davilman, a new level of absurdity is reached as in this exchange between W and his mom, Barbara Bush, about an Iraqi flag:

> "Where is Dad?" asks George.
> He holds out a flag.
> "I got this for him."
>
> "He does not want
> that flag, George,"
> says Bar.
> "If he did he would have gotten one himself."
> But I will put it in the den with all
> The other chazerai."

The piece de resistance of Bush-era parody is, however, not a send-up of a particular book, but rather of a genre of biography for juveniles, *Young Dick Cheney: Great American* by Bruce Kluger and David Slavin (illustrated by Tim Foley). This rather lengthy text, punctuated by smart line drawings of a pudgy Cheney, takes the reader on an odyssey, from the first time the young Dick put his finger in oil, ". . .a small, sparkling black puddle, creating the most beautiful rainbow," he'd ever seen. "He was drawn to it, like a kitten to a dish of really dark milk." It ends when he rigged his first big ballot for his high school pageant. "'After reviewing the votes,' Dick told the committee, casually setting fire to the pageant ballots and tossing them into a small wastebasket, 'I regret to inform you of a voting irregularity. It appears that art student Chad Broward's unique 'horsefly ballot' confused many students, and now we have... a three-way tie for the winner.'" Although ham-fisted at times, the humor is nonetheless a tonic for those who endured Bush-Cheney for eight years.

Of course, no parody actually changes the political world, but it provides a way to vent. Using children's images and stories also makes the critiques more accessible and thereby more human.

NO WAR ON IRAQ
No Blood For Oil
WHO SAYS THERE'S NO REST FOR THE WICKED?
SK
Dreamland
The sleep through the night mattress

The Model President: George W. Bush Advertising Star

When was the last time a sitting president of the United States was a model for a commercial advertising campaign? The answer is: Never! After all, there are protocols that prevent commanders-in-chief from shilling for products. As leaders of the capitalist free world, while in elected office presidents are not CEOs, they are spokespeople for all American goods, therefore ethically prevented from throwing their weight behind any single product. Other than the occasional public service announcement, presidents must be above the promotion and public relations fray. Once they are out of office, well, even then they are not free to hawk commercial wares. It's just not dignified. In the United States this is an unwritten regulation, yet elsewhere in the world there are no such restrictions. This is not say American ex-presidents supplement their retirement incomes by making commercials abroad. Still, that doesn't stop advertisers from co-opting the images of sitting or retired presidents. During George W. Bush's last term (2004 – 2008) he may not (to paraphrase Lyndon B. Johnson) have sought nor did he accept advertising jobs, but his image was nonetheless employed in scores of foreign campaigns for organizations like Amnesty International, media conglomerates, including newspapers and television stations, and even commercial products, like Lipton Tea, Arno Blenders, and Daimler Chrysler's Smart Car, which featured a photo of W under the headline "Still looking for weapons of mass destruction. Not smart."

Arguably, it is an invasion of even his high-profile life to exploit W's stature in order to pitch retail commodities (unless it is somehow done as parody or social comment). But an entirely different tenet applies when using him as a symbol. In recent years, there has been a trend, of sorts, to juxtapose W with other world symbols—or other world figures who represent a range of unsavory policies and acts—in order to illustrate distinct points of world view often related to his policies. Although it is common to satirize politicians in political or topical cartooning, using advertisements to make or exploit a political statement is a relatively recent practice (Oliviero Toscani and Tibor Kalman's advertisements for Benetton in the mid-1990s took on social issues, but they never used an American president's visage). So when a company like SK Bedding advertises its "Dreamland" mattress with a portrait of Bush collaged among photos of burned babies, flag-draped coffins, and images of Abu Ghraib, under the title: "Who Says There's No Rest for the Wicked?" the conventional rules have obviously been changed. Additionally, this campaign also includes depictions of Kim Jong Il and Robert Mugabe. The idea that the leader of the free world would be ideologically lumped together with murderous dictators gives one pause. Was this just an anomaly or is this how people view the United States and its leader?

Politics and commerce are not such strange bedfellows after all. A campaign for the newspaper *Milenio* may not be such an overt condemnation of Bush as SK Bedding, but its conceptual conceit forces critical comparisons. The campaign's big idea is based on an equation (A + B = C). For example, Fidel Castro + a mariachi band = Hugo Chavez. Another shows a gorilla + razor = Arnold Schwarzenegger. The pièce de résistance shows Homer Simpson + John Wayne = (a scowling) Bush. The juxtapositions here are very revealing. Likewise ads for Paintpark, a recreational venue in Great Britain for paintball shooting, use characters wearing Bush, Saddam, and Bin Laden masks—the concept is pretty obvious. While the image is benign enough, under the headline "War Games: Recruit your Company For a Game of Paintball," the idea that Bush is thrown together with Saddam is disturbingly humorous. Another odd one is the series of poster-like advertisements for Dogotel, a Mexican kennel, playing off the Mexican translation of the word dogotel, meaning "low life." Bush, Bin Laden, and Castro are rendered separately in incriminating vignettes. The Bush iteration, admittedly a shoddy rendering, shows him against mushroom clouds and missiles.

The ad for Arno blenders may not be as biting as this but is decidedly humiliating. It shows a photo of President George Bush I in a blender with a picture of Alfred E. Newman; next to the blender, presumably after it was blended, is a glass with a photo of George Bush (in all fairness they also have a similar one with Bill Clinton). The Marmite Squeezy syrup ad shows a marmite portrait of W with the tag line, "You either love it or hate it" (meaning the syrup, of course). That's pretty benign, but the Lipton Tea advertisements, however, are surprisingly impertinent: In its parody of a newspaper front page (titled *The Daily Focus*) a lead story with a photograph of Bush drinking water sits next to the headline "George W. Bush successfully names all 50 US states." A similarly goofy photograph of Kim Jong-Il as a Pee Wee Herman-look-alike accompanies the headline "Kim Jong-Il Chooses not to Spank His Dog." While these stories are more silly than offensive, the idea that Bush has parity with Kim is of interest. Conversely, the ad for *Cape Times* newspaper lands a more directly offensive blow. Its papier-mâché effigy of W under the heading "Public enemy No, 1?" is a pretty strong indictment. *Egoista* magazine's "Bushit" advertisement simply takes a swat, showing W with a splat of pigeon poop on his shoulder with the caption "since 1945 there have been only 26 days of peace in the world."

Other advertisements are less about being critical of Bush than exploiting his familiar face. The SIC News Channel's campaign shows various world leaders having conversations where a fly is on the nose of one of the conversers (i.e. on George W. Bush)—its hard to say what the point of that one is. In the ad for IPPU, a label printer, Bush is arm-in-arm with a smiling Fidel Castro, which, of course, is just plain silly. And speaking of silly, to promote its smaller size newspaper, the German *Welt Kompakt* campaign shows baby versions of world leaders, like Bush, Angela Merkel, and Pope Benedict under the headline "BIG NEWS. Small Size." The World Association for Newspapers' campaign pairs world foes together (under "Hide & Seek" is a collage of Bush seeking out Bin Laden).

The most damning ads are predictably from political advocacy organizations, like Amnesty International, which produced a series of enlarged commemorative stamps attacking torture in dictatorial regimes including those in Myanmar, Iran, and Zimbabwe with portraits of their leaders. The last stamp in the series, to "stamp out torture," includes President Bush. Another Amnesty campaign, "Make Some Noise for Human Rights" concert, includes photographs of world leaders, including Bush, Kim Jong Il, and Mugabe holding their ears. And in Amnesty's "The Power of Your Voice" campaign, Bush is linked to Presidents Putin and Ahmadinejad.

Never before in the history of advertising has an American president been recurrently portrayed in this kind of advertising (even going back to the nineteenth century). One reason may be the increase in "social commentary" ads by companies like Benetton, Kenneth Cole, Ben & Jerry's, and others. Maybe another reason is that as a form of entertainment, advertising is taking more rule-busting chances. Still, one wonders, if U.S. policy had not lost its long-held positive stature and President Bush were more popular elsewhere in the world, would this trend be happening today? What's most telling is that advertising reflects what the masses know and understand. In this crop of campaigns apparently the world seems to hold this leader of the free world in fairly low esteem.

Where Have You Gone, R. Cobb?

In 1968 the two most influential underground newspaper cartoonists in America were R. Crumb, whom most everyone knows today, and R. Cobb, whom sadly many do not. Crumb devastated establishment pieties while Cobb attacked the establishment's devastation of rights and liberties. Both made an indelible impression on my impressionable generation.

Crumb, who lives in the south of France today, survived the 1960s to become a bona fide culture hero with films, books, and exhibitions celebrating his creative madness. Cobb, who lives in Australia, left the ephemeral art of cartooning for a career as a concept designer and art director in television and films, including *The Abyss*, *Aliens*, *True Lies*, *Total Recall*, *Rocketeer*, and many more. But for me, Cobb's weekly single panel cartoon with its bold pen line and intricate cross-hatching featured in the *Los Angeles Free Press* has the most resonance. His blunt portrayals of scowling helmeted LA police branded this breed of law enforcer as robotic instruments of raw power years before the film *Robocop*, while his bearded everymen, survivors of nuclear winter who find shelter amid the post-apocalypse rubble of LA, are cautionary comic beings that underscored a collective fear of the endgame.

Los Angeles native Ron Cobb (b. 1937) was the Vietnam War and civil rights-era's Herblock (the editorial cartoonist for the *Washington Post* who courageously attacked McCarthyism and the Cold War). Herblock made the H-bomb a specter of horror through depictions of a sneering, menacing bomb with a five-o'clock shadow. Likewise, Cobb underscored America's growing environmental crisis through a repertory of dazed lost souls, like the one holding the plug of a broken portable television, aimlessly looking for an electrical outlet against the backdrop of total environmental annihilation. He also designed the widely used Ecology

symbol made from the lower-case letter e combined with an o (e for environment and o for organism), which he explained in analytic detail in an October 25, 1969 cartoon.

Cobb, a former inker for Disney Studios and later a U.S. Army signal corps artist in Vietnam, emerged into the underground in 1965 when he started contributing cartoons to Art Kunkin's *Los Angeles Free Press* (Freep) that were quickly picked up by the Underground Press Syndicate (UPS) and distributed free to other undergrounds (including a couple I worked on). The cartoons, reminiscent of MAD's Will Elder, were not funny in the goofy sense, although some of his characterizations were comically exaggerated in the prevailing style, but decidedly serious in tone and texture. Still, they were nothing like Jules Feiffer's shorthand renderings or Robert Osborn's expressionist visuals. They did, however, elicit uneasy laughter from the viewer. His 1968 cartoon addressing postwar real estate development shows a sign in a forest of ancient trees that reads: "Soon to be erected on this site: Sequoia Square. Shopping Center and 300 Unit Hotel-Motel Complex." In light of all the forests and parks that have succumbed to speculation this was a prescient warning. A jarringly poignant issue that

conflates race relations and the environment shows an Apollo 58 landing craft on the moon with two black men in space suits cleaning up all the debris left by the previous 57 missions. And a detailed rendering of manmade waste along a highway reveals rows of billboards showing bucolic scenes with a sign that reads: "Scenic Drive Next 2 Miles."

I still have his album cover for Jefferson Airplane's *After Bathing at Baxter's* and recently rediscovered two of his three books (published in 1971 by Price/Stern/Sloan): *Raw Sewage*, cartoons about the environment, and *My Fellow Americans*, "patriotic cartoons," which serve as jaundiced but nonetheless precise histories of the late 1960s and early 1970s political and social angst and attitudes. While the book cover lettering suggests the period when they were published (and the musty smell of decaying pages is noticeable), the images have not lost their potency. In "Progress" two cavemen in one panel are threateningly brandishing bones at each other, while in the second, a man in a suit shoots another through the heart with a gun. In another cartoon, a working GI Joe-like replica of a "Leatherneck," which the toy box says "Puts You in the Action," walks away with a bloody bayonet after stabbing the little boy who was playing with it. And in a futuristic vision of the law and order state, two men on a bench marked "for B Citizens Only" under the watchful eyes of both surveillance camera and police officers in a tank, one of whom says, "Well, at least we don't have to worry about anarchy anymore."

Crumb's comics were brilliant comedies, but Cobb's cartoons brilliantly distilled issues into icons, and served as rallying points for those engaged who questioned government and its leaders. They were right for the times, but when the epoch came to an end, when the LA Freep closed down in the early 1970s, Cobb's cartoons ended too.

Mad Music

Visual art is one vehicle for satire. Music is another powerful weapon. In 1962 I spent hours listening to *MAD* magazine's first LP (Big Top Records), *MAD "Twists" Rock 'N' Roll.* Playing it over and over, I learned every inane lyric by heart. "When My Pimples Turned to Dimples (that say I love you)," "Please Betty Jane (shave your legs)," and the existential "(She's Got A) Nose Job," with the refrain "now she's the prettiest girl in town," were imbedded in that part of my cerebral cortex that surprisingly even today sparks atwitter when I am idly waiting for take-out food or a prescription to be filled. (And if asked nicely I will gladly belt out each tune in two-part harmony.) So worn out was the vinyl of my first copy of "Twists" (it was the era of the twist), that I bought two additional copies, which probably sent the record straight to #102 on the Billboard charts (without the proverbial bullet).

The album was the first time a magazine crossed platforms (now a common occurrence) transmuting from art to music and spawning such cultural treasures over a decade later as *The National Lampoon's Radio Dinner* album and scores of other such multimedia productions. It made a lot of sense too: *MAD*'s sarcastic humor was as much about verbal as visual wit—and in pre-Beatles 1960s rock 'n' roll numerous clichés were ripe for parody. Making fun of the ever-popular "my baby died in a car crash" genre with "(All I Have Left Is) My Johnny's Hub Cap," and the "my baby was caught doing it with someone else" genre with "Somebody Else's Dandruff (On My Lover-baby's Shirt)" or "I Found Her Telephone Number Written On The Boys Bathroom Wall" may sound puerile today but who knew from puerility back then. Humor was not over-analyzed; it just occurred like a bodily function. *MAD* was a slap at pop commercial culture that has been perfected in the twenty-first century by the likes of Jon Stewart and Stephen Colbert.

MAD *"Twists" Rock 'n' Roll* was written and produced by Norm Blagman and Stan Bobrick (whose names sounded like *MAD* characters). The songs were sung in true doo-wop syncopation by Jeanne Hayes, Mike Russo, and The Dellwoods (Saul Zeskand, bass, Mike Ellis, first tenor, Andy Ventura, second tenor, C. Victor Buccellato, lead singer, and Amadeo Tese, baritone). I so wanted to be a Dellwood that I made my mom buy Dellwood Milk. The cover of the LP featured that classic moron, Alfred E. Newman, painted by Norman Mingo (a logo more recognizable at one time than the Swoosh). Owning the record made me feel part of a club, which later evolved into the sardonic, ironic 1960s youth culture.

So why am I writing about this album when it's not even an major anniversary (forty-seven years old this year)? I could reflect on the fact that LPs and CDs will soon be totally obsolete, but that's not the reason. More to the point, I recently came across the cover for this album and it sparked the notion that every generation has some definitive object that triggers memories—some of these are visual, others visual and oral. For me songs like "(Even if I live to be 22) I'll Always Remember Being Young" and "Let's Do the Pretzel (And End Up Like One)" bring me back to a time before art, design, and humor had to be sophisticated to be good.

Covering *Weirdo* (Magazine)

MAD was my satiric bible until I hit puberty. Then came *Weirdo* edited by R. Crumb—the next generation

Weirdo was Crumb's brainchild, a vehicle for channeling the comics that molded his method and expressed his innermost kooky and screwball visions (as if he really needed another such outlet). As originally conceived *Weirdo* would feature original comic book stories both personal and socially critical. Like *RAW*, it would also include independent artists—known and unknown. Crumb's secret passion for photo-funnies, through which he indulged some of his sexual fantasies in the tradition of a popular format once found in girlie magazines, was also played out (like with the cover for *Weirdo* #6, which barely resembles anything Crumb had done before).

Weirdo was published as a quarterly by Last Gasp. Its first issue premiered in spring 1981. With its illuminated border—an homage to Kurtzman's original *MAD* magazine—and smoking masthead/logo hanging in the air above his Basil Wolverton-inspired character Etaoin Shrdlu (the letters made by linotype operators at the end of a galley of typesetting), this was clearly a magazine that owed much to comics and other popular culture.

Crumb, however, apparently took little joy in editing *Weirdo*, noted Peter Bagge, who took over the editorship in 1983. Crumb remained a contributor, creating most of the covers, while Bagge did nine issues, and then Aline Kominsky-Crumb took over for the final nine issues, which ended officially in 1993. Crumb's most satisfying act was making *Weirdo*'s covers, and it was clear why. Inspired by *MAD* and *Humbug*, he was could pay homage while expanding the legacy. His masthead logos, alone, which morphed each issue from high to low tech, organic to mechanical, vintage

to unprecedented, were done with great appreciation for the lettering arts. "I always thought covers was the most important part of any magazine, in making each issue a powerful artifact in its own right, as well as bring part of a strong series," Crumb told interviewer Jean-Pierre Mercier.

And it is his collected covers that are both the most memorable and surprising of the *Weirdo* run. The best had that retro look, but they were never entirely old fashioned. And the most inventive were definitely Crumb's excuse for making playful boarders and quirky logos. For the connoisseur of magazine covers—and I consider myself one—*Weirdo* should be in the pantheon. Because it is a comic book, it's too easily overlooked by the design historical establishment—and I consider myself part of that, too—but it should not be ignored. In fact, covers rarely get any better than this.

INDEX

Books from Allworth Press

Allworth Press is an imprint of Allworth Communications, Inc. Selected titles are listed below.

Design Disasters: Great Designers, Fabulous Failures, and Lessons Learned
edited by Steven Heller (6 x 9, 240 pages, paperback, $24.95)

How to Think Like a Great Graphic Designer
by Debbie Millman (6 x 9, 248 pages, paperback, $24.95)

Designers Don't Read
by Austin Howe (5 ½ x 8 ½, 224 pages, paperback, $24.95)

Design Literacy: Understanding Graphic Design, Revised Edition
by Steven Heller (6 x 9, 464 pages, paperback, $24.95)

Graphic Design Time Line: A Century of Design Milestones, Revised Edition
by Steven Heller and Elinor Pettit (6 ¾ x 9 7/8, 256 pages, paperback, $29.95)

Graphic Design History
edited by Steven Heller and Georgette Ballance (6 ¾ x 9 ¾, 352 pages, paperback, $29.95)

Design Dialogues
by Steven Heller and Elinor Pettit (6 ¾ x 10, 192 pages, paperback, $24.95)

Green Graphic Design
By Brian Dougherty with Celery Design Collaborative (6 x 9, 212 pages, paperback, $24.95)

Citizen Designer: Perspectives on Design Responsibility
edited by Steven Heller and Véronique Vienne (6 x 9, 272 pages, paperback, $19.95)

Design Humor: The Art of Graphic Wit
by Steven Heller (6 ¾ x 9 7/8, 240 pages, paperback, $24.95)

Swastika: Symbol Beyond Redemption?
by Steven Heller (6 x 9, 184 pages, paperback, $19.95)

Looking Closer 5
edited by Michael Bierut, William Drenttel, and Steven Heller (6 ¾ x 9 7/8, 256 pages, paperback, $21.95)

To request a free catalog or order books by credit card, call 1-800-491-2808. To see our complete catalog on the World Wide Web, or to order online, please visit *www.allworth.com*.

OCT 2 1 2010